# BETWEEN LOVING AND LEAVING

# BETWEEN
## LOVING AND LEAVING

### Essays on the New Midwestern History

Edited by
JON K. LAUCK

UNIVERSITY OF OKLAHOMA PRESS : NORMAN

Publication of this book is made possible in part through the generosity of Edith Kinney Gaylord.

Library of Congress Control Number: 2024060691

ISBN: 978-0-8061-9602-2 (hardcover)

The paper in this book meets the guidelines for permanence and durability of the Committee on Production Guidelines for Book Longevity of the Council on Library Resources, Inc. ∞

The manufacturer's authorized representative in the EU for product safety is Mare Nostrum Group B.V., Mauritskade 21D, 1091 GC Amsterdam, The Netherlands, email: gpsr@mare-nostrum.co.uk.

To the memory of a Midwestern farmer,
Dale W. Lauck, 1932–2022

# CONTENTS

JON K. LAUCK

# INTRODUCTION

## The Guerrilla War for Midwestern Studies

The voice of the Midwest in American historical studies is getting louder, and it is being heard in more quarters of American intellectual life. It needs to be louder, however, because voices from the American interior can still be hard to hear in the din of national culture. The recent progress the field of Midwestern history has made is reported here and, given its steady and grinding gains, it should be celebrated. But the good news is reported alongside an accounting of the various setbacks the field has suffered of late and, given the obstacles still to be overcome, a word of caution is provided. Within the chapters in this book, amid all this back-and-forth for the field and the prevailing conditions of academic turmoil, varied scholars carry the conversation further and examine the state of an array of subtopics within Midwestern studies. These contributors offer their own thoughts on the matters at hand and sketch out an agenda for research and, one hopes, provide a roadmap for more progress in the field.

Midwestern history still needs some megaphones in the form of new institutional supports that can amplify the diverse voices of the field in the coming decades and give the nation's understudied midsection its due. Without larger institutional support, however—if reinforcements never arrive—the battle can still be fought, the cause carried on, and the voices of the center of the country strengthened if those committed to the field continue to work together to build an audience for Midwestern history and provide this audience with the essential stories of the region. Whether presented grandly and loudly with official fanfare via a more robust institutional infrastructure or communicated more sporadically via scattershot voices and guerrilla organizing, the cause is just if one believes in giving the nation's center proportionate representation in the historical record and in advancing a thorough and comprehensive understanding of the American past.

The most significant development for Midwestern studies in the past decade has been the inception of a more sustained and organized discourse about the region. The Michigan-based meetings of the Midwestern History Association (MHA) each May, which started in 2015 and were free and open to the public due to the generosity of the Hauenstein Center at Grand Valley State University, have been crucial to fostering a discussion about the region and giving scholars a platform to talk about their research. The launch of *Middle West Review* in 2014, the same year that the MHA was created, then provided scholars with a place to publish their work where it would remain permanently accessible and a continuing part of the dialogue within the field.[1] *Middle West Review* also published special symposia on topics such as African American history, Native American history, Jewish history, environmental history, reform politics, geography, women's history, regionalism, German history, and major books about the Midwest to provide deeper dives into various aspects of Midwestern history.[2] The work presented at the MHA sometimes found its way into various edited collections about Midwestern history that further advanced thinking about the region.[3] The first MHA conference, for example, yielded a suggestive collection of essays that gave some shape to the field, which increasingly marched under the banner of the New Midwestern History.[4] The emergence of new publications parallel to *Middle West Review* also benefited the field, especially *The New Territory* (which focused on the southwestern Midwest), the *Cleveland Review of Books*, Ursuline College's *Rust Belt Studies*, and *Belt Magazine* (as in "Rust Belt"). The latter was connected to Belt Publishing, which publishes books about the Midwest, including a series on Midwestern cities stretching from Youngstown to Sioux Falls.[5]

In addition to these newer publications, the field benefited from older outlets, including the half-century of work by the Society for the Study of Midwestern Literature and its journals *MidAmerica* and *Midwestern Miscellany*. State historical society journals and university presses also do essential work. The latter include Kent State University Press, Michigan State University Press, the University of Nebraska Press, the University Press of Kansas, the University of Missouri Press, the University of Wisconsin Press, Southern Illinois University Press, and others, including the presses run by state historical societies such as the Indiana Historical Society Press, Minnesota Historical Society Press, the South Dakota Historical Society Press, and the Wisconsin Historical Society Press. Some university presses maintain series on the Midwest, such as the Iowa and the Midwest Experience series at the University of Iowa Press, the Minnesota and the Upper Midwest series at the University of Minnesota Press, the New Approaches to Midwestern Studies series at Ohio University Press, the new Heartland History series at Indiana University Press, and the Latinos in Chicago and the Midwest series at the University of Illinois Press. The University of Oklahoma Press has taken a particular interest in American regionalism more generally and has also published books about Midwestern subregions.[6] This included *North Country*, which focused on the northern lake country and its forests, mining, and fishing.[7] Literary journals that publish reviews and nonfiction essays also support the field of Midwestern studies and give regional voices a platform from which to be heard. These include *Midwest Review* at the University of Wisconsin-Stevens Point, the *Chicago Review of Books*, *Great Lakes Review*, and *Local Culture*, run by Front Porch Republic, which was organized to promote regionalism.

As encouraging as these advances and continuing publishing efforts are for the field, the signs of backsliding must also be recognized. The most destructive blows to the field come in the form of cutbacks in Midwestern history departments, which have been hobbled by downsizings.[8] These reductions mean there are a lot fewer historians employed in the Midwest near regional archival collections and capable of diving into Midwestern history projects. Some professors who have survived the age of budget cuts are departing academia on their own, as described in the grim and growing body of "quit lit," leaving behind interrupted research agendas and books unwritten.[9] The overall precarity of the profession mitigates against the sort of long-term, deeply researched book projects that once were the bone and sinew of the field of history. Formerly vibrant forums for presenting work on the Midwest have also been terminated. This includes both the Missouri Valley History Conference and the Mid-America Conference on History, which over the years generated thousands of research papers that commonly led to journal articles.[10] The graduate students who used to present papers at these conferences are also thinner on the ground due to the diminishment of Midwestern PhD programs in history.[11]

Publishing outlets have also suffered. The online journal *Studies in Midwestern History* petered out when the pandemic hit and remains dormant. Truman State University Press in Missouri died as did, in earlier years, Iowa State University Press, the University of South Dakota Press, Bowling Green State University Press in Ohio, and Sunflower University Press in Manhattan, Kansas. Most recently, the University of Cincinnati Press shut down. The University of Missouri Press and the University Press of Kansas were both targeted for closure but rallied support and survived.[12] Northern Illinois University Press weathered a storm after campus bureaucrats deemed it "nonessential" and carried on by becoming an imprint of Cornell University Press, a not ideal result for those who want to see Midwestern outlets assert some independence, promote cultural regionalism, and generally escape Eastern control.[13] Some journals that once took an interest in Midwestern topics, such as the old *Minnesota Review*, have lost all connection to the region.[14] Other Midwest-focused journals have straight-up died: *Upper Midwest History, Midwest Review, Mid-America, The Old Northwest, Chicago Books in Review, Heritage of the Great Plains, Midwest Gothic, Old Northwest Review, Wapsipinicon Almanac,* and *Flyover Country Review.*[15] In early 2025, news spread that the journals *Annals of Iowa* and *Ohio History* were being shuttered.

As bad as the loss of journals is for regional studies, even worse is the closure of colleges in the region which could potentially house journals and employ article-writing professors. Closed colleges include Finlandia University in northern Michigan, which had a specialization in Finnish and Nordic studies geared toward the Upper Peninsula; Presentation College in South Dakota, which was home to a professor active in regional studies; Iowa Wesleyan University in Mt. Pleasant; Cardinal Stritch University in Milwaukee; Fontbonne University in St. Louis; three branches of the University of Wisconsin system; and, in Ohio, Chatfield College, Notre Dame College, and a satellite of Ohio University in Proctorville.[16] In a related matter, no Midwestern university is known as a home for doctoral work focused on the Midwest, especially after the termination of the graduate program in history at Iowa State University.[17]

Examining the advances and setbacks in the field and attempting to determine the degree of progress that has been made or the level of backsliding suffered requires the use of measurements that yield imprecise findings. Whatever the calculus, and despite many hard-won victories for the field, one cannot shake the feeling of being, in the end, up against it. In comparison to the Midwest, the field of Southern studies is massive and supported by dozens of major titles surveying the history of the region. So is Western history, which has exploded since the "New Western History" battles of the 1980s. While many universities, including in the Midwest, offer courses on Southern history and Western history, the number of courses offered on the history of the Midwest hovers between slim and none, *even in the Midwest*.[18] The fields of Southern and Western history also benefit from a powerful archipelago of research institutes and academic centers that aid their fields by providing fellowships and writing time for scholars and by hosting conferences, seminars, and workshops where research can be discussed and refined. The absence of college courses and research centers within the Midwest is a major problem because hoping for assistance from outside the region is unlikely to be a winning strategy. The trade publishers of New York, for example, who exert much power in the wider culture, are unlikely to boost the field.[19] The owner of The Raven Book Store in Lawrence, Kansas, when the University Press of Kansas was in danger of closing, noted how "corporate publishing has long held a coastal bias" and highlighted the "number of literary novels set in Brooklyn" when making the case for keeping Midwestern university presses going.[20] Literary agents and New York's commercial publishers are not combing the interior of the country desperately searching for the next hot book on Midwestern history.

To counteract these forces and limited resources and overcome decades of neglect, Midwestern studies needs a forceful institutional intervention. This could come in the form of a new Institute for Midwestern Studies, an entity for promoting culture that now does not exist in the region. The South and West, as noted, benefit from several such entities that actively promote the study of their respective regions while the Midwest lags far behind. If such a center could be established, it could promote the exploration of all angles of Midwestern history and create a platform for a variety of the region's voices. It could also host a new *Midwest Review of Books*, comparable to *The New York Review of Books*, the *London Review of Books*, or the *Los Angeles Review of Books*. While it would discuss books and intellectual life generally, the *Midwest Review of Books* would pay particular attention to books and writing about the Midwest and bring to such discussions a Midwestern sensibility, thereby injecting an important perspective into the national dialogue. The Institute for Midwestern Studies could also fund fellowships designed to promote the study of the region, similar to a program run by the Newberry Library in the 1950s. The institute could also host conferences, house visiting research scholars, and organize, edit, and publish important books about the Midwest. The more resources that were available, the more ambitious the plans could be.

While awaiting our Lafayette, who might never arrive, the battle must continue. Reinforcements would be a most welcome relief, but those seeking to build the field do have, in historical and comparative terms, a fair number of assets to draw on, along with the ennobling energies of a just cause. It would not be a shock to most observers that Midwestern history needs attention and that bit of conventional wisdom is essential to the theory of the case for building bigger platforms for Midwestern studies. Addressing this problem of neglect can take on some needed urgency with a dose of anticolonial passion ginned up by the realities of our distorted national culture, which is barbell-like, heavy on both ends and thin in the middle. For too long the Midwest has been dependent on coastal tastemakers, and resistance to this dynamic has supplied the necessary ardor for past bursts of cultural regionalism and can do so again.[21] Defiance of outside domination can be a powerful force, and it can galvanize our efforts to bolster and build the field, similar to embracing Simone Weil's theories of localism, rootedness, and paying attention, along with promoting the virtues of tending to the marginalized and forgotten. While larger history departments and more regional journals would be helpful, we can carry on with our existing infrastructure, relying, in particular, on the meetings of the Midwestern History Association and the Society for the Study of Midwestern Literature, along with state-oriented history conferences that persist in Ohio, Indiana, Missouri, Michigan, and South Dakota. We can also build our alliance by bringing into the fold bookstores such as Raven in Lawrence, Prairie Lights in Iowa City, and Boswell Books in Milwaukee, as well as bookseller associations such as the Great Lakes Independent Booksellers Association and the Midwest Independent Booksellers Association. So too with libraries and librarians (including presidential: Eisenhower, Ford, Hoover, Obama, Truman), museums and museum directors, historical societies, graduate students, high school teachers, social and civic clubs and churches, and various parties interested in the region who can come from any walk of life.

It can be a guerrilla effort, tapping grassroots localist energies and relying on whatever resources people and groups can give, and it can persist as long as this stage of organizing needs to continue. We can also tap the power of social media to spread the word of our efforts, a powerful organizational tool that regionalists in previous decades never conceived of using. Making clear our wishes is another important step, and the list should include the revival of conferences that have been allowed to lapse and the creation of positions in Midwestern studies at large research institutions such as the University of Minnesota and the University of Michigan. All colleges in the region should join this alliance too, however. Budgets are tight and travel money is thin so scholars at smaller institutions should cast down their bucket where they are, as Booker T. Washington said, and provide crucial leadership to this effort, reconnecting to their places and injecting needed life into the regionalist cause.[22]

When marching forward, with minimal resources or with maximalist institutional support or with something in between, some questions rise to the surface in terms of importance. What makes the Midwest distinct and different is the first among such questions and should be a guiding principle in Midwestern studies research that helps a wider public see how the Midwest compares to other regions.[23] A related matter is the boundaries of the Midwest, or the search for a general consensus about the territorial limits of the region.[24] Recent polling has greatly aided this discussion.[25] The early history of the territory that would become the Midwest, the Native American tribes of the region, exploration, the Great Power wars of the eighteenth century, the American Revolution, the founding charters and early state-making in the Midwest, and sectional tensions and ultimately the Civil War will also remain foundational issues in Midwestern studies. The nature of agrarian settlement, small-town life, civic culture, reform movements, race relations, immigration, industrialization, the emergence of stronger forms of regional identity, and the impact of world wars, depressions, and mass culture—or how modernity slammed into the traditional Midwest—will also remain critical matters for researchers to address, especially in a manner that compares Midwestern experiences to other regions. The story of Midwestern writers and intellectuals and how the region shaped their thinking and the emergence of a Midwestern sensibility provides another rich mine for inquiry.[26] Environmental history should also be a focus, especially on a micro-scale, with particular attention to subregional variations in topography that can yield smaller but critical histories of river valleys and other natural formations.[27]

Such micro-histories are a reminder of the importance of tending to smaller-scale details, to complexity, to facts on the ground, and otherwise avoiding abstractions that blind us to the smaller wrinkles of Midwestern life. One of the signature features of the New Midwestern History could be an emphasis on empiricism and transcending the theory wave and re-embracing a commitment to evidence-driven research. This common-sense Midwestern approach would help alleviate some of the problems that now beset the academy. *Middle West Review* has cut a path in this direction by adopting its "Statement of Principles" (September 2023), committing itself to free speech, open inquiry, and a heavy reliance on research and evidence.

Advancing the cause of the New Midwestern History is dependent on individual authors working in concert, as in this volume. The authors assembled here serve as learned guides to existing scholarship, provide new thinking on old questions, and offer roadmaps to future work. In chapter 1, veteran historian R. Douglas Hurt tackles the central role of farming in Midwestern life and surveys the major topics in Midwestern agricultural history from the late eighteenth to the early twenty-first century. Hurt addresses the cultures of immigrant and utopian communities and discusses the effects of ethnic labor on the meat-packing industry, vegetable fields, and agriculturally based communities, as well as noting the development of an agricultural underclass in the region. He assesses the contributions of women in organizational and policy developments in Midwestern agricultural politics and explains that the Midwest provided the economic reasons for the founding of many political organizations, both conservative and radical. His chapter suggests areas for needed research such as Native American and African American agriculture, the effects of science and technology on the environment, and the significance of twenty-first-century agricultural policy to farm families. Hurt also urges attention to oral histories to capture the experiences of late twentieth and twenty-first-century farm men and women in the age of declining farm population, increasing capital expenses, and growing farm sizes, as well as international market and government dependency.

Another foundational element of Midwestern studies is the Native American history of the region. In his chapter on Native American historiography, historian Joshua Jeffers highlights intersections in Native American and Midwestern history in order to examine the ways in which recent studies in Native American history inform the New Midwestern History. Focusing primarily on studies of removal, race, and labor, Jeffers observes that Native histories tend to use ana-lytical lenses other than that of the Midwest, which he attributes to a conceptual antagonism associated with popular narratives of Midwestern history. He argues that scholarship on Native American history offers insight into the character of Midwestern history that is often obscured in popular renderings of the region's past. Thus, a primary challenge for the New Midwestern History, Jeffers argues, is transforming popular ideas about the history and culture of the Midwest to reflect the histories of exploitation and violence that shaped the region's past and continue to inform its present. In an effort to begin to reconcile popular under-standings with the historical development of the region, Jeffers calls for a more nuanced popular representation of the Midwestern past that includes its histories of exploitation and their role in shaping the historical development of the region.

Some of the issues raised in Midwestern Native American historiography are relevant to the study of African Americans in the Midwest, who are the focus of the next three chapters. In her chapter, Ashley Howard challenges how scholars see the Midwest by locating the region within a Black Midwestern intellectual tradition. Drawing on autobiography, expressive writing, music, and other forms of vernacular expression, Howard argues that the entire field of Midwestern studies can be enriched by taking seriously the experiences and intellectual frameworks of Black Midwesterners. This critical intervention dis-pels what many think of as a discordant identity, asserting that race and region are equally influential in Black Midwesterners' expression of self. In taking this intersectional identity seriously, scholars can employ new lenses through which to "see" the Midwest, grappling with the "in-betweenness" of Black Midwestern identity. This shift brings to light not only intraregional migration but also a range of Black experiences from the horrific to the joyous, and every banal moment in between. In so doing, Howard suggests that scholars can and should cultivate new Black histories of the Midwest that neither cater to the white gaze nor care much about it. For Howard, music offers a unique avenue to explore alternative Black epistemologies given the reciprocal impact of region and race on Black culture. By identifying the racialized political economy in Midwestern cities like Dayton, Ohio, Howard argues that the lived experiences of Black people not only incubated new forms of Black culture, but that these musical forms were an assertion of Black agency within the region. Howard's Midwest contains more than meets the eye. In truly "seeing" Black Midwestern-ers, including their views, contributions, and experiential knowledge, scholars arrive at a more expansive vision of what the Midwest can be.

Moving from Howard's more modern musical forms, E. James West returns to Black cultural forms that were foundational to the Midwest. In his chapter, West focuses on the history of the development of the Black Midwestern press and its positionality within Midwestern history and African American studies. West is guided by two key concerns. First, how have Midwestern historians understood and interrogated the role of Black people (generally) and the Black press (specifically) in the region's development? Second, how have scholars of Black history (generally) and the Black press (specifically) reflected on and written about the relationship between Black Midwestern periodicals and the region they inhabited? In the period since the publication of Henry Lewis Suggs's 1996 collection *The Black Press in the Middle West*, parallel waves of scholarship have helped to reshape the fields of Midwestern history and African American studies. Focusing in particular on the Chicago *Defender* and the Omaha *Star*, but making reference to a diverse cast of Black journalists and publications, this chapter explores the productive possibilities of placing these bodies of scholarship in closer conversation. West demonstrates how, in the three decades that have passed since the publication of Suggs's landmark text, an increasing attentiveness to locality and regionality, and the transformative impact of periodical digitization and greater archival access, have helped usher in a new wave of scholarship on the Black Midwestern press. Most pressingly, West argues for the need to recenter the Black press within Midwestern history and African American studies. In doing so, West emphasizes the enduring significance of the Black press in the Midwest and the role of the region's Black periodicals in making it "the Black media capital of America and the world."

The broader world and the role of Black Midwesterners in it is the focus of Olivia Hagedorn and Erik McDuffie in their chapter about the Midwest and the African Diaspora. Hagedorn and McDuffie trace the life, activism, and overseas travels of Christine Johnson (1909–99), a brilliant and charismatic Chicago-based community organizer, teacher, writer, and world traveler. Her associates included the preeminent Black nationalist Malcolm X; Nation of Islam leader Elijah Muhammad; cultural figure Margaret Burroughs; Chicago labor activist and Communist Party leader Ishmael Flory; and Kwame Nkrumah, the founder of the West African nation of Ghana. Johnson's life reveals the history of the "diasporic Midwest." This framing resists notions of Midwestern provinciality; extends the spatial, temporal, and analytical study of the African Diaspora beyond the Atlantic Seaboard; and positions the Midwest as a germinal center of Black transnational thought, movement formation, and political action.

Johnson's work and global travels also elucidate "diasporic cultural feminism," which describes the politics and subject position of Black women cultural workers like Johnson, who used cultural politics to center working-class women within Black liberation movements worldwide. Accordingly, diasporic cultural feminism sheds light on the transnational lives and feminist practice of Johnson as she struggled to envisage global Black liberation and intersectional justice. Combined, the diasporic Midwest and diasporic cultural feminism frameworks foreground how local, regional, and global forces converged to make Chicago an epicenter of Black women's international activism. Johnson's life and globetrotting holds important implications for rethinking and dispensing with prevailing (mis)perceptions of the twentieth-century Midwest as white, heteropatriarchal, provincial flyover country. Her life locates Chicago as a site of generative potential, a space where African American women forged cutting-edge transnational movements and advocated transformative social change locally and globally. Johnson's life reminds us that the Midwest is inextricably linked to the Black world and beyond. Telling her story requires us to jettison masculinist and nationally bounded narratives of African American Midwestern history.

The call to locate the Midwest in a global context is echoed by Timothy Dean Draper in his chapter examining the place of contemporary Midwestern regional and historical scholarship in transnational historiography, especially that promoted by the Organization of American Historians' La Pietra project of the late 1990s and early twenty-first century. Since the 1990s, both the Organization of American Historians and the American Historical Association have promoted scholarship, professional development, and instructional curriculum exploring global narratives, and, as Draper argues, the question needs to be answered of not whether but *where* is the place for regional and local studies in such scholarship. After briefly reviewing the history of La Pietra and late twentieth and early twenty-first-century transnational studies, Draper discusses the revival of Midwest studies, which predated the transnational "turn" but mostly began to attract professional notice in the 2010s. Drawing on Turnerian historiography, Draper argues that there has long been a transnational element to Midwestern historiography and that there are three foundational areas of Midwestern studies that have global implications. The first such area is that of the colonial Midwest, where Native Americans, Europeans (particularly the French and English), and Africans met and negotiated power and cultural relationships from the seventeenth through late eighteenth centuries. Boundaries—both cultural and geographic—represent a second area of analysis, including the frontier and state-making of the Old Northwest and the commercial and transportation significance of the Great Lakes. The third and final area of investigation is that of immigration, where early studies of Europeans in the Midwest helped shape the fields of immigration and ethnic historiography, and more recent works, especially on Latinos in the region, reflect the changing demographics of the region and nation. Finally, Draper suggests areas through which to link the Midwest to transnational scholarship, including mission work, agriculture, science, technology, and architecture.

Emiliano Aguilar's chapter follows up on Draper's call for more attention to Latino immigration and explains how the increasing numbers of Latinas/os in the Midwest offer the field an opportunity for reflection and inclusion. While the site of recent and large migrations of Mexican, Central American, and Caribbean communities in the twenty-first century, the Midwest has served as a site of placemaking since the late nineteenth and early twentieth centuries for some Latina/o communities. In Midwestern history, however, the history of Midwestern Latina/o communities is often absent or neglected. This chapter briefly summarizes the innovative turning points the subfield has made since 2010 in reconceptualizing the place of race in the Midwest. Then the chapter discusses and briefly overviews the historiography of Latina/o Midwest scholarship. While this is not an exhaustive retelling, the chapter aims to serve as a first step in bridging the gap between Midwestern and Latina/o history. The chapter focuses on the work of early twentieth-century social scientists, such as Paul S. Taylor, and the boom in studies that coincided with the civil rights movement of the 1960s and 1970s. Aguilar argues that in reconceptualizing race in the Midwest, the field should not omit the decades-long study of the region's Latina/o demographic. The chapter highlights the urgency and need for more historiographical work that could bridge the scholarship of the Midwest with that of its Latina/o community. Ideally, this work would serve as a primer for a new generation of scholars and for an opportunity to incorporate scholarship into existing pedagogical practices and research.

In her chapter, Sara Egge moves the discussion from race and ethnicity to gender, exploring how gender defined and organized life in the Midwest. She argues that gender was elastic and that gender roles were weak, allowing people to bend norms and defy assumptions. Midwesterners demonstrated and performed contradictory gender norms easily and often, without explanations or qualms that doing so was messy or uncomfortable. This gender fluidity existed even as many Midwesterners ascribed to heteronormative or patriarchal systems. In this way, gender elasticity emerged at the intersection of divergent notions of an essential Midwest, ideas that called the region both anti-capitalist and capitalist, nurturing and rugged, communal and individualist, relational and isolated, innovative and bland. Egge unravels this history by focusing on a household in Chicago. A widow and her two wards lived together because gender shaped how regional residents understood where and with whom they could live. Gender also helped to create the built environment in which the trio lived, with its railroads, stock yards, agricultural fairgrounds, and parks all part of a landscape forged by patriarchal designs about space. Educational, religious, and civic cultures also emerged out of gender constructs, and Egge documents how gender created both segregated and integrated institutions, like libraries, opera houses, and settlement houses. People living across the Midwest formed organizations that built public spaces like these, and Egge takes us beyond Illinois with examples from across the region. Finally, Egge showcases how queer Midwesterners blazed trails of protest using the press, local politics, and the body to challenge, sometimes by only their presence, the white masculinist assumptions linked to the region. Protest became an essential quality of the region because queer people spoke out against inequality, state-supported violence, and exclusionary policies.

After a focus on race, ethnicity, and gender, the book moves into a discussion of various subfields in Midwestern studies that focus on the region's literature and art, its geography and regional identity, its environmental history, its iconic small towns, and, finally, its recent intellectual history. In her chapter, Marcia Noe adapts the feminist studies concept of the three waves of the women's movement to analyze the trajectory of developments in Midwestern literary studies over the past sixty-two years. Noe argues that first-wave work focused on identifying the essential characteristics of the Midwest and how this project could not achieve its goal given the diversity, complexity, and paradoxical elements of the Midwest. While second-wave recovery work of little-known Midwestern authors is valuable and ongoing, third-wave work, intersectional and outward looking, has taken twenty-first-century Midwestern literary scholars in four directions: using poststructuralist critical approaches; applying methodologies from other disciplines; exploring how the Midwest intersects with other regions and nations; and participating in the critical turn in recent regional scholarship. Noe discusses fourteen such works of regional scholarship published during the past twenty years and identifies several common emphases: nostalgia; amorphous regional identity; the destructive societal consequences of the death of the agrarian dream; and a commitment to a communitarian ethos and a spiritual connection to nature as remedies for the region's ills. Several of these works of scholarship discuss the novels of Nebraskan Willa Cather, emphasizing these novels' commitment to community and nature and their consequent inspirational impact.

Noe's focus on nature is carried forward by Camden Burd, who explores the development of the field of environmental history and its relation to the Midwest. Burd demonstrates that regional topics have been central in shaping the contours of environmental history, often serving as the basis for many field-defining works. This is due, he argues, to the unique social, economic, and ecological realities of the Midwest. Additionally, Burd outlines the several themes that have come to define Midwestern environmental history: agriculture; extraction; conservation/environmentalism/recreation; and industry/urbanity. Finally, he reflects on the development of Midwestern regional studies and proposes that scholars interested in further developing the field must consider its environmental history. Believing that there is an environmental lens through which to understand the social, political, and cultural histories of the region, Burd argues that historians of the Midwest must more thoroughly dive into the unique relationships Midwesterners have had with the natural world. Ultimately, Burd's chapter serves as an important resource for organizing the vast field of Midwestern environmental history while offering thoughtful prompts to consider for those interested in developing the broader field of Midwestern studies.

Midwestern environmental history is directly related to the region's geography. In his chapter, the geographer Timothy Anderson examines some of the powerful images, tropes, and discourses associated with the Midwest, a place that for many Americans is at once real and perceived, both concrete and imagined. He argues that a number of these discourses and images are deeply embedded in the nation's psyche and its idealized identities. These concepts are examined through a synopsis of how cultural and historical geographers in particular have approached the Midwest as a place. First, leading authors and dominant research themes in the geographic literature on the region since roughly the 1920s are identified. This is followed by a discussion of some of the central concepts arising from the long tradition of geographic scholarship concerning the Midwest. Finally, an overview of recent critiques of these "traditional" studies by a new generation of geographers over the past two decades is presented. Prior to about 1980, cultural and historical geographers focused their research on defining and delimiting the Midwest as a distinctive subcultural region and then documenting its characteristic cultural landscape features. Such scholarship was preoccupied with the analysis of folk cultural landscape elements and charting landscape changes stemming from successive episodes of settlement. After 1980, geographers studying the Midwest shifted much of their attention to identifying and mapping migration streams into the region from East Coast locales during the early modern period in an effort to better understand large-scale social and historical settlement processes at work in inter-regional migrations. Most recently, technological advances have allowed the compilation of very large electronic databases of genealogical and genetic data that a newer generation of geographers is using to develop more accurate spatial-temporal models of intergenerational migration across North America. The Midwest once again figures prominently in these newer studies, playing a central role as the staging ground for transregional migration streams that linked the East and West coasts.

Anderson's focus on Midwestern boundaries and regional identity receives additional attention from Zachary Michael Jack. For more than a half-century, Jack explains in his chapter, innovative interdisciplinary scholars have searched for datasets capable of ascertaining and recording the ebb and flow of regional identity and prominence. Though he regarded his data as inadequate, pioneering cultural geographer James R. Shortridge cautiously mapped regional affiliations in the 1980s based on more than ten thousand third-party consumer warranty cards in which purchasers were asked to identify their home region as Midwest, South, East, or West. Decades later in December 2010, Google released its eagerly awaited Google Ngram Viewer, an online search engine capable of charting frequencies of search strings using a yearly count of words found in digitized print sources published between 1800 and 2019. Early studies by Jean-Baptiste Michel at Harvard claimed it would be a game-changing technology in what Michel called "culturomics," the statistical study of linguistic and cultural phenomena. Culturomics, Michel and his coauthors claimed, would "extend the boundaries of rigorous quantitative inquiry to a wide array of new phenomena spanning the social sciences and the humanities," including cultural geography.[28] Google's Ngram Viewer sheds light on many of the questions Shortridge and his colleagues attempted to answer with the limited datasets of the 1980s, this time with the benefit of an estimated half a trillion words across more than fifteen million scanned publications searched by Google Ngram. While the Ngram Viewer cannot necessarily address the emotional and subjective resonances implicit in regional identity, it can determine when regional calling cards such as "Midwest" and "Heartland" began appearing in books and periodicals in statistically significant ways; graphically illustrate the use of specified words over time (including pinpointing the years in which use of the word "Midwest" peaked and valleyed in the corpus of American English); and extrapolate future trends (if the Ngram Viewer shows a particular term rising or falling in percentage use from 2000 to 2019, for instance, it would be possible to project near-future gains or losses). Culturomics can help concretize the feeling among many contemporary scholars that the Midwest has quietly become a "lost" or forgotten region, in as much as the Ngram Viewer graphically illustrates a decades-long decline in the use of "Midwest" and adjacent regional metonymic expressions such as "Heartland" and "Heartland values."

Environmental history, geography, and Midwestern regional identity are directly tied to the critical role of the land itself in Midwestern studies. As the art historian Jason Weems explains in his chapter, the Midwestern landscape has been frequently analogized to the human figure, so much so that the transposition of the two forms is arguably foundational to Midwestern identity. Pioneers likened the open horizon to the human spirit and the plow-resistant sod to their own hardened bodies and determination. A generation later, the anthropomorphized landscape became a cipher for the experiences of economic, technological, and social modernization. Still today, artists evoke the humanity of the land to unearth the possibilities and foreclosures of the Midwestern social body in relation to issues of gender, race, and belonging. Weems asks how and to what degree has this Midwestern analogy of human figure to landform (and vice versa) constituted the region, and more importantly to what ends? Working across the region's post Euro-American settlement history, Weems unpacks the landscape to human figure analogy to offer a new critical understanding of Midwestern identity and, moreover, a call for a more subtle and multifaceted anatomization of the ways that we perceive the region and shape our understanding of its past, present, and future. Weems asks what might be gained if we moved beyond analogy and metaphor and take seriously the possibilities of analyzing the region—in addition to and alongside its inhabitants—as a materially defined and embodied subject and how we might redraw the relationship between the region's human, living nonhuman, and nonliving elements. The propensity of Midwestern image makers to envision the region as a living and often anthropomorphized form is born of an array of unusually visceral and psychologically laden affinities that arise when a landscape and its inhabitants act upon each other in equally constitutive and often ineffable ways. In other words, to really capture the history and meaning of the Midwest requires more than simply recognizing that a tight connection exists between people and the land. Instead, Weems argues that we must unlock this relationship through recognition of its two-way nature. This means moving beyond frameworks that focus only on human authority over the land to instead perceive how the land also exerts power over and sometimes against its human inhabitants, and how those inhabitants respond to its capacity to do so.

If the land has been central to Midwestern imagery and identity, so has the small town. By the middle of the twentieth century, Jason Stacy explains in his chapter, the Midwestern small town had become representative of the nation itself in the popular mind. Stacy's chapter traces three trends that laid a foundation for this synecdoche: the formation of "Main Streets" out of Midwestern settlement patterns; the maturation of the Midwestern industrial-agricultural economy in the late nineteenth century; and two literary trends that emerged during the generation that bridged the nineteenth and twentieth centuries. Stacy then analyzes the way this synecdoche proved adaptable after 1945 and offered both a bulwark of American identity against economic and social flux, as well as a seat for self-actualization in the face of a supposedly repressive dominant culture. Finally, Stacy briefly considers the "othering" of the small town in twenty-first-century popular media. Throughout, Stacy traces the ways in which popular culture confected economic and social changes into tropes where the Midwestern small town proved normative as a place both wholesomely American and wholly repressive. Unpacking this myth's origins, life-cycle, decline, and modern variants advances an accurate and robust Midwestern history by situating the mythologized Midwestern town within its historical context and thereby undermines the seeming timelessness of its claims.

Finally, in his chapter, Andrew Seal surveys intellectual life in the Midwest since the 2010s and finds that it has been both tumultuous and productive. Several new print and digital publications and publishers have given more Midwesterners space to explore the region from new angles. Events of national or global significance occurring in the Midwest have brought greater attention from outside and have prompted Midwesterners to reckon more seriously with the region's histories of racism and violence. Yet Midwestern writers still struggle with the question of how to explain what is distinctive and important about their region to non-Midwesterners. Reacting to what they perceive as condescension (especially from coastal elites), Midwestern writers often end up anticipating arguments that have not been made and answering questions that have not been asked. Seal's chapter points out how Midwestern writers' concern with the imagined opinions of outsiders prevents their own books, essays, and other cultural products from fully exploring their own experiences of, attitudes toward, and position in, the Midwest. But it also looks to several emerging writers whose work points toward new possibilities for thinking about Midwestern identity and Midwestern history. These writers have tapped into their own ambivalence about growing up in and continuing to live in the Midwest. Neither suppressing their feelings of alienation nor using them as a reason to abandon the region, these writers instead reflect on the causes of their alienation as conditions that are shared among many people. They feel that they are attached to but not fully accepted by their hometown or home state or home region, and they have the humility and perspicacity to recognize that many other Midwesterners—and many people outside the Midwest—experience something very similar.

The issues raised and the questions asked in *Between Loving and Leaving* are designed to keep the field active and vibrant for another ten years when, one hopes, more stock will be taken and more advances in the field will be recognized. The hazardous state of academe and the chronic need for additional resources makes this future hopeful day less than certain, however. More victories for the field will require a steady effort, with whatever resources can be found, and with some hard work and a few breaks more Americans will hear the voices of Midwestern studies and better understand the center of the country.

## NOTES

1. Jon K. Lauck, "The Origins and Progress of the Midwestern History Association, 2013–2016," *Studies in Midwestern History* 2, no. 11 (2016): 139–49.

2. *Middle West Review* offered, for example, symposia about books such as David McCullough's *The Pioneers* (vol. 7, no. 1, 2020), Russell Nye's *Midwestern Progressive Politics* (vol. 8, no. 1, 2021), Britt Halvorson and Joshua Reno's *Imagining the Heartland* (vol. 9, no. 1, 2022 and vol. 9, no. 2, 2023), and Tom Schaller and Paul Waldman's *White Rural Rage* (vol. 11, no. 1, 2024), as well as a symposium on "Fargo" (both the film and the series) (vol. 5, no. 2, 2019). The journal also published many review essays connecting similar books together and interviewed prominent Midwestern intellectuals and writers.

3. See Jon K. Lauck, ed., *The Midwestern Moment: The Forgotten World of Early Twentieth-Century Midwestern Regionalism, 1880–1940* (Hastings College Press, 2017) and Lauck, ed., *The Making of the Midwest: Essays on the Formation of Midwestern Identity, 1787–1900* (Hastings College Press, 2020).

4. Jon K. Lauck, Gleaves Whitney, and Joseph Hogan, eds., *Finding a New Midwestern History* (University of Nebraska Press, 2018).

5. Claire Kirch, "Belt Publishing Celebrates the Industrial Midwest," *Publishers Weekly*, July 23, 2015.

6. Alexander Finkelstein and Anne F. Hyde, eds., *Reconsidering Regions in an Era of New Nationalism* (University of Nebraska Press, 2023).

7. Jon K. Lauck and Gleaves Whitney, eds., *North Country: Essays on the Upper Midwest and Regional Identity* (University of Oklahoma Press, 2023).

8. Jon K. Lauck, "The Ongoing History Crisis," *Middle West Review* 9, no. 1 (2022): vii–xii. See also the "Symposium on the History Jobs Crisis" in *Middle West Review* 9, no. 2 (2023): 177–92.

9. Lukas Moe, "Love's Labor, Lost and Found: Academia, 'Quit Lit,' and the Great Resignation," *Los Angeles Review of Books*, June 7, 2022. See also Anna Thompson Hajdik, "Teaching the Midwest in an Era of Precarity," *Middle West Review* 10, no. 2 (2024): 77–83.

10. On the history of these long-running conferences, see James Giglio, "A History of the Mid-America Conference on History," *Studies in Midwestern History* 1, no. 10 (2015): 89–101 and Oliver B. Pollak and Harl A. Dalstrom, "Omaha's Missouri Valley History Conference, 1958–2009: An Intellectual History," *Studies in Midwestern History* 2, no. 2 (2016): 13–32.

11. Jon K. Lauck, "The Contraction of History Ph.D. Programs in the Midwest," *Middle West Review* 11, no. 1 (2024): xi–xiii.

12. John Eligon, "Plan to Close University of Missouri Press Stirs Anger," *New York Times*, July 17, 2012; Danny Caine, "Why Kansans Must Not Allow Budget Cuts to Close the University Press of Kansas," *Kansas Reflector*, February 14, 2021.

13. Scott Jaschik, "When a University Press Is Deemed 'Nonessential,'" *Inside Higher Ed*, May 23, 2016; Calvin Reid, "Northern Illinois University Press Partners with Cornell University Press," *Publishers Weekly*, April 4, 2019.

14. Jon K. Lauck, "How Regionalism Dies: The Intellectual Journey of *The Minnesota Review*," *MidAmerica* 41 (2014): 80–87.

15. On the demise of *The Old Northwest* and *Mid-America*, see David M. Fahey, "The Rise and Fall of a Midwestern Studies Journal: *The Old Northwest*, 1975–1992," *Studies in Midwestern History* 1, no. 9 (2018): 84–88 and Theodore J. Karamanski, "A Catholic History of the Heartland: The Rise and Fall of *MidAmerica: An Historical Review*," *Studies in Midwestern History* 2, no. 1 (2018): 1–12. In 2017, when focusing on the work of *Midwest Gothic, Neat Magazine, Old Northwest Review*, and the book series New Stories from the Midwest, Patricia Oman noted the "current renaissance in Midwestern literature." All of these publications have now ceased operations. Oman, "Publishing from Flyover Country: The Rejection of Heartland Iconography by Contemporary Midwestern Literary Magazines," *Midwestern Miscellany* 45 (Spring 2017), 64.

16. Jeff Bremer, "The Death of a Midwestern College," *Middle West Review* 10, no. 1 (2023): 211–18.

17. Roger Riley, "Cuts Makes History a Thing of the Past at Iowa State," *WHO13 Des Moines News*, June 6, 2022; Pamela Riney-Kehrberg, "The Future of Midwestern History: A Gloomy View from the Middle Land," *Middle West Review* 10, no. 2 (2024):

159–64. Northwestern University in Chicago has focused to a certain extent on Chicago history and is interested in broadening its focus to the larger Midwest.

18. Kevin Mason, "In the Shadow of the South and West: Centering Studies of Midwestern History," *Middle West Review* 10, no. 1 (2023): 237–41.

19. Patricia Nelson Limerick's book on the American West, *Legacy of Conquest: The Unbroken Past of the American West* (W. W. Norton, 1987), was published by a major New York publisher and thus helped define the field of Western history for a broad audience, which was already amenable and conditioned to buying books about the field via Western movies, television shows, and pulp fiction. See Jon K. Lauck, "An Interview with Patricia Nelson Limerick," *Middle West Review* 10, no. 2 (2024): 301–68.

20. Caine, "Why Kansans Must Not Allow Budget Cuts."

21. On earlier episodes of Midwestern regionalism, see Robert L. Dorman, *Revolt of the Provinces: The Regionalist Movement in America, 1920–1945* (University of North Carolina Press, 1993) and Jon K. Lauck, *From Warm Center to Ragged Edge: The Erosion of Midwestern Literary and Historical Regionalism, 1920–1965* (University of Iowa Press, 2017).

22. David B. Danbom, "'Cast Down Your Bucket Where You Are': Professional Historians and Local History," *South Dakota History* 33, no. 3 (2003): 263–73.

23. See, for example, Jon K. Lauck, "Not the South: A Critical Angle on Midwestern History," *Great Lakes Review*, July 2023.

24. For treatments of three Midwestern borders, see Jon K. Lauck, ed., *The Interior Borderlands: Regional Identity in the Midwest and Great Plains* (Center for Western Studies, 2019); Jon K. Lauck and Gleaves Whitney, eds., *Where the East Meets the Midwest: Essays on a Regional Borderland* (Kent State University Press, 2025); and Lauck and Whitney, *North Country*. The crucial next step is a volume on the Midwestern/Southern borderlands.

25. Jon K. Lauck, "Finding the Boundaries of the American Midwest," *Middle West Review* 10, no. 2 (2024): xi–xx.

26. See Joseph Hogan, Jon K. Lauck, Paul Murphy, Andrew Seal, and Gleaves Whitney, eds., *The Sower and the Seer: Perspectives on the Intellectual History of the American Midwest* (Wisconsin State Historical Society Press, 2021).

27. See, for example, David S. Faldet, *Oneota Flow: The Upper Iowa River and Its People* (University of Iowa Press, 2009); Jon K. Lauck, ed., *Heartland River: A Cultural and Environmental History of the Big Sioux River Valley* (Center for Western Studies, 2022); Cheri Register, *The Big Marsh: The Story of a Lost Landscape* (Minnesota Historical Society Press, 2016); Ryan Schnurr, *In the Watershed: A Journey Down the Maumee River* (Belt Publishing, 2017); Lisa Knopp, *What the River Carries: Encounters with the Mississippi, Missouri, and Platte* (University of Nebraska Press, 2012); Ryan Allen and Brian T. Hazlett, eds., *On Common Ground: Learning and Living in the Loess Hills* (Ice Cube Press, 2023).

28. Jean Baptiste Michel et al, "Quantitative Analysis of Culture Using Millions of Digitized Books," *Science* 331, no. 6014 (2010): 176.

R. DOUGLAS HURT

**1**

# MIDWESTERN FARMING

## Past and Present

The agricultural history of the Midwest often inadvertently implies an isolated self-centeredness. The Midwest, however, has always been connected to national and world markets since the first flatboat loaded with Western Reserve cheese and butter descended the Ohio River for New Orleans in the late eighteenth century followed by cargoes of wheat loaded on steamboats at Minneapolis in 1823, and wind-driven freighters carrying barrels of pork and flour from the Upper Midwest to Buffalo beginning in 1825 for transshipment on the Erie Canal to markets in New York City and the world beyond. All of these economic developments belie the stereotype of regional economic isolation that led to political isolationism. While the assumption of economic isolation is demonstrably incorrect, the latter has more than a grain of truth depending on time and place, both of which indicate the dangers of linking the findings of one state's history across centuries to a subsection of the region.[1]

Although settlers began claiming land west and north of the Ohio River during the late eighteenth and early nineteenth centuries, not until the Treaty of Ghent ended the War of 1812 did they rapidly and aggressively take up the land, legally and illegally. Many succeeded and others failed, but land ownership promised the possibility of independence and economic security. Northerners and Southerners mixed their cultures and their agricultural methods. Soon a host of immigrants from abroad contributed to agricultural life in the countryside. In time, new developments in science and technology transformed agriculture and enabled the settlement of lands west of the Missouri River in Kansas and Nebraska and into the prairie lands of eastern South and North Dakota. The blending of cultures, settlement to the western and northern areas of the Midwest, and the economic, social, and political development of small communities, as well as ethnic clannishness and amalgamation mark much of the region's history into the early twentieth century. By the twenty-first century, Midwestern agricultural and rural life had become simpler because of less crop diversity and fewer farms, people, and viable communities. It also became more complex with large-scale farms, off-the-farm employment, particularly for women, and an increasing reliance on expensive science and technology to maintain, if not increase, production.[2]

These developments essentially ended Native American agriculture in the Midwest east of the Mississippi River, except for subsistence production, such as the raising of wild rice by the Menominee. The removal of the Native cultural groups during the early and mid-nineteenth century and their relocation in the Great Plains substantially failed due to the environment and the vacuous promises of agricultural support by the federal government. Much has been written about the Indian boarding schools and rudimentary agricultural education for Indian boys, as well as the efforts of the Bureau of Indian Affairs to promote cattle raising on the reservations in the Great Plains. However, histories are needed of the social and economic aspects of Native American agriculture, including livestock raising in the post–New Deal period, particularly during the late twentieth and early twenty-first centuries.[3]

Moreover, much research remains to be done concerning the agriculture of African American farmers during the late nineteenth and early twentieth centuries. The general parameters of African American agriculture in the Midwest often begins with Black migration into the region from the post–Civil War South during the late nineteenth century. The settlement of the Exodusters in Kansas during the late 1870s and early 1880s gave freedom, economic opportunity, and security to a select few who fled racism in the Reconstruction South. African Americans established farm communities in every Midwestern state. Some squatted on public lands, purchased small acreages, or rented. Although land ownership provided economic advantages for these farmers, increasing commercialization and costly agricultural specialization during the late nineteenth century limited their possibilities. This agricultural population aged, and the children looked beyond the farm for better opportunities. Marginal farmers often sold out and moved on, but others stayed, holding fast to the land and their way of life. They lived relatively isolated lives and had limited contact with neighboring white communities, and racial discrimination remained an ever-present burden. Neither rich nor poor, they enjoyed financial security and stability, but they were out of mainstream Midwestern agricultural and rural life by the late twentieth century. Specialty production for niche, local markets and government programs that provided monetary support, however, helped many African American farmers remain on the land. The few Black farmers who had large acreages invested in fertilizers, pesticides, hybrid seeds, and machinery like their white peers. Many, if not most, African American farmers measured success not by acreages and machinery owned or individual wealth but by their rural lifestyle and close community interactions.[4]

Immigrant farm men and women tended to settle close together during the nineteenth century for mutual support. These settlers established tightly knit communities that maintained their cultural traditions, adapted to the Midwestern environment, and selectively participated in a market economy. By the twentieth century, these settlements remained marked by town and family names and usually a Lutheran or Catholic church long after the inhabitants no longer spoke the native language of their parents and grandparents. In some cases, immigrants established utopian, communal settlements, such as the Shakers in Ohio, New Harmony, Indiana, the Amana communities in Iowa, the Bishop Hill Commune in Illinois, and Zoar, Ohio. These communities often had been founded for the purposes of practicing religious or individual freedom, but their success depended on agriculture. Utopian settlements along with the inclusion of the various German, Scandinavian, and Irish settlements, among others, merit inclusion in any synthesis of Midwestern history.[5]

By the late twentieth century, the newly emerging field of environmental history increasingly influenced the history of Midwestern agriculture. From the Dust Bowl to inorganic chemical fertilizers, pesticides, and herbicides, to genetically modified crops, historians began to study the relationship of farmers with the natural environment. Midwestern farmers adopted land-transforming technologies, both chemical and hardware, that changed the land and economy as well as the social and cultural lives of farm men and women. A resurgence of public interest in organic agriculture during the late twentieth and early twenty-first centuries also encouraged scholars to investigate the tensions between commercial producers and organic, often noncommercial, farmers. One group believed that it alone could produce a Green Revolution via capital-intensive agriculture based on chemicals and hybrid and genetically modified seeds, and the other contended that it could be achieved only by preserving the health of the land by eschewing the application of inorganic chemicals to the soil.[6]

Regarding the industrialization of Midwestern agriculture, the meatpacking industry changed significantly during the nineteenth century. During the early 1820s, for example, Cincinnati earned the sobriquet of "Porkopolis." The city drew upon the emerging Corn Belt for an abundant supply of hogs and the Ohio and Mississippi Rivers provided cheap transportation to market. As the settlement of the Midwest expanded, other river towns along the Wabash, Illinois, and Missouri Rivers developed smaller-scale meatpacking industries. By the late nineteenth century, however, five meatpacking companies in Chicago dominated the Midwestern meatpacking industry, and meatpacking drove industrial-agricultural production and employment in other regional cities. By 1900, the Chicago plants of Armor, Swift, and Morris ranked among the major employers of the nation.[7]

After the turn of the twentieth century, smaller, independent meatpackers began purchasing livestock from farmers directly at local auctions. Hogs and later cattle could be transported cheaper by truck than by railroad. Iowa, Minnesota, and Wisconsin became major locations for the direct buying of hogs and the location of packing plants. By 1950, employment at the terminal meatpackers had declined significantly. As the meatpacking industry moved west, corporate consolidations eliminated most small-scale businesses. The packers increasingly specialized in the purchase and slaughter of hogs. Beef processors moved to the Great Plains area of Nebraska, Colorado, and Kansas where they drew upon large-scale cattle feedlots to which farmers sold grain, alfalfa, and cattle. Vertical integration enabled the packers to raise and slaughter cattle efficiently and transport precut, frozen, boxed beef to grocery stores and restaurants across the nation. The days of sending chilled carcasses to butchers in distant towns and cities soon lay in the distant past. As the meatpackers moved west to capitalize on irrigated feed grains and an abundant supply of stocker cattle, they also relied on cheap immigrant labor, primarily Latinx, then increasingly African and Asian.[8]

African Americans, Irish, Germans, and Eastern European immigrants dominated the workforce of the meatpackers in Chicago, Omaha, Kansas City, East St. Louis, and Milwaukee during the late nineteenth and early twentieth centuries. Native-born whites held most of the meatpacking jobs in the smaller stockyard cities in Iowa, Minnesota, Wisconsin, and Kansas. In 1911, white women held 11 percent of the meatpacking jobs in Chicago. Ethnic and racial tensions prevented a strong union movement in the meatpacking industry until the late 1930s and early 1940s when the Congress of Industrial Organizations (CIO) organized the Big Four packing plants in the major terminal marketing cities. The CIO Packinghouse Workers Organizing Committee, succeeded by the United Packinghouse Workers of America (UPWA), improved working conditions, hours, and benefits for workers. By 1953, white women constituted 13 percent and Black women 7 percent of UPWA membership, and they gained leadership roles in the union.[9]

Mexican, Latinx, and Southeast Asian agricultural workers increasingly replaced local, white workers during the twentieth and early twenty-first centuries. Between 1980 and 2005, 20 percent of the immigrants who moved to the Midwest came from Latin America. Many took jobs in the meatpacking industries. In 1986, the Immigration Reform and Control Act extended naturalization for more than two million migrants, and it served as a catalyst for Hispanic migration. By 2000, Latinx and Asian workers dominated the agriculturally related workforce. The pork packing industry remained centered in Iowa but here, too, Latinx and Southeast Asian workers predominated; however, the meatpackers successfully weakened and broke unionization efforts among these workers.[10]

During the late twentieth and early twenty-first centuries, refugees, a collective term for men and women, often in families, fleeing violence, sought a better life in the Midwest. The meatpacking industry also attracted them with jobs that did not require skills or knowledge of English. Only strong arms and backs and a willingness to work in a difficult and dangerous environment were required for employment, but the meatpacking plants offered them safety, economic security, and the dignity of work, as well as the peace of the Midwestern environment. The Catholic Church and the mosques became their sanctuary and safe harbor where religion, race, and circumstance bound them in supportive social groups. Intercultural living with native-born whites has proved challenging. Although meatpackers and non-white labor from distant lands have saved the economy and the existence of many small, Midwestern towns, and while native-born whites are friendly and helpful, even welcoming, they have felt a loss of whiteness and racial homogeneity in their communities. Racism in the sense of a reluctance or inability to reject whiteness as a superior, defining mark of exceptionalism in Midwestern life, particularly related to agriculture and the meatpacking industry, still prevails among many native-born Midwesterners. A cultural and economic tension prevails between the white community outside the meatpacking plants and the non-white community who work within them. Refugees in the Midwest live precarious lives in the meatpacking towns, and they cling to their culture and religion for a sense of security and belonging.[11]

The meatpackers stimulated the local Midwestern economies by creating trade, service, and banking centers. Retail stores, restaurants, and motels benefited. This stimulation of local economies, however, was based on low-paying, dangerous jobs. Meatpacking wages kept workers near or below the poverty line, and the industry attracted the unskilled, working poor. As a result, the meatpacking industry contributed to the rapid expansion of poverty in the rural Midwest. Language barriers and uncertain legal status reinforced and perpetuated this underclass. Towns and cities that host the meatpackers often cannot provide adequate city services, education, and housing for these workers. Community leaders, however, have sought the multiplier benefits to the local economy from the location of a meatpacking plant nearby despite its foundation on low-wage, unskilled, poorly educated, immigrant, and refugee labor. Consequently, city officials who sought the economic boost of a meatpacking plant have struggled with the need to provide adequate housing, sewage and trash collection services, medical care, religious services, as well as addressing the problems of crowded schools where English often is not the first language of the students. Workers in the Midwestern meatpacking plants do not have the opportunities for upward mobility and increased purchasing power that would enhance their standard of living. They remain a voiceless, vulnerable, underclass inextricably linked by poverty in one of the most productive agricultural regions on earth.[12]

During the twentieth century, Mexican, Mexican American, and Latinx workers followed the crops, thinning and topping sugar beets, detasseling hybrid seed corn, and picking tomatoes, berries, and other fruits and vegetables. In 1967 the Farm Labor Organizing Committee (FLOC) organized in the Midwest to improve the wages and working conditions of migrant and seasonal farmworkers and help eliminate poverty and powerlessness. It achieved limited success in Ohio and Michigan, particularly among the tomato processors and cucumber farmers. During the 1980s, the FLOC negotiated contracts with corporate growers to establish minimum wages, eliminate child labor, provide unemployment and workers' compensation, and provide social security payments. The tomato processors, such as Campbell's and Libby, however, sought to break the FLOC by requiring tomato farmers to pick their crop mechanically, thereby avoiding strikes during harvest time. If farmers wanted to raise tomatoes for sale to a major processor, they had to have a contract, and a contract required the mechanical picking of tomatoes. This requirement significantly limited the organizational work of the FLOC in the Midwest. Migrant workers, however, continue to provide important agricultural labor for the cultivation of other crops in the region.[13]

The political history of the Midwest often has emphasized the grievances of farmers. Historians of Midwestern agrarian politics have focused on the origin, development, and activities of the National Grange of the Patrons of Husbandry, National Farmers' Alliance and Industrial Union, National Farmers' Alliance, and the People's Party. While these organizations sought economic and political reform and attracted considerable attention in the Great Plains, farmers in the seven Midwestern states not part of the Great Plains pursued less vitriolic political agendas because of their voting traditions within the Democratic and Republican parties and their comparative economic security.[14]

The twentieth-century political history of the Midwest has emphasized the careers and achievements of state politicians, such as progressive Republicans Joseph L. Bristow, Peter Norbeck, Gilbert N. Haugen, and George Norris. Political biographies of Midwestern politicians who have influenced regional and national agriculture policy are probably relegated to the past, with a few exceptions, because publishers want to appeal to a wide market of general readers, and specialized studies that emphasize the life and times of agricultural leaders do not meet that marketing goal. A biography of Secretary of Agriculture Tom Visak would be a notable exception, but until his papers are available only time will tell. The new political history of Midwestern women includes their activism in agricultural organizations such as the Farm Bureau, Farmers' Union, and National Farmers Organization, as well as local and state organizations. These women earned the reputation of being strong "agrarian feminists" who have made a difference within their economic, social, and political subculture.[15]

Economic hardship has remained an important subject for the study of Midwestern agriculture. The effects of the grain embargo to the Soviet Union by the Carter administration remains controversial but not substantially or critically investigated by historians. The 1980s farm crisis has been carefully investigated in Iowa, but the effects of the economic crash for the farm community have not been substantially pursued for other Midwestern states. Important economic studies of Midwestern livestock raising that emphasize commercialization and specialization have focused on hog and cattle raising, but a comprehensive investigation of the transformations of poultry raising from the barnyard to vertically integrated agricultural enterprises remains largely unstudied. Commodity histories that focus on Midwestern crops, such as corn, sugar, beets, and soybeans, have helped broaden our knowledge of the commercialization and specialization of Midwestern agriculture as well as improved our understanding of the technological and scientific requirements to produce these crops. Studies of water mining and its ramifications for the agricultural economy and urban and rural communities in the Central Great Plains have emphasized the drawdown of the Ogallala Aquifer in Kansas and Nebraska. Recent research also has focused on the drying up of Great Plains rivers, such as the Cimarron in southwest Kansas and its effects on farming and communities in the region. Groundwater exploitation resulting in conflicts between urban and agricultural areas regarding development, access, and use, as well as regulation, remains an important subject for further research.[16]

The history of agricultural policy that applies to the Midwest can be traced in general studies that emphasize the New Deal and its legacies. Contemporary agricultural policy has changed the emphasis of providing a safety net for farmers that diverges, at least theoretically, from New Deal–based production, price support, and marketing programs. Current income guaranties provided by crop insurance and production averaging to protect farmers from an economic disaster still have their foundation in past policy, but the study of current agricultural policy remains essential to determining which policy options have benefited Midwestern farm families the most.[17]

If recent studies are indicative of future work, we can expect to see agroecology influencing the agricultural history of the Midwest. The developments in genetic engineering, livestock disease control and eradication, and state and regional histories of veterinary medicine also offer important possibilities for investigation, as do the multiplicity of linkages between the farm and commercial food processing industries. More research also needs to be done on oral history. As the farm population continues to decline, agricultural historians need to record and publish the experiences of farm families over time as they adjusted to economic, social, and political changes in the late twentieth and early twenty-first centuries.

Although few Midwestern scholars self-identify as agricultural historians because of academic job requirements for teaching, many conduct specialized research and publication in various agricultural history topics that enhance promotion in rank and their reputation as scholars. Agricultural history courses, however, are offered by only a few Midwestern universities; often they are not land-grant universities or within departments of history. The agricultural history course taught at Fort Hays State University within the Department of Agriculture is a notable example. Midwestern history departments cater to urban and suburban students, although where agricultural history is taught the classes draw students, particularly if they are given a curriculum checkoff for some coursework requirements related to science, technology, or social history. Even where the emphasis on the training of historians in agricultural history had become an important institutional identifier at Iowa State University, however, administrative decisions terminated the graduate program in Agricultural History and Rural Studies based on weak arguments of economic necessity. Put differently, the training of historians to pursue the study of Midwestern agricultural history remains the responsibility of supportive major professors working with dedicated students, but this is the way agricultural historians have been trained in the past. Faculty in history departments that do not have a graduate program can do much to increase the learning of Midwestern agricultural history by discussing various topics that relate to appropriate subject courses. Overall, the study of Midwestern agricultural history has limitless possibilities for teaching, research, and publication. Much remains to be done.[18]

## NOTES

1. Kristin L. Hoganson, *The Heartland: An American History* (Penguin Press, 2019); R. Douglas Hurt, *The Great Plains During World War II* (University of Nebraska Press, 2008); R. Douglas Hurt, *The Big Empty: The Great Plains in the Twentieth Century* (University of Arizona Press, 2011).

2. Foundational studies of the agricultural and rural history of the Midwest include R. Carlyle Buley, *The Old Northwest: Pioneer Period, 1815–1840*, 2 vols. (Indiana University Press, 1950); John G. Clark, *The Grain Trade in the Old Northwest* (University of Illinois

Press, 1966); Allan G. Bogue, *From Prairie to Corn Belt: Farming on the Illinois and Iowa Prairies in the Nineteenth Century* (Iowa State University Press, 1963); John Mack Faragher, *Sugar Creek: Life on the Illinois Prairie* (Yale University Press, 1986); David E. Schwob, *Hired Hands and Plowboys: Farm Labor in the Midwest, 1815–60* (University of Illinois Press, 1975); J. Sanford Rikoon, *Threshing in the Midwest, 1820–1940: A Study of Traditional Culture and Technological Change* (Indiana University Press, 1988); Glenda Riley, *The Female Frontier: A Comparative View of Women on the Prairie and the Plains* (University Press of Kansas, 1998); Nicole Etcheson, *The Emerging Midwest: Upland Southerners and the Political Culture of the Old Northwest, 1787–1861* (Indiana University Press, 1996); and John C. Hudson, *Making the Corn Belt: A Geographical History of Middle-Western Agriculture* (Indiana University Press, 1994). For recent studies of Midwestern agriculture and rural life, see J. L. Anderson, "Making the Rural Midwest: Commodities and Communities," in *A Companion to American Agricultural History*, ed. R. Douglas Hurt (Wiley-Blackwell, 2022) and R. Douglas Hurt, *Agriculture in the Midwest, 1815–1900* (University of Nebraska Press, 2023).

3. R. Douglas Hurt, *Indian Agriculture in America: Prehistory to the Present* (University Press of Kansas, 1987).

4. Nell Irvin Painter, *Exodusters: Black Migration to Kansas after Reconstruction* (Norton, 1989). Major works on African American farming and rural communities include Stephen A. Vincent, *Southern Seed, Northern Soil: African-American Farm Communities in the Midwest, 1765–1900* (Indiana University Press, 1999). For recent studies see Debra A. Reid, "Land Ownership and the Color Line: African American Farmers in the Heartland, 1870s–1920," in *Beyond Forty Acres and a Mule: African American Landowning Families Since Reconstruction*, ed. Debra A. Reid and Evan P. Bennett (University Press of Florida, 2012); Debra A. Reid, "The Whitest of Occupations"? African Americans in the Rural Midwest, 1940–2010," in *The Rural Midwest Since World War II*, ed. J. L. Anderson (Northern Illinois University Press, 2014); Anna Lisa Cox, "What If Manasseh Cuttler Were Black? The History of Diverse Pioneers Who Created Ohio," in *Settling Ohio: First Peoples and Beyond*, ed. Timothy G. Anderson and Brian Schoen (Ohio University Press, 2023).

5. Foundational studies for the settlement of immigrant communities include Jon Gjerde, *The Minds of the West: Ethnocultural Evolution in the Rural Midwest, 1830–1917* (University of North Carolina Press, 1997); James P. Shannon, *Catholic Colonization on the Western Frontier* (Yale University, 1957); and D. Aidan McQuillan, *Prevailing Over Time: Ethnic Adjustment on the Kansas Prairies, 1875–1925* (University of Nebraska Press, 1990). For a recent history of Zoar that includes agriculture as part of community development, see Kathleen M. Fernandez, *Zoar: The Story of an Intentional Community* (Kent State University Press, 2019).

6. Donald Worster, *Dust Bowl: The Southern Plains in the 1930s*, 25th anniversary ed. (Oxford University Press, 2004); J. L. Anderson, *Industrializing the Corn Belt: Agriculture, Technology, and Environment, 1945–1972* (Northern Illinois University Press, 2009); David D. Vail, *Chemical Lands: Pesticides, Aerial Spraying, and Health in North America's Grasslands Since 1945* (University of Alabama Press, 2018).

7. Essential studies of the Midwestern meatpacking industry include Margaret Walsh, *The Rise of the Midwestern Meat Packing Industry* (University Press of Kentucky, 1982); Wilson J. Warren, *Tied to the Great Packing Machine: The Midwest and Meat Packing* (University of Iowa Press, 2007); Wilson J. Warren, *Struggling with "Iowa's Pride": Labor Relations, Unionism, and Politics in the Rural Midwest since 1877* (University of Iowa Press, 2000); Rick Halpern, *Down on the Killing Floor: Black and White Workers in Chicago's Packinghouses, 1904–1954* (University of Illinois Press, 1997); and Dennis A. Deslippe, *Tights, Not Roses!": Unions and the Rise of Working-Class Feminism, 1945–80* (University of Illinois Press, 2000). See also William Cronon, *Nature's Metropolis: Chicago and the Great West* (Norton, 1991); Louise Carroll Wade, *Chicago's Pride: The Stockyards, Packingtown, and Environs in the Nineteenth Century* (University of Illinois Press, 1987); and Deborah Fink, *Cutting into the Meatpacking Line: Workers and Change in the Rural Midwest* (University of North Carolina Press, 1998). For a study of Mayan women meatpacking workers in Nebraska, see Ann L. Sittig and Martha Florinda González, *The Mayans Among Us: Migrant Women and the Meat Packing Industry on the Great Plains* (University of Nebraska Press, 2016).

8. John C. Hudson, *Making the Corn Belt: A Geographical History of Middle-Western Agriculture* (Indiana University Press, 1994).

9. Michael Innis-Jiménez, *The Great Migration to South Chicago, 1915–1940* (New York University Press, 2013); Roger Davis, "Hispanics in the Midwest," *Middle West Review* 6 (2019): 205–13; Sergio Gonzales, *Mexicans in Wisconsin* (Wisconsin State Historical Society Press, 2017); June Juffer, *Intimacy Across Borders: Race, Religion, and Migration in the U.S. Middle West* (Temple University Press, 2013); Anne V. Millard and Jorge Chapa, *Apple Pie and Enchiladas: Latin Newcomers in the Rural Midwest* (University of Texas Press, 2004); Lilia Fernandez, *Brown in the Windy City: Mexican and Puerto Ricans in Postwar Chicago* (University of Chicago Press, 2014); Sook Wilkinson and Victor Jew, eds., *Asian Americans in Michigan: Voices from the Midwest* (Wayne State University Press, 2015).

10. Foundational studies include Juan R. García, *Mexicans in the Midwest, 1900–1932* (University of Arizona Press, 1996); Dennis Nordin Valdés, *Al Norte: Agricultural Workers in the Great Lakes Region, 1917–1970* (University of Texas Press, 1991); and W. K. Barger and Ernesto M. Raza, *The Farm Labor Movement in the Midwest: Social Change and Adoption among Migrant Farm Workers* (University of Texas Press, 1994). See also Jim Norris, *North for the Harvest: Mexican Workers, Growers and the Sugar Beet Industry* (Minnesota Historical Society Press, 2009). For the sugar beet industry in Michigan, see Kathleen Mapes, *Sweet Tyranny: Migrant Labor, Industrial Agriculture, and Imperial Politics* (University of Illinois Press, 2009). See also Jim Norris, "Hispanics in the Midwest Since World War II," in *The Rural Midwest Since World War II*, ed. J. L. Anderson (Northern Illinois University Press, 2014).

11. Kristy Nabhan-Warren, *Meatpacking America: How Migration, Work, and Faith Unite and Divide the Heartland* (University of North Carolina Press, 2021).

12. Hudson, *Making the Corn Belt*; Fink, *Cutting into the Meatpacking Line*; Hurt, *The Big Empty*.

13. R, Douglas Hurt, *Agricultural Technology in the Twentieth Century* (Sunflower University Press, 1991).

14. John D. Hicks, *The Populist Revolt* (University of Minnesota Press, 1933); Robert C. McMath Jr., *Populist Vanguard: A History of the Southern Farmers' Alliance* (University of North Carolina Press, 1976); Jeffrey Ostler, *Prairie Populism: The Fate of Agrarian Radicalism in Kansas, Nebraska, and Iowa, 1880–1892* (University Press of Kansas, 1993); R. Alton Lee, *Principle over Party: The Farmers' Alliance and Populism in South Dakota, 1880–1900* (South Dakota State Historical Society Press, 2011); Thomas A. Woods, *Knights of the Plow: Oliver Hudson Kelly and the Origins of the Grange in Republican Ideology* (Iowa State University Press, 1991); Hurt, *Agriculture in the Midwest*.

15. Russel B. Nye, *Midwestern Progressive Politics: A Historical Study of Its Origins and Development, 1870–1958* (Michigan State University Press, 1959); Gilbert C. Fite, *Peter Norbeck: Prairie Statesman* (University of Missouri Press, 1948); Jon K. Lauck, *Thune vs Daschle: Anatomy of a High-Plains Senate Race* (University of Oklahoma Press, 2007); Jon K. Lauck, John E. Miller, and Paula M. Nelson, *The Plains Political Tradition* (South Dakota Historical Society Press, 2018); Jon K. Lauck and Catherine McNicol Stock, *The Conservative Heartland: A Political History of the Postwar American Midwest* (University Press of Kansas, 2020); Lucy Eldersveld Murphy and Wendy Venet, *Midwestern Women: Work, Community, and Leadership at the Crossroads* (Indiana University Press, 1997); Nancy K. Berlage, *Farmers Helping Farmers: The Rise of the Farm and Home Bureaus, 1914–1935* (Louisiana State University Press, 2016); Jenny Barker Devine, *On Behalf of the Family Farm: Iowa Farm Women's Activism since 1945* (University of Iowa Press, 2013); Sara Egge, *Woman Suffrage and Citizenship in the Midwest, 1870–1920* (University of Iowa Press, 2018).

16. Pamela Riney-Kehrberg, *When a Dream Dies: Agriculture, Iowa, and the Farm Crisis of the 1980s* (University Press of Kansas, 2022); Hudson, *Making the Corn Belt*; J. L. Anderson, *Capitalist Pigs: Pigs, Pork, and Power in America* (West Virginia University Press, 2019); John Opie, *Ogallala: Water for a Dry Land*, 3rd ed. (University of Nebraska Press, 2018); Lucas Bessire, *Running Out: In Search of Water on the High Plains* (Princeton University Press, 2022); Burke W. Griggs, "Irrigation Communities, Political Cultures, and the Public in the Age of Depletion," in *Bridging the Distance: Common Issues of the Rural West*, ed. David B. Danbom (University of Utah Press, 2015).

17. Jonathan Coppess, *The Fault Lines of Farm Policy: A Legislative and Political History of the Farm Bill* (University of Nebraska Press, 2018); R. Douglas Hurt, *Problems of Plenty: The American Farmer the Twentieth Century* (Ivan R. Dee, 2002).

18. Riney-Kehrberg, "Future of Midwestern History" (see introduction, n. 17); R. Douglas Hurt, "Teaching Agricultural History at Land-Grant Universities," in *Quintessentially American: Land-Grant Universities and the Making and Shaping of the Modern World, 1920–2015*, ed. Alan I. Marcus (University of Alabama Press, 2016).

JOSHUA J. JEFFERS

2

# NATIVE HISTORY, POPULAR MEMORY, AND THE NEW MIDWESTERN HISTORIOGRAPHY

During the last quarter century, numerous studies have examined Native American history in the region now known as the Midwest, but few are written as Midwestern histories. They are *in* the Midwest but not *of* the Midwest.[1] Similarly, there is a growing body of literature on Native history in the fields of labor history, urban history, the histories of race, gender, and ethnicity, and the history of tourism and activism, among others, but these studies typically do not employ the lens of Midwestern history.[2] The Native American historiography that does exist on the region focuses heavily on the colonial and early national periods, prior to the existence of a Midwest,[3] and "falls off in the middle decades of the nineteenth century."[4] Thus, despite notable exceptions, including publications in *Middle West Review* and *Ohio Valley History*, Midwestern history and Native-American-history-in-the-Midwest remain adjacent rather than integrated historiographies.

The reasons for this lie largely with the emergence and application of settler-colonial theory since 2000 or so. Settler-colonial theory contends that settler societies are framed by a "logic of elimination" that includes military conquest and occupation but also ongoing processes of legitimization and memorialization. "Invasion is a structure not an event."[5] Thus claiming the land, conquering its inhabitants, and physically occupying it is simply one facet of a larger process of destruction and creation. In other words, settler colonization is "not a relic of the past but a historical condition remade at particular moments of conflict" in the service of perpetually constructing legitimacy.[6] Settler colonialism thus involves making homelands at least as much as destroying them. Settler societies perpetually affirm their indigeneity, in part through the appropriation of Native histories and spaces. Historian Stephen Pearson, for example, describes "the settler-colonial process of indigenization" among twentieth and twenty-first century white Appalachians, which both "provides settlers with identities that imbue their lives with meaning" and allows them to position themselves as indigenous victims of American colonialism. This foundational aspect of settler colonialism is "driven by the crucial need to transform an historical tie ('we came here') into a natural one ('the land made us')."[7] While in Pearson's case the process of indigenization has come full circle, transforming settler ownership of the land into an act of decolonization, settlers in the early Midwest made the forms and processes of colonization—frontier warfare, squatting, clearing the land—the attributes of indigeneity. Through the elision of a Native American presence and the construction of the history and memory of settlement, settler societies forge indigeneity by creating historical traditions linking them to the landscape.[8] Out of this process emerges what cultural theorist Mark Rifkin labels "settler common sense—the ways the legal and political structures that enable nonnative access to indigenous territories come to be lived as given, as simply the unmarked, generic conditions of possibility for occupancy, association, history, and personhood."[9]

This framework for understanding the history of American colonialism fundamentally conflicts with powerful and ubiquitous popular beliefs concerning the Midwestern past. As anthropologist A. Lynn Smith observes, "it can be dangerous to consider Euro-American settler and Native memoryscapes in the same frame [as] settler-colonial memorials often assert a vantage point diametrically opposed to a Native one, and in the battle for dominance on a 'public theatre of memory,' memory entrepreneurs may dismiss, attempt to obliterate, or even incorporate and 'cannibalize' previously hegemonic historical traditions, resulting in a settler-colonial memoryscape that *is at war with its Indigenous counterparts.*" This "ambivalent and oppositional relationship between Euro-American and Native American memoryscapes" is at the heart of the incongruence of Native American historiography and popular understandings of the Midwestern past.[10]

In his 2017 essay, "Notes from the West to the Midwest," historian William Deverell observed that the New Western History marked a transformative historiographical shift "because it so aggressively destabilized foundations of nonacademic understandings of the West."[11] A similar destabilization in popular understandings of the Midwest remains elusive. While scholars have for decades challenged the traditional understanding of Midwestern history, a narrative of "settlement" that "obscures histories of Native presence and power" and masks the history of conquest and exploitation that underwrote regional growth has retained "considerable explanatory authority, especially at the level of popular discourse and public memory."[12] The "enduring power" of this narrative to erase Native people and obscure exploitation and violence remains "considerable and deeply problematic."[13] More than simply clearing land and building cabins, the settlement narrative is intimately bound up with specific beliefs about the culture and history of the Midwest, and it is distinctive for its selectivity and discursive power.[14] Historian Mary Lethert Wingerd notes, for example, the evidence of Native history in Minnesota—in the names of towns, schools, and rivers, in popular literature, advertising, and parks containing mounds and earthworks. But for most Minnesotans, Native people were "no more part of the making of Minnesota than dancing bears and squirrels hawking beer."[15] In this way, Native history haunts more than informs popular ideas about the Midwest.

The settlement narrative emerged from celebratory nineteenth-century histories that include a lot of biography, local lore, and town and state histories. They are the bedrock of the traditional Midwestern narrative, the Turner thesis writ small. White Americans have continually "imagined the possibility of creating a white yeoman's republic," and the settlement narrative offers a heroic origin story that obscures histories of exploitation and serves as a powerful instrument of colonization, dispossession, and erasure.[16] And it provides the foundation for the "Heartland Myth," a twentieth-century iteration in which the Midwest is the "quintessential home" of the nation, a place of "nostalgic yearnings" and "prelapsarian innocence." Like the settlement narrative, the Heartland Myth "refers to values as much as to place," and it tends to obscure the role and legacy of institutionalized forms of inequality, exploitation, violence, and dispossession in the historical development of the region.[17] But Midwestern historical development can no more be separated from histories of violence and exploitation than from its cornfields and county fairs. This impasse may help to explain why Native historiography remains largely distinct from Midwestern historiography.

Native histories in the Midwest are often counterpoints to the claims of freedom, justice, and opportunity at the core of the Heartland Myth. Moreover, historical markers, place names, and all manner of local heritage reveal the enormous "psychic investment in a highly ideological tapestry of collective (mis)memory" that is built into the Midwestern landscape in the form of street, business, school, and place names, festivals, local lore, and other markers of public memory.[18] In this way, "the frontier has erased its tracks," making it extremely difficult to transform this popular understanding even as counter-histories pile up.[19] Recent intersections in Native American and Midwestern historiography highlight the possible contours of an integrated history but also the considerable challenges that remain. Historians must find ways to broaden popular awareness of "how the romanticized past continues to influence" ideas about Midwestern history, as well as offer a more nuanced narrative of the region's past that reconciles its history of "settlement" with its history of exploitation and violence.[20] In short, the Midwest requires a more honest popular narrative of its past. Some of the heaviest lifting involves recovering lost stories and applying new perspectives to well-known events, perspectives that may well completely transform the popular understanding of those events. Consider, for example, the massacre at Bad Axe often considered the last battle east of the Mississippi. Here historians must correct the fiction that Bad Axe was a "military engagement" rather than a massacre, as well as address the layers of cultural heritage based on these flawed beliefs.[21] Recent histories of removal, race, and labor, in particular, offer clues to how Native Midwestern history might help to frame a more nuanced popular narrative of the Midwestern past.

Far more localized and fragmented than removals in the Southeast, removals north of the Ohio River took place over many years and witnessed a spectrum of struggle and perseverance. These removals helped to establish the myth of a vacant landscape but also highlight the "adaptive resistance" of Native people as they confronted American expansion.[22] At the same time, they reveal the continuation of settler colonialism through legal and extra-legal means. In the years following the War of 1812, Native leaders advanced commercial agriculture and welcomed Protestant missionaries in an effort to "create the conditions that would allow them to remain."[23] As Native communities in Ohio worked to accommodate American demands to "civilize," they faced harassment, poaching on their lands, and attacks on their homes. Confronted with the persistence of Native leaders, American negotiators turned to bribes and manipulation to secure land cessions.[24] As clamor among whites for removal intensified during the 1830s, all lands were ultimately ceded.[25] These histories make visible Native efforts to remain in the Midwest, challenge claims concerning the inevitability of Indian removal, and reveal the marriage of extra-legal violence and state pressure that characterized expansion.

In *Land Too Good for Indians: Northern Indian Removal*, historian John Bowes argues that removal represents an ongoing ethnic cleansing that manifested in a variety of ways, from "civilization" efforts and termination policies to mob violence and narratives of "victimless settlement."[26] While Bowes employs a national lens, the implications are that the Midwest emerged from an enduring, tripartite project of Indian dispossession, resource extraction, and state-building, and thus removal was a constitutive element in the processes of both regional and state formation. In this way, Bowes highlights the structural legacy of removal—regional consolidation and historical forgetting.[27] Historian Michael Witgen's *Seeing Red: Indigenous Land, American Expansion, and the Political Economy of Plunder in North America* characterizes the history of the early Midwest as a story of sacrifice and squander in which the natural resources of Anishinaabewaki, the Anishinaabeg homeland, served the emergence of an "economically successful and politically viable post-Revolutionary United States" only to be "used up and squandered" as part of a decades-long "political economy of plunder." Witgen's analysis turns the settlement narrative on its head, emphasizing the waste and destructiveness of colonization and the protracted transfer of wealth and resources.[28] The political economy of plunder, he writes, "subsidized white property ownership."[29] Witgen forces us to interrogate the freedom and opportunity so closely associated with popular ideas about the Midwest from the perspective of those for whom the narrative of Midwestern history is one of loss. The New Midwestern History must interrogate and work to communicate how the inclusion of such perspectives alters our understanding of the region's character, stereotypes, and legacy.

During the nineteenth century, concerted efforts to exploit Native timber resources introduced new forms of dispossession as the "lumber frontier's variation of settler colonialism" employed a "bewildering legal and extralegal thicket that facilitated the plunder of the region's most marketable resource." In the decades following the Civil War, local leaders raised taxes on forest lands some thirty-fold, forcing many Native landholders into foreclosure. Fraud outfits, known as "timber sharks," filed claims on Native timberlands. If the landowner did not appear at the required hearing, the land was transferred. A victim could appeal, and many did, but as complaints moved through the bureaucracy the land was stripped of timber.[30] Meanwhile, Anishinaabeg faced sustained hostility from local authorities who saw little reason to protect Native lands and resources. Viewed against the backdrop of earlier struggles by Ohio Shawnees, Wyandots, and others against removal, the assault on Anishinaabeg timber highlights the persistent, generation-over-generation nature of settler-colonial invasion and the ways in which the culture and structures of settler colonialism serve one another in the processes of dispossession.

The structures of race and racism are a case in point.[31] While recent studies highlight the malleability of race, with African American and Native American identities at times melding into one another, they also show that fixing racial categories often pitted non-whites against one another. The mid-nineteenth-century concept of race in the Midwest tended to associate "whiteness" and "civilized," which created a sociopolitical space for Natives of mixed ancestry willing to uphold the tenets of white supremacy. These "Moccasin Democrats," a powerful faction of the Minnesota Democratic Party during this period, "exercised political power in the Upper Midwest" frequently at the expense of Black people and Native traditionalists.[32] Similarly, Reverend John Stewart's early nineteenth-century missionary efforts to the Wyandots highlight how turn-of-the-twentieth-century Black progressives contrasted calls for Black citizenship with "Native American savagery." Reverend Stewart acted as an agent of cultural elimination, attacking Native traditions as a wicked affront to God, and in doing so participated in a broader project of erasure that included not only Native people but also Stewart himself and the presence of Black and mixed-race communities in the region.[33]

In Wisconsin, "contests over belonging and transitions to racialized thinking" similarly worked to efface mixed-race people. But despite a growing insistence on rigid racial lines, mixed-blood families persisted, and their histories offer an opportunity for viewing the Midwest from outside the narrative of racial fixity, where shape-shifting was a common occurrence. In her study of the "Revels kindred," historian Jennifer Kirsten Stinson observes that mixed-race families often did not separate themselves into Black, white, or Indian. But as racial categories hardened, "national anxieties" about race and citizenship brought efforts to erase multi-racial Americans and solidify racial distinctions. In the hysteria following the 1862 "Sioux Uprising," for example, "racial identity was no longer malleable." Indian ancestry "was not only reviled, it was dangerous," and Natives of mixed ancestry pursued a variety of avenues to "expunge all trace of their Indian roots." The "people in-between," once the "lynchpin of Euro-American and Indian coexistence," now only "muddied the invented narrative of civilization's harmonious triumph over a romantic but primitive and ahistorical world."[34] The presence of individuals of ambiguous racial status "belied the logic of racial distinctiveness and white purity," and thus members of the Revels family had to become "White," "Black," or "Indian."[35] While the one-drop rule prevented most Revels kindred from claiming whiteness, blood quantum prevented them from claiming Indianness. For Revels men, the loss of whiteness meant the loss of manhood, which meant the loss of citizenship. In the following decades, the imposition of racial categories restructured the "everyday derogations and kinship and social patterns" of the Revels kindred. The institutions that had once united the families of Forest County, Wisconsin were fractured along lines laid down by the cultural insistence on race fixing. Gossip and social stigma associated with darker complexions and passing by light-skinned individuals proliferated. As a result, mixed-race communities divided racially as, for many, race became thicker than blood.[36] By the twentieth century, racial categories had hardened around a biological understanding of whiteness, and mixed-bloodedness "became the post-frontier version of the Vanishing Indian."[37]

The Revels' story challenges the perception of the Midwest as monolithic, homogeneous, and white, but also illustrates the profound impact of racialization and its accrual over time. During the mid-nineteenth century, the Revels kindred "forge[d] belonging through indigenous kinship, clustered landholding, religiously inspired abolitionism, and commercial agriculture." They came to "embody the midwestern agrarian dream." By century's end, however, they were "insecurely white, problematically black, and not officially Indian," split by the racial distinctions imposed upon them.[38] The obliteration of Native and African American communities is "especially problematic" in cases like Reverend Stewart and the Revels kindred because their "presence and experiences attest to African American and Native American founders of the region."[39] During the nineteenth century, racial toleration and the possibility for racial ambiguity "diminished over time" as race became central to the "production of whites' midwesternness."[40] White beliefs about race inform how the Midwestern past and Midwestern-ness have been historically defined and understood. Thus, for

Black, Native, and mixed-race Midwesterners "shaping one's own place and narrative in the heartland . . . hinged upon how much one fit within or chafed against standard white narratives."[41]

Such histories rewrite the settlement story as a narrative of loss but also of adaptation and reinvention, a tension at the core of Native American historiography more generally.[42] In the field of Native labor history, for example, historian Chantal Norrgard's *Seasons of Change: Labor, Treaty Rights, and Ojibwe Nationhood* examines work and community among Ojibwes in Minnesota. She emphasizes the "vital connection between Ojibwe livelihoods and their political autonomy" in order to highlight labor and sovereignty as sites of colonial struggle.[43] Norrgard emphasizes the "role that labor has played in American Indian adaptability and perseverance" by "facilitat[ing] cultural production and community among Native peoples rather than a loss of identity." For Norrgard, it is a story of economic adaptation and resistance that "was intertwined with [Ojibwe] sovereignty and self-determination." Ojibwe men often took up wage labor in the timber industry, while others turned traditional activities, such as harvesting fish, berries, wild rice, and maple sugar, to commodified ends. Once the region's lumber had been cut, its minerals extracted, and fisheries depleted, tourism filled the economic void as governments shifted toward policies of conservation and recreation. Meanwhile, however, Ojibwe treaty rights eroded as state governments extended jurisdiction over Ojibwe resources and restricted Ojibwe economic activities. It was in this context that "Ojibwe economic activities took on new meaning" as a form of resistance and assertion of sovereignty against state encroachment.[44] While Norrgard emphasizes adaptation, resistance, and perseverance in the face of settler colonialism, one cannot help but see a story of destruction and colonial subjugation. Ojibwe adaptation and resistance offer examples of remarkable resilience, but their struggles highlight the precariousness of federal treaties protecting Native resources and the perniciousness of state-level actors in seeking to undermine those protections. Berrying, for example, continued merely as a vestige of the past, long replaced by a mechanized produce industry. The land was stripped of its lumber and minerals, and the challenges to Ojibwe fishing rights continue unabated.

Historian Brenda Child cautions that Native agency should not be overstated and thereby obscure the difficult and often unforgiving realities Native people faced. Drawing on her experiences and those of her extended family at Red Lake Indian Reservation, Child describes the reservation as a place of "precarious survival" that "rarely felt like freedom or sovereignty." She offers a history of life in Minnesota from an Ojibwe perspective, and the view is not one of burgeoning economic growth, but rather a hostile, dispossessed landscape of pillaged resources, unemployment, and poverty. The use of trespass laws enabled authorities to circumvent treaty rights, while game laws "criminalized the seasonal round" to protect the "lifeways and desires of sportsmen and tourists." Government-backed industrial enterprises "established a way of life destructive to the wild rice habitat," further pushing Ojibwe people to the margins.[45] Nevertheless, Child offers an intimate examination of the economic life of Ojibwe people, the roles they "ingeniously juggled," and the "extraordinarily difficult choices" required "to endure and pursue self-determination." Despite their differences, these works highlight the intersection of Native American, Midwestern, and working-class history. The social and economic challenges confronted by Native Midwesterners are often broadly experienced by working-class people; thus, working-class histories may offer a framework for a shared Midwestern past.

The related field of urban history has, for the twentieth century in particular, developed a robust Native historiography, and scholars have examined a variety of Midwestern cities, highlighting identity, community building, activism, and urban life among Native people.[46] As with Native labor histories, Native urban histories reveal creative adaptation and resilience alongside structural inequality and oppression. In *Indians on the Move: Native American Mobility and Urbanization in the Twentieth Century*, historian Douglas Miller highlights this duality, arguing that while urban Natives faced enormous challenges moving into the "belly of the settler-colonial beast," "Indianness" and urbanity are not incompatible. Rather, cities were "places of reinvention" where a "portable and pliable brand of tribal citizenship and Indigeneity" emerged, and Native migrants "achieved a degree of decolonization."[47] While Miller is telling a national story, Midwestern cities loom large. In places like Minneapolis–St. Paul, Cincinnati, Cleveland, Chicago, St. Louis, Rapid City, and others, Native people confronted the challenges and opportunities of urban life. It is for historians of the Midwest to map these stories as Midwestern, to grapple with what such adaptations and sacrifices reveal about relations of power, and to evaluate what those power relations suggest concerning the historical development of Midwestern culture and institutions. After all, from what did they "achieve a degree of decolonization?"

The field of settler-colonial urbanism seeks to "shed new light on the ways that settler constituencies produced and reinforced a racialized economy of power in the second half of the twentieth century . . . [and] to illuminate how settler prosperity, entitlement, and advantage have been realized and secured."[48] Drawing on the paradigm of indigenous decolonization, historian David Hugill argues that "postwar urban strategies and political developments (suburbanization, the expansion of the middle class, interstate construction, and inner-city devalorization)" divided urban space, "producing and sustaining discrete zones of privilege and deprivation" and cementing the "structured advantage" of some and the exclusion of others. These "settler colonial legacies, material distributions, and knowledge practices *continue* to shape collective forms of togetherness," and "moving toward anything like a politics of decolonization" demands that we actively work to undermine the "machinery of enforcement" that secures unequal material advantages and is so often invisible to those who benefit from it.[49]

This spectrum of new histories brings fundamental challenges to Midwestern history and augers for new assumptions about the character of Midwestern history and culture. As Fletcher et al. observe in the introduction to the *Ohio Valley History* special issue on Black and indigenous histories, "there is both historical and moral value in destabilizing harmful myths: revealing how the romance of the "First West" is a story of settler-colonial displacement and genocide, [but] this fable-busting must involve not only challenging the old, but creating the new: striving to salvage, contextualize, and center marginalized voices."[50] After nearly five decades of New Indian History, the old Turnerian teleology has become an ideological lens rather than a framework for understanding the past.[51] This shift transformed both the scholarship on Native American history and the popular narrative of United States history.[52] Like the New Indian History, Native Midwestern histories have broadened our understanding of the Midwest and its past, prompting new questions, debates, and challenges. While a paradigm shift on the order of the New Indian History remains beyond the horizon, Native histories in the Midwest challenge fundamental assumptions about the Midwest, its attributes, and legacy, and they highlight the chasm between what many Americans generally believe about the Midwest and what new Midwestern histories have revealed. Native American scholarship stresses the persistence, adaptation, and innovation of Native peoples in their efforts to navigate removal, adapt to rapid economic changes, and defend their sovereignty, lands, and resources. It has also made visible the dynamic structures of racism, capitalism, and settler colonialism as they manifested in the Midwest. As Midwestern histories, these studies highlight a central challenge for New

Midwestern History to bring popular beliefs about the Midwestern past in line with the historical development of the region. In her recent book, *Memory Wars: Settlers and Natives Remember Washington's Sullivan Expedition of 1779*, anthropologist A. Lynn Smith offers a history of memory making that perhaps provides a model for reconciling Native American and Midwestern historiographies. Less concerned with the veracity of specific claims in the memorials of the Sullivan expedition, Smith focuses on the "salience over time" of those stories and how they have shaped the popular historical consciousness of specific local contexts.[53] By making visible the construction of popular historical consciousness in this way, she creates space for local communities to question and evaluate long-held assumptions about the past. Moreover, the book includes examination of Native histories of these events, which highlights the convergences and divergences of these different but overlapping and simultaneous historical traditions. Smith's research provides a compelling example of integrating popular memory, local history, and Native American history that may offer a model for future Midwestern histories.

## NOTES

1. Doug Kiel, "Untaming the Mild Frontier: In Search of New Midwestern Histories," *Middle West Review* 1, no. 1 (2014): 9–38, 12; recent examples include Chantal Norrgard, *Seasons of Change: Labor, Treaty Rights, and Ojibwe Nationhood* (University of North Carolina Press, 2014); Gunlog Fur, "Indians and Immigrants—Entangled Histories," *Journal of American Ethnic History* 33, no. 3 (2014): 55–76; John P. Bowes, *Land Too Good for Indians: Northern Indian Removal* (University of Oklahoma Press, 2016); Carla Joinson, *Vanished in Hiawatha: The Story of the Canton Asylum for Insane Indians* (Nebraska University Press, 2016); Douglas K. Miller, *Indians on the Move: Native American Mobility and Urbanization in the Twentieth Century* (University of North Carolina Press, 2019); Jeffrey Ostler, *Surviving Genocide: Native Nations and the United States from the American Revolution to Bleeding Kansas* (Yale University Press, 2019); Samantha Seeley, *Race, Removal, and the Right to Remain: Migration and the Making of the United States* (University of North Carolina Press, 2021); and Michael Witgen, *Seeing Red: Indigenous Land, American Expansion, and the Political Economy of Plunder in North America* (University of North Carolina Press, 2022).

2. While the literature on race, gender, and ethnicity in the Midwest is too extensive to list here, for a summary see Jeffrey Helgeson, "Thoughts on a Critical Regional History of the Midwest: Examining the Legacies of the Dream of a White Yeoman's Republic," *Middle West Review* 5, no. 2 (2019): 33–39. On tourism and activism, see Katrina Phillips, *Staging Indigeneity: Salvage Tourism and the Performance of Native American History* (University of North Carolina Press, 2021); Katrina Phillips, "When

Grandma Went to Washington: Ojibwa Activism and the Battle over the Apostle Islands National Lakeshore," *NAIS: Journal of the Native American and Indigenous Studies Association* 8, no. 2 (2021): 29–61; Nick Estes and Jaskiran Dhillon, eds., *Standing with Standing Rock: Voices from the #NoDAPL Movement* (University of Minnesota Press, 2019); David Vivian, "Searching for Histories of Tourism in the Ohio Valley," *Ohio Valley History* 19, no. 3 (2019): 3–6; Rosalyn R. LaPier and David R. M. Beck, *City Indian: Native American Activism in Chicago, 1893–1934* (University of Nebraska Press, 2015); Julie Davis, *Survival Schools: The American Indian Movement and Community Education in the Twin Cities* (University of Minnesota Press, 2013); Melissa Rohde, "Labor and Leisure in the "Enchanted Summer Land": Anishinaabe Women's Work and the Growth of Wisconsin Tourism, 1900–1940," in *Indigenous Women and Work: From Labor to Activism*, ed. Carol Williams (University of Illinois Press, 2012).

3. I am asserting that the Midwest did not exist prior to the nineteenth century. Miamis at Kekionga in 1720 were not living in "the Midwest," for such a place did not exist. Midwest is "not an Indigenous maker of place, but rather a US spatial category that is defined, in part, by the national project of replacing Indigenous societies." Doug Kiel and James F. Brooks, "Introduction: Reframing and Reclaiming Indigenous Midwests," *Middle West Review* 2, no. 2 (2016): vii–x, vii. Samantha Seeley suggests that Americans in the early nineteenth century would have understood the region encompassing the Mid-Atlantic states and the Ohio Valley "as a coherent region, linked by migration from East to West," and it was the failure of a movement to colonize African-Americans in Ohio Country, followed by a sharp increase in white migrants and a national project of removal that brought about the emergence of the Midwest as a distinct region in the minds of Americans. Seeley, *Race, Removal, and the Right to Remain*, 17.

4. Charlene J. Fletcher, Alessandra LaRocca Link, and Matthew E. Stanley, "Introduction: Black and Indigenous Histories of the Ohio Valley," *Ohio Valley History* 20, no. 5 (2020): 1–7, 6; the editors noted that the journal had yet to publish a twentieth-century Native history.

5. Patrick Wolfe, *Settler Colonialism and the Transformation of Anthropology: The Politics and Poetics of an Ethnographic Event* (Cassell, 1999), 2.

6. Alyosha Goldstein, "Where the Nation Takes Place: Proprietary Regimes, Antistatism, and U.S. Settler Colonialism," *South Atlantic Quarterly* 107, no. 4 (2008): 833–61, 835.

7. Stephen Pearson, "'The Last Bastion of Colonialism': Appalachian Settler Colonialism and Self-Indigenization," *American Indian Culture and Research Journal* 37, no. 2 (2013): 166, 167; Lorenzo Veracini, *Settler Colonialism: A Theoretical Overview* (Palgrave Macmillan UK, 2010), 21–22, 46. In her discussion of the pillars of white supremacy, theorist Andrea Smith links the process of indigenization to that of genocide, writing that "through this logic of genocide, non-Native peoples then become the rightful inheritors of all that was indigenous—land, resources, indigenous spirituality, and culture." Andrea Smith, "Indigeneity, Settler Colonialism, White Supremacy," cited in Pearson, "'The Last Bastion of Colonialism,'" 177.

8. Patrick Wolfe, "Settler Colonialism and the Elimination of the Native," *Journal of Genocide Research* 8, no. 4 (2006): 387–409, 389–90.

9. Mark Rifkin, *Settler Common Sense: Queerness and Everyday Colonialism in the American Renaissance* (University of Minnesota Press, 2014), xvi–xvii.

10. A. Lynn Smith, *Memory Wars: Settlers and Natives Remember Washinton's Sullivan Expedition of 1779* (University of Nebraska Press, 2023), 39, emphasis mine.

11. William Deverell, "Notes from the West to the Midwest," *Middle West Review* 4, no. 1 (2017): 33–40, 33–34.

12. Fletcher et al., "Introduction," 3, 5–6.

13. Rebecca Kugel, "Planning to Stay: Native Strategies to Remain in the Great Lakes, Post-War of 1812," *Middle West Review* 2, no. 2 (2016): 1–26, 2.

14. James Loewen, *Sundown Towns: A Hidden Dimension of American Racism* (New Press, 2005); Brent Campney, *Hostile Heartland: Racism, Repression, and Resistance in the Midwest* (University of Illinois Press, 2019); James Joseph Buss, *Winning the West with Words: Language and Conquest in the Lower Great Lakes* (University of Oklahoma Press, 2011).

15. Mary Lethert Wingerd, *North Country: The Making of Minnesota* (University of Minnesota Press, 2010), xii.

16. Helgeson, "Thoughts on a Critical Regional History of the Midwest," 33, 34, 37. On erasure, see Hoganson, *The Heartland*, 15–17 (see chapter 1, n. 1); Patrick Wolfe, *Traces of History: Elementary Structures of Race* (Verso, 2016), esp. chapter 5; James Joseph Buss, "Appealing to the Great Spirit: Foundational Fictions and Settler Histories," *Middle West Review* 2, no. 2 (2016): 143–67; Jean M. O'Brien and Lisa Blee, "What Is a Monument to Massasoit Doing in Kansas City? The Memory Work of Monuments and Place in Public Displays of History," *Ethnohistory* 61, no. 4 (2014): 635–53; Buss, *Winning the West with Words*; Lorenzo Veracini, "The Imagined Geographies of Settler Colonialism," in *Making Settler Colonial Space: Perspectives on Race, Place, and Identity*, ed. Tracey Mar and Penelope Edmonds (Palgrave Macmillan UK, 2010); Jean O'Brien, *Firsting and Lasting: Writing Indians out of Existence in New England* (University of Minnesota Press, 2010); Laurie Hovell McMillin, *Buried Indians: Digging Up the Past in a Midwestern Town* (University of Wisconsin Press, 2006); Patrick Wolfe, "Settler Colonialism"; for history as a site of colonization and dispossession, see Joshua J. Jeffers, "Colonizing the Indigenous Past: Settler-Colonial Place-Making and the Ancient Landscape of the Early Midwest," in Lauck, *The Making of the Midwest* (see introduction, n. 3); Terry A. Barnhart, *American Antiquities: Revisiting the Origins of American Archaeology* (University of Nebraska Press, 2015); Terry Barnhart, "'A Common Feeling': Regional Identity and Historical Consciousness in the Old Northwest, 1820–1860," *Michigan Historical Review* 29, no. 1 (2003): 39–70; Gordon Sayre, "The Mound Builders and the Imagination of American Antiquity in Jefferson, Bartram, and Chateaubriand," *Early American Literature* 33 (1998): 225–49.

17. Hoganson, *The Heartland*, xiv.

18. Nicholas A. Brown and Sarah E. Kanouse, *Re-Collecting Black Hawk: Landscape, Memory, and Power in the American Midwest* (University of Pittsburgh Press, 2015), 3.

19. Kiel, "Untaming the Mild Frontier," 13–14; Kiel and Brooks, "Introduction."

20. Fletcher et al., "Introduction," 3.

21. Brown and Kanouse, *Re-Collecting Black Hawk*, 3. Issues associated with memory and memorialization are certainly not unique to the Midwest; see anthropologist A. Lynn Smith's discussion of the "so-called Battle of Chemung" in *Memory Wars*, 295. But for the Midwest, memory is the primary chasm separating these historiographies.

22. Bowes, *Land Too Good for Indians*, 13.

23. Kugel, "Planning to Stay," 3.

24. Stephen Warren, "The Ohio Shawnees' Struggle against Removal, 1814–1830," in *Enduring Nations: Native Americans in the Midwest*, ed. R. David Edmunds (University of Illinois Press, 2008), 83, 84.

25. Kugel, "Planning to Stay," 7, 18.

26. Bowes, *Land Too Good for Indians*, 11–13; Buss, *Winning the West with Words*, 6; Buss, "Appealing to the Great Spirit"; Susan E. Grey, "Native Americans and Midwestern History," in *Finding a New Midwestern History*, ed. Jon K. Lauck, Gleaves Whitney, and Joseph Hogan (University of Nebraska Press, 2018), 56.

27. On settler colonialism and state formation, see also Bethel Saler, *The Settler's Empire: Colonialism and State Formation in America's Old Northwest* (University of Pennsylvania Press, 2015); William H. Bergmann, *American National State and the Early West* (Cambridge University Press, 2012).

28. Witgen, *Seeing Red*, vii, 20–22, 33–34, 89.

29. Witgen, *Seeing Red*, 253.

30. Theodore Karamanski, "Settler Colonial Strategies and Indigenous Resistance on the Great Lakes Lumber Frontier," *Middle West Review* 2, no. 2 (2016): 27–51, 27, 40–42.

31. On the fluidity of Native identity in the Midwest during the early nineteenth century, see Michael Leonard Cox, "Isaac Walker and the Complexities of Midwestern Native American Identity," in Lauck, *The Making of the Midwest*, 289–303; Jennifer Kirsten Stinson, "African American, African Indian, *and* Midwestern," *Middle West Review* 7, no. 1 (2020): 57–67; Jennifer Kirsten Stinson, "Becoming Black, White, and Indian in Wisconsin Farm Country, 1850s–1910s," *Middle West Review* 2, no. 2 (2016): 53–84; Lucy Eldersveld Murphy, *Great Lakes Creoles: A French-Indian Community on the Northern Borderlands, Prairie Du Chien, 1750–1860* (Cambridge University Press, 2014); Bradley J. Birzer, "Jean Baptiste Richardville: Miami Metis" and Susan Sleeper-Smith, "Resistance to Removal: The 'White Indian,' Frances Slocum," both in *Enduring Nations: Native Americans in the Midwest*, ed. R. David Edmunds (University of Illinois Press, 2008); Donald H. Gaff, "Three Men from Three Rivers: Navigating Between Native and American Indian Identity in the Old Northwest Territory," in *The Boundaries Between Us: Natives and Newcomers along the Frontiers of the Old Northwest, 1750–1850*, ed. Daniel Barr (Kent State University Press, 2006).

32. Jameson Sweet, "Race, Citizenship, and Dakota Indians in the Upper Midwest," *Journal of the Early Republic* 39, no. 1 (2019): 99–109, 99, 104, 105.

33. See Hughes's discussion of "Negrotown," a free Black community known as "a haven for escaped slaves" and home to a variety of mixed-race families. As Hughes

notes, the website for the church contains no mention of its founder, John Stewart, his importance to generations of Black Christians, or the racist violence that transformed the area. Sakina Hughes, "The Community Became an Almost Civilized and Christian One: John Stewart's Mission to the Wyandots and Religious Colonialism as African American Racial Uplift," *NAIS: Journal of the Native American and Indigenous Studies Association* 3, no. 1 (2016): 24–45, 24–25, 32, 40–41.

34. Wingerd, *North Country*, 231, 351–2.

35. Stinson, "Becoming Black, White, and Indian," 54, 60, 68–69.

36. Stinson, "Becoming Black, White, and Indian," 68–69.

37. Lee, *Masters of the Middle Waters*; Wolfe, *Traces of History*, 173.

38. Stinson, "Becoming Black, White, and Indian," 77.

39. Hughes, "The Community Became an Almost Civilized and Christian One," 41.

40. Jennifer Kirsten Stinson, "Race, Family, and Region in the Nineteenth-Century Upper Midwest: A History of African, Indian, and European Communities in the Heartland" (PhD diss., Indiana University, 2009), 1.

41. Stinson, "African American, African Indian, *and* Midwestern," 57.

42. There is an extensive literature on Anishinaabeg history, labor, and reservation life in the Midwest; see Brenda J. Child, *My Grandfather's Knocking Sticks: Ojibwe Family Life and Labor on the Reservation* (Minnesota Historical Society Press, 2014); Brenda J. Child, "A New Seasonal Round: Government Boarding Schools, Federal Work Programs, and Ojibwe Family Life during the Great Depression" and Melissa Meyer, "White Earth Women and Social Welfare," both in Edmunds, *Enduring Nations: Native Americans in the Midwest*; Brenda J. Child, "Wilma's Jingle Dress: Ojibwe Women and Healing in the Early Twentieth Century," in *Reflections on American Indian History: Honoring the Past, Building a Future*, ed. Albert L. Hurtado and Wilma Mankiller (University of Oklahoma Press, 2008); Rohde, "Labor and Leisure;" Brenda J. Child, "Politically Purposeful Work: Ojibwe Women's Labor and Leadership in Postwar Minneapolis," in Williams, *Indigenous Women and Work*; Brenda J. Child and Colin Calloway, *Holding Our World Together: Ojibwe Women and the Survival of Community* (Penguin Publishing Group, 2012); Chantal Norrgard, *Seasons of Change*; Erik M. Redix, *The Murder of Joe White: Ojibwe Leadership and Colonialism in Wisconsin* (Michigan State University Press, 2014); Larry Nesper, *The Walleye War: The Struggle for Ojibwe Spearfishing and Treaty Rights* (University of Nebraska Press, 2002); and Brenda J. Child, *Boarding School Seasons American Indian Families, 1900–1940* (University of Nebraska Press, 1998).

43. Norrgard, *Seasons of Change*, 2.

44. Norrgard, *Seasons of Change*, 2, 4, 8; see also Edmund Jefferson Danziger, *Great Lakes Indian Accommodation and Resistance During the Early Reservation Years, 1850–1900* (University of Michigan Press, 2009).

45. Child, *My Grandfather's Knocking Sticks*, 3–4, 170–72.

46. See Estes and Dhillon, *Standing with Standing Rock*; Kyle T. Mays, "Pontiac's Ghost in the Motor City: Indigeneity and the Discursive Construction of Modern Detroit," *Middle West Review* 2, no. 2 (2016): 115–42; David Hugill, "Metropolitan Transformation and the Colonial Relation: The Making of an 'Indian Neighborhood'

in Postwar Minneapolis," *Middle West Review* 2, no. 2 (2016): 169–99; John N. Low, *Imprints: The Pokagon Band of Potawatomi in Chicago* (Michigan State University Press, 2016); LaPier and Beck, *City Indian*; Davis, *Survival Schools*; James B. LaGrand, *Indian Metropolis: Native Americans in Chicago, 1945–75* (University of Illinois Press, 2005).

47. Miller, *Indians on the Move*, 5, 6, 44, 69, 195.

48. David Hugill, *Settler Colonial City: Racism and Inequity in Postwar Minneapolis* (University of Minnesota Press, 2021), 3, 6. See Nathan McClintock and Stéphane Guimont Marceau, "Settler-Colonial Urbanisms: Convergences, Divergences, Limits, Contestations," *Urban Geography* (2022): 1–5; Libby Porter and Oren Yiftachel, "Urbanizing Settler-Colonial Studies: Introduction to the Special Issue," *Settler Colonial Studies* 9 (2019): 177–86; Heather Dorries, Robert Henry, David Hugill, Tyler McCreary, and Julie Tomiak, *Settler City Limits: Indigenous Resurgence and Colonial Violence in the Urban Prairie West* (University of Manitoba Press, 2019); Nathan McClintock, "Urban Agriculture, Racial Capitalism, and Resistance in the Settler-Colonial City," *Geography Compass* 12 (2018): 1–16; David Hugill, "What is a Settler-Colonial City?" *Geography Compass* 11 (2017): 1–11; Hugill, "Metropolitan Transformation"; David Hugill, "Settler Colonial Urbanism: Notes from Minneapolis and the Life of Thomas Barlow Walker," *Settler Colonial Studies* 6 (2016): 265–78. On settler colonialism, see Lorenzo Veracini, "Settler Colonialism as a Distinct Mode of Domination," in *The Routledge Handbook of the History of Settler Colonialism*, ed. Edward Cavanaugh and Lorenzo Veracini (Routledge, 2016); Walter Hixon, *American Settler Colonialism: A History* (Palgrave Macmillan, 2013); Veracini, *Settler Colonialism*; and Wolfe, *Settler Colonialism*.

49. Hugill, "Metropolitan Transformation," 171, 172, 194 (emphasis in the original); for decolonization paradigm, see Susan A. Miller, "Native America Writes Back: The Origin of the Indigenous Paradigm in Historiography," *Wicazo Sa Review* 23, no. 2 (2008): 9–28; Susan A. Miller, "Native Historians Write Back: The Indigenous Paradigm in American Indian Historiography," *Wicazo Sa Review* 24, no. 1 (2009): 25–45; and Donna L. Akers, "Decolonizing the Master Narrative," *Wicazo Sa Review* 29, no. 1 (2014): 58–76.

50. Fletcher et al., "Introduction," 1–7, 5–6.

51. Andrew Isenberg and Thomas Richards Jr., "Alternative Wests," *Pacific Historical Review* 86, no. 1 (2017): 4–17; Thomas Richards Jr., "Farewell to America," *Pacific Historical Review* 86, no. 1 (2017): 114–52; Bruce E. Johansen, "Donald Trump, Andrew Jackson, Lebensraum, and Manifest Destiny," *American Indian Culture & Research Journal* 41, no. 4 (2017): 115–22; Paul Frymer, *Building an American Empire: The Era of Territorial and Political Expansion* (Princeton University Press, 2017); Philip J. Deloria, "American Master Narratives and the Problem of Indian Citizenship in the Gilded Age and Progressive Era," *Journal of the Gilded Age & Progressive Era* 14, no. 1 (2015): 3–12.

52. For the New Indian History, see Robert Berkhofer, "The Political Context of a New Indian History," *Pacific Historical Review* 40: 357–82. On the field of Native American history, see Donald Fixico, ed., *Rethinking American Indian History* (University of New Mexico Press, 1997), esp. chapters 1–3; Russell Thornton, ed., *Studying Native America: Problems and Prospects* (University of Wisconsin Press, 1998), esp.

chapters 8 and 9; R. David Edmonds, "Blazing New Trails or Burning Bridges: Native American History Comes of Age," *The Western Historical Quarterly* 39, no. 1 (2008): 6–16; Frederick Hoxie, ed., *The Oxford Handbook of American Indian History* (Oxford University Press, 2016), "Introduction," esp. 3–6; and James R. Allison, "Beyond it All: Surveying the Intersections of Modern American Indian, Environmental, and Western Histories," *History Compass* 16, no. 4 (2018): 1–11.

53. Smith, *Memory Wars*, 34.

**3**

# "WE WANT THE FUNK"

## On Knowing and Seeing Black Midwestern History

I have a tradition. Every Midwest History Association conference, I proudly rock my "Yes, There Are Black People in Iowa" t-shirt. A vibrant blue, it's not my funkiest look, but it is one that helps me feel "seen." Much like my other favorite Raygun t-shirt, "Black History is Nebraska History," these statement pieces reflect what Black Midwesterners like myself have long known. We exist. Our experiences matter. And our stories are an integral part of this region's history and self-conception. As senior editor of *Zora* magazine Morgan Jenkins affirms, Black Midwesterners "do exist—abundantly and vibrantly."[1] Yet so frequently the inclusion of our stories are "value-added" narratives, fitting Black people in "without the story crumbling apart."[2] While research that recovers the contributions of Midwesterners of color are critical, scholars must also work to decenter laudatory or exceptional narratives to capture the full spectrum of the Black Midwestern experience, including anti-Black violence, Black joy, and everyday Black life.[3] To do so, scholars must broaden their archive and method.

By centering not only African American embodied experiences but also Black studies praxis, scholars can arrive at new histories of the Midwest. Through this disruption, innovative insights arise about the region and the nature of historical inquiry itself.

Black history is frequently told from the margins. Black Midwestern history is at the margin of the margins, a grand irony considering the region's historic and geographic centrality. As African Americans are frequently understood to be *in* and not *of* the Midwest, careful attention must be paid to the particulars of if, where, and how Black actors appear in the archive. At times it is difficult to locate the ideologies and impacts of African Americans in what has been imagined to be a discordant place. But the abundant scholarship detailing the limits of the archive when documenting Black experiences paves a way forward.[4]

As a complement to scholarly and textual evidence, regional knowledge must also be located among the people themselves. By including alternative forms of knowledge, including songs, poetry, photography, and other forms of vernacular expression, regional study can align with Black studies disciplinary commitments and become fuller because of it. I argue that the integration of Black studies approaches can enrich the entirety of Midwestern studies. Specifically, through the deployment of a Black Midwestern intellectual tradition, interdisciplinary, intersectional, diasporic, and multi-racial narratives can be mobilized in "seeing" the Midwest, offering a more complete account of the region.

## BLACK INTELLECTUAL HISTORY

Over the first two decades of the twenty-first century, the field of Black intellectual history experienced tremendous growth. The field centers Black people's ideas, situating African Americans as producers of knowledge, not just objects of inquiry. This orientation is particularly important as Black intellectual history embodies "the twin objectives of defining and defending Black humanity."[5] Scholars who undertake this intellectual orientation upend mainstream perceptions of a region racialized as exclusively white. Moreover, by centering how Black Midwesterners have defined and defended their identities, not only to white regional counterparts who deny their Midwesternness but also their racial counterparts who doubt Black people's affinity to America's heartland, a more capacious narrative emerges.

In the aftermath of the 2016 election, numerous commentators looked to the Midwest to interpret Donald Trump's unexpected victory. Four years later,

Brookings Institute researcher John C. Austin asked, "Will voters in the Midwest's struggling communities decide again?"[6] In his subsequent research he found that it was not working-class white residents that determined the 2020 presidential election but the large turnout of Black voters in Michigan and Wisconsin.[7] That only white Midwesterners are included in the composition of "once-mighty, currently hollowed-out manufacturing communities" speaks volumes of the rhetorical power of the imagined Midwest.[8] By centering Black ideas and ideology, researchers might have answered a more important question: why did Black Midwesterners, who experience greater economic marginalization, overwhelmingly vote against President Trump?[9] In thinking about the origins and impact of this flipped script, Black Midwesterners challenge dominant understandings of the region's meaning (hardworking white bootstrappers) to more critically consider the relationship between region, race, and ideology.

Scholars have much to learn in seeing political, social, and historical phenomena from the vantage point of different and forgotten interlocutors. As historian Manning Marable elaborates, that act "is essentially the Black intellectual tradition, the critical thought and perspectives of intellectuals of African descent and scholars of black America, and Africa, and the black diaspora."[10] I employ a more expansive definition of intellectuals to include the street-corner poets, hair-braiding philosophers, and porch-sitting griots. Thus, the intellectual production at barbershops, kitchen tables, and quasi-formal sites like churches and fraternal organizations are just as important as Historically Black Colleges and Universities (HBCUs) like Lincoln University in Missouri and Wilberforce University in Ohio. Black people have built this intellectual tradition among themselves through music, literature, films, and the entirety of discourses emerging from Black life. "From its inception," historian Brandon Byrd argues, "Black Studies refused the artificial separation of art and life, the physical and metaphysical, and ideas and experience."[11] Framing Black studies as a "counterhegemonic enterprise," I take up Byrd's call for intellectual historians and apply it here: when conceptualizing the Black Midwest, "who produces knowledge and what is knowledge for?"[12]

Alternative epistemologies become particularly useful in decentering the dominant Midwestern canon. Patricia Hill Collins argues that "far from being the apolitical study of truth, epistemology points to the ways in which power relations shape who is believed and why."[13] Black Midwesterners have come to know certain things about this region because of their dual responsibility of defining and defending. From this vantage point, unconventional regional knowledge emerges. As literary scholar Mary Burger argued in 1975, "I think it is safe to say that nowhere else in America—North, South, East or West—can the black so consistently see and experience so much inconsistency."[14] Navigating both the hopes and hazards of the Midwest, African Americans create "independent self-definitions and self-valuations," mobilizing "music, literature, daily conversations, and everyday behavior as important locations for constructing [an alternative] consciousness."[15] From this distinctive standpoint of the Black Midwest, scholars identify more expansive regional epistemologies.

## TRADITIONAL STUDIES OF THE BLACK MIDWEST

When considering the published scholarship, an essential component of these works has been the declaration of Black Midwestern existence. As such, these accounts often align with familiar narratives within mainstream American history. Canonical texts like Quintard Taylor's *In Search of the Racial Frontier* and Bruce A. Glasrud and Charles A. Braithwaite's *African Americans on the Great Plains* are essential readings for reinscribing Black life into the region.[16] More recent accounts like Melissa Ford's *A Brick and a Bible* and Jennifer Harbour's *Organizing Freedom* offer gendered and regional analyses of Black organizing and resistance.[17] Other works like Jack Blocker's *A Little More Freedom* and Brent Campney's *Hostile Heartland* document not only the impact of African Americans but also the white response to their presence in the region.[18] The vast majority of books on the Midwestern African American experience, however, are narratives told at the local or state level. These comprise some of the most thoughtful and deep histories on the experiences of Black people in the Midwest with work by Richard Breaux, Nikki Taylor, and William Green among the best.[19] But while such essential texts locate and document the Black experience in places like Iowa, Ohio, and Minnesota, they do not offer a theorization of the region in its entirety.[20]

In addition to historical monographs, there are numerous texts targeting audiences in search of general information. These are frequently part of collections about the racial, ethnic, and religious history of local "others." While these recovery efforts are vital, they often fit into well-worn regional narratives, glossing over difficult histories and including only the most exceptional community members and touchstones.[21] Limited early histories written by government researchers[22] and statistical portraits of Black life represent two other popular genres.[23] Finally, there are several well-researched oral history collections that gather testimony on the Black Midwest.[24] Collectively, these projects preserve invaluable insight to the lived experiences of Black people but are again limited to municipal or state-level inquiry.

## NEW STORIES OF THE BLACK MIDWEST

To find new ways of telling Midwestern stories, we must center the Black Midwestern intellectual tradition. The sources for this endeavor are manifold, as Black intellectual history is the "critical examination of what the group—historians, novelists, theologians, sociologists, psychologists, and others—were thinking and saying."[25] Autobiography, as one of the original sources of Black intellectual history, is a particularly fruitful place to begin imagining the Black Midwest at the regional level.[26] Black Midwestern autobiography echoes themes in broader African American literature but is differentiated by "the duality [that] comes out of living with the uneasy tolerance of middle America, and the in-betweenness from forming an idea of self and race in such an ambivalent atmosphere."[27] These narratives provide unique insights into how Black people center themselves, their identities, and their experiences within the Midwest. They also capture the diversity of Black Midwestern life across time and place. Walking alongside lynching survivor James Cameron in his traumatic account or peeking into Margo Jefferson's privileged childhood or Tanisha Ford's stylish closet broadens our understanding of Black Midwestern life from the harrowing to the sublime, illuminating the unique ways that Black Midwesterners center themselves.[28]

As evidenced in their personal accounts, African Americans frequently moved between Midwestern hubs, providing a comparative lens through which to understand the region. Consider the painter Aaron Douglas. Born in 1899 in Topeka, Kansas, he moved to Detroit after graduating from high school and before attending the University of Nebraska. After being denied the opportunity to serve in the Student Army Training Corps (SATC), he transferred to the University of Minnesota, where he earned the rank of corporal in their program.[29] *American Daughter* author and *Ebony* magazine editor Era Bell Thompson found home in Iowa, North Dakota, and Illinois.[30] Malcolm X also lived an intraregional Midwestern life. The child of United Negro Improvement Association organizers, X was born in Omaha and moved with his parents to Milwaukee, Wisconsin; East Chicago, Indiana; and then Lansing, Michigan.[31] Prominent communist Harry Haywood left Omaha for Minneapolis after a racist attack on his father, and then finally relocated to Chicago.[32] When taken as a whole, these life narratives offer perspective to the variations of Black life within the Midwest by highlighting the extant networks, intraregional migrations, and community institutions that provided the context for these individuals' life trajectories.

Expressive writing offers a particularly valuable lens through which to understand the Midwestern experience. Despite their unique insights, Black Midwestern authors are often "de-regionalized," a by-product of lingering misconceptions about race and region. As poet and author Hanif Abdurraqib details, for Black Midwestern authors to gain acknowledgment it "would require a reckoning with the multitudinous nature of Blackness . . . it requires a deconstruction of an idea about what the Midwest is and how it, like so much of the fantasy of America, relies on people who cast bad faith blankets over regions."[33] But this limiting view of Blackness and region is not only mobilized by those who choose to imagine the Midwest as an exclusively white place. Literature scholar Lisa Long articulates the uniquely Black Midwestern struggle as individuals "are either invisible in the region, or their experiences are deemed inauthentic—both because their credentials as true African Americans are somehow neutralized by their Midwesternness, and their Midwesternness is suspect because they are African American."[34] The Midwest renders Black authors illegible just as their racial perspective renders their regional experiences unrecognizable to others. This is no more evident than in the erasure of some of the Midwest's most iconic authors from their regional origins.

For many, including Black Americans, the heartland represents an opportunity to live the American Dream. But Black people's knowledge of this region highlights the tension between promise and reality. Specifically, by investigating Black prose we locate "Mid-America's in-betweenness—its benevolent racism, its patronizing exploitation."[35] In a close reading of Richard Wright's *Black Boy* and *Native Son*, Ronald Primeau notes "although freedom is the goal, its realization falls short of expectation."[36] Wright himself describes the letdown of the Midwestern promise, directly influencing the "Bigger Thomases" of the world to react violently: "it was not that Chicago segregated Negroes more than the South, but that Chicago had more to offer . . . did so much more to dazzle the mind with a taunting sense of possible achievement that the segregation it did impose brought forth from Bigger a reaction more obstreperous of that in the South."[37] Contemporary writer Roxanne Gay offers a similar assessment: "I say that the Midwest is home even if this home does not always embrace me, and that the Midwest is a vibrant, necessary place. I say I can be a writer anywhere, and as an academic, I go where the work takes me. Or, I said these things. Now, I am simply weary."[38] Or as Minneapolis poet Danez Smith queries succinctly, "Do you know what it's like to live someplace that loves you back?"[39] Without a doubt, exclusion, isolation, and oppression are a part of the Black Midwestern experience, but it is not the only experience.

In a tribute essay following Toni Morrison's death, Abdurraqib wrote lovingly of her ability to draw vast, complicated portraits of Black people: "I think of this often, but especially when Black people in the Midwest are flattened by those who don't live in these places or have never been."[40] The Black Midwest holds meaning as family, opportunity, and home as much as, if not more so than, a place of harm. Writer Saeed Jones says of moving to Columbus, Ohio, from New York City: "There was just an ease that, as a writer, frees up my creativity. It frees up all of the daydreams and ideas and random things in my head, so I can spend time cultivating art."[41] Black Midwestern people maintain a lush interior life, one that is not constantly in conversation with oppression. Consider poet laureate Rita Dove's *Thomas and Belulah*, which recounts the ups and downs of a Midwestern Black couple's seven decades together. Loosely based on Dove's own grandparents, the collection recounts the banality of parenting alongside the guilt of a friend's tragic death.[42] Gwendolyn Brook's 1956 children's book *Bronzeville Boys and Girls* similarly offers brief poetic portraits of Black children playing, dreaming, and occasionally being naughty.[43] Black spaces and thinkers are not consumed with being "othered," but rather cultivate deeper meditations on the human condition outside of the white gaze. That some of the most iconic Black Midwestern writers are ripped from their regional roots is no accident. Blackness is misunderstood as a separate stand-alone category, one that is frequently told only in reference to suffering. But in centering Black ways of knowing, the connection between region and identity ceases to be a unilateral one. Rather, the long-standing presence of African Americans and their significant social, cultural, and intellectual contributions are "instrumental in defining the distinct flavor of the Midwestern regional identity."[44]

By centering Black Midwesterners as agents of knowledge, their intellectual resonance emerges in wide-ranging forms including language, art, style, and music. This vernacular knowledge is also alive in oral traditions and other outlets that speak directly to Black audiences. Comedians Richard Pryor, Dick Gregory, and Amber Ruffin have been keen observers of Midwestern life.[45] The first three independent nonprofit Black history museums were in the Midwest.[46] Films like *The Homesteader* (1919), Oscar-nominated documentary *A Time for*

*Burning* (1966), and *Crossroad Stories* (2014) all tell narratives of resilience and what it means for Black people to be in a place grappling with their presence.[47] Photographers of Black life, like John Johnson and Gordon Parks, capture with their viewfinders what Smithsonian curator Michèle Gates Moresi describes as "a time and a place where African-Americans were treated as second-class citizens but lived their lives with dignity."[48] These sources are but a brief glimpse into the possibility that lies beyond traditional ways of seeing the Black Midwest. Taken as a whole, these sources tell us just as much about the African Americans who inhabited this place as it does the region itself.

Through the incorporation of alternative Black epistemologies, the reciprocal impact of African Americans and regional identity becomes even more apparent. Through this expansion of the archive, scholars can move beyond the accepted tropes of Black Midwestern locations and contributions to consider the fluidity of the Black Midwestern experience and its ongoing salience. The sounds of the Black Midwest are born from the specific context in which its creators lived. Kansas City had a jazz scene that rivaled the "gilt palaces and funky butt dance halls" of New Orleans's Storyville neighborhood because the city's location as a transportation hub provided stable employment and a concentration of talent, yet was far enough removed from market pressures that musicians could innovate.[49] The "Minneapolis sound," a rock funk mash-up best exemplified by Prince and associated acts, producers Jimmy Jam and Terry Lewis, and the group Morris Day and the Time, is also a product at the intersection of race and region. As children these artists participated in a "school integration program that bussed North Minneapolis kids to the south side, exposing them to mainstream rock, and white fashion and culture in the process," as well as art initiatives and the Black cultural hubs in their own communities.[50] Thus, music becomes an essential entry point for understanding the cultural landscape of the twentieth century.

In Midwestern cities, overlapping factors of residential segregation, disposable income, and intraregional networks translated trying conditions into new American artforms, and Dayton, Ohio, was its epicenter. The "Land of Funk," as it came to be known, was so dubbed because fourteen of Dayton's funk bands secured recording contracts with major labels.[51] Moreover between 1968 and 1999, thirteen of those groups produced 143 songs that landed on Billboard's R&B/soul music charts.[52] Like Kansas City jazz, Minneapolis rock, or even the Chicago blues, the built environment and regional experiences of Black people led directly to the development of this new artistic form. But in the case of Ohio, it was also what funk came to signify. Portia Maultsby argues that the development of this new music was rooted in the same disaffection that Bigger Thomas felt: "the optimism that once prevailed in the middle class transformed into feelings of ambivalence, and the unemployed expressed their disillusionment at the system that had failed them."[53] These musical stylings came as Black people responded to their environment and reasserted worth in themselves and their work. Tony Bolden argues that "the funk" became a distinct form of Black vernacular epistemology, as the ethos registered "nothing on the $x$ axis of white signification, and everything on the $y$ axis of blackness."[54] Through funk music, Black folk in Dayton, Detroit, and Des Moines flipped regionalized racial stereotypes into a form of cultural resistance.

This way of Black Midwesterners, knowing themselves and "signifyin'(g)," is perfectly encapsulated by Prince's first appearance on *American Bandstand* in 1980. After performing "I Wanna Be Your Lover," Dick Clark bantered incredulously with the artist: "Where did you learn to do this in Minneapolis? . . . This isn't the kind of music that comes out of Minneapolis!"[55] Prince just shakes his head at Clark's ignorance, offering his own retort behind sly, knowing eyes, "No?" The outlandish costumes, elaborate set designs, and sheer pleasure of the groove all provided alternative ways of Black Midwesterners seeing themselves and being seen in the American context. A direct outgrowth of the disbelief that Minneapolis or anywhere else in the Midwest could, in fact, be so damn funky.

## CONCLUSION

As the Black Midwest Initiative declares in their mission statement, "We [Black Midwesterners] understand that the various forms of oppression and marginalization that we struggle against are not the sum total of our existence. Just as we have known pain and suffering and struggle, we have known joy and love and care. So we fight—because we know that we are worth fighting for."[56] New approaches to Black Midwestern studies must honor the commitment of the Black intellectual tradition by embracing the complexity, beauty, horror, and promise that this region holds for people of African descent. The reframing of these experiences must affirm Black Midwesterners' humanity and their rightful places in broader regional histories. But it is not enough that histories grow from the charge of "define and defend," as this still represents a partial knowledge. Rewriting Black people into these spaces cannot just be token inclusion in extant narratives but new stories that center Black people and their intellectual traditions. By reimagining the ways of knowing the Midwest and broadening the sources, methods, and chroniclers, Black Midwestern narratives enrich the entire region, sharing our abundance and vibrancy.

## NOTES

1. Morgan Jenkins, "The Midwest Has Meaning for More Than Just Whites," *Zora*, October 29, 2019. https://zora.medium.com/the-midwest-has-meaning-for-more-than -just-whites-e1655bc6f050.

2. Vincent Harding, "History: White, Negro, and Black," in "No More Moanin': Voices of Southern Struggle," ed. Sue Thrasher, special issue, *Southern Exposure* 1 (Winter 1974): 52.

3. My discussion of the study of race and ethnicity in Iowa history can be found in Ashley Howard, "Race and Iowa History," *The Annals of Iowa* 80, no. 4 (2021): 377–83.

4. Ashley D. Farmer, "Disorderly Distribution: The Dispersal of Queen Mother Audley Moore's Archives and the Illegibility of Black Women Intellectuals," *The Black Scholar* 52, no. 4 (2022): 5–15; Marisa J. Fuentes, *Dispossessed Lives: Enslaved Women, Violence, and the Archive* (University of Pennsylvania Press, 2016); Saidiya Hartman, *Wayward, Beautiful Experiments: Intimate Histories of Riotous Black Girls, Troublesome Women, and Queer Radicals* (W. W. Norton, 2020).

5. Derrick P. Aldridge, Cornelius L. Bynum, and James B. Stewart, "Introduction," in *African American Thought in the Twentieth Century*, ed. Derrick P. Aldridge, Cornelius L. Bynum, and James B. Stewart (University of Illinois Press, 2021), 2.

6. John C. Austin, "Will Voters in the Midwest's Struggling Communities Decide the Election Again?" *Brookings Institute*, October 6, 2020, https://www.brookings.edu /blog/the-avenue/2020/10/06/will-voters-in-the-midwests-struggling-communities -decide-the-election-again/.

7. John C. Austin, "Where Midwesterners Struggle, Trumpism Lives On," *Brookings Institute*, November 23, 2020, https://www.brookings.edu/blog/the-avenue/2020/11 /23/where-midwesterners-struggle-trumpism-lives-on/.

8. Austin, "Where Midwesterners Struggle."

9. Colin Gordon, *Race in the Heartland: Equity, Opportunity, and Public Policy in the Midwest* (University of Iowa and Iowa Policy Project, 2019), 8–10.

10. Manning Marable, "Introduction: Black Studies and the Racial Mountain," in *Dispatches from the Ebony Tower: Intellectuals Confront the African American Experience*, ed. Manning Marable (Columbia University Press, 2000), 1–2.

11. Brandon R. Byrd, "The Rise of African American Intellectual History," *Modern Intellectual History* 18, no. 3 (2021): 849.

12. Byrd, "African American Intellectual History."

13. Patricia Hill Collins, *Black Feminist Thought: Knowledge, Consciousness, and the Politics of Empowerment*, 2nd ed. (Routledge, 2000), 252.

14. Mary W. Burger, "I, Too, Sing America: The Black Autobiographer's Response to Life in the Midwest and Mid-Plains," *Kansas Quarterly* 7, no. 3 (1975): 54.

15. Collins, *Black Feminist Thought*, 251.

16. Bruce A. Glasrud and Charles Braithwaite, eds., *African Americans on the Great Plains: An Anthology* (University of Nebraska Press, 2009); Quintard Taylor, *In Search of the Racial Frontier: African Americans in the American West 1528–1990*, new ed. (W. W. Norton, 1999).

17. Melissa Ford, *A Brick and a Bible: Black Women's Radical Activism in the Midwest During the Great Depression* (Southern Illinois Press, 2022); Jennifer R. Harbour, *Organizing Freedom: Black Emancipation Activism in the Civil War Midwest* (Southern Illinois University Press, 2020).

18. Jack S. Blocker, *A Little More Freedom: African Americans Enter the Urban Midwest, 1860–1930* (Ohio State University Press, 2008); Campney, *Hostile Heartland* (see chapter 2, n. 14). Other works that take a regional approach include Anna-Lisa Cox, *The Bone and Sinew of the Land: America's Forgotten Black Pioneers and the Struggle for Equality* (Hachette Press, 2018); Erik S. McDuffie, "The Diasporic Journeys of Louise Little: Grassroots Garveyism, the Midwest, and Community Feminism," *Women, Gender, and Families of Color* 4, no. 2 (2016): 146–70; Leslie A. Schwalm, *Emancipation's Diaspora: Race and Reconstruction in the Upper Midwest* (University of North Carolina Press, 2000); Henry Lewis Suggs, *The Black Press in the Middle West, 1865–1985* (Greenword Press, 1996); and V. Jacque Voegeli, *Free but Not Equal: The Midwest and the Negro During the Civil War* (University of Chicago Press, 1967).

19. Richard Breaux, "To the Uplift and Protection of Young Womanhood": African American Women at Iowa Private Colleges and the University of Iowa, 1878–1928," *History of Education Quarterly* 50, no. 2 (May 2010): 159–81; William D. Green, *Degrees of Freedom: The Origins of Civil Rights in Minnesota, 1865–1912* (University of Minnesota Press, 2015); Nikki M. Taylor, *Frontiers of Freedom: Cincinnati's Black Community 1802–1868* (Ohio University Press, 2005).

20. Other local and state histories include Rachelle Chase, *Creating the Black Utopia of Buxton, Iowa* (History Press, 2019); Christy Clark-Pujara, "CONTESTED: Black Suffrage in Early Wisconsin," *The Wisconsin Magazine of History* 100, no. 4 (2017): 21–27; Keona Ervin, *Gateway to Equality: Black Women and the Struggle for Economic Justice in St. Louis* (University of Kentucky Press, 2017); Crystal Moten, *Continually Working: Black Women, Community Intellectualism, and Economic Justice in Postwar Milwaukee* (Vanderbilt University Press, 2023); Nell Irvin Painter, *Exodusters: Black Migration to Kansas After Reconstruction* (W. W. Norton, 1992); Kimberley L. Phillips, *AlabamaNorth: African-American Migrants, Community, and Working-Class Activism in Cleveland, 1915–1945* (University of Illinois Press, 1999); Richard B. Pierce, *Polite Protest: The Political Economy of Race in Indianapolis, 1920–1970* (Indiana University Press, 2005); and Joe W. Trotter Jr., *Black Milwaukee: The Making of an Industrial Proletariat, 1915–1945* (University of Illinois, 2007), as well as numerous articles, master's theses, and doctoral dissertations.

21. Arcadia Publishing's Black America series best exemplifies this trend, which includes *Cleveland's Gospel Music* (2003), *Black at Bradley, 1897–2000* (2001), *Black Baseball in Kansas City* (2000), *Another Ann Arbor* (2006), and *Iowa's Black Legacy* (1999).

22. John M. Robb, *The Black Coal Miner of Southeast Kansas* (Commission on Civil Rights, 1969); Earl Spangler, *The Negro in Minnesota* (T. S. Dennison, 1961); Thomas Earl Sullenger and J. Harvey Kerns, *The Negro in Omaha: A Social Study of Negro Development* (Municipal University of Omaha, 1931); Emma Lou Thornbrough, *The Negro in Indiana: A Study of a Minority* (Indiana Historical Bureau 1957); and Leola Nelson Bergmann, *The Negro in Iowa* (State Historical Society, 1969).

23. Rex R. Campbell and Peter R. Robertson, *Negroes in Missouri: A Compilation of Statistical Data from the 1960 U.S. Census of Population* (Missouri Commission on Human Rights, 1967); Chicago Commission on Race Relations, *The Negro in Chicago: A Study of Race Relations and Race Riot* (University of Chicago Press, 1922); Everett Clapsy, *The Negro in Southwestern Michigan: Negroes in the North in a Rural Environment* (Dowagiac, MI, 1967); Wendell Phillips Dabny, *Cincinnati's Colored Citizens* (Dabny Publishing Company, 1926).

24. Examples include March on Milwaukee Project, Detroit '67 Oral History Project, Black Women in the Midwest Project, Rondo Oral History Project (Minnesota), the Black Oral History in Nebraska, and the Yellow Springs Oral History project (Ohio).

25. John Hope Franklin, "Foreword," in *Black Intellectuals: Race and Responsibility in American Life*, ed. William Banks (New York, 1996), ix.

26. V. P. Franklin, *Living Our Stories, Telling Our Truths: Autobiography and the Making of the African-American Intellectual Tradition* (Oxford University Press, 1995), 11.

27. Burger, "The Black Autobiographer's Response," 43–44.

28. James Cameron, *A Time of Terror: A Survivor's Story* (Life Writes Press, 2016); Margo Jefferson, *Negroland: A Memoir* (Vintage, 2015); Tanisha Ford, *Dressed in Dreams: A Black Girl's Love Letter to the Power of Fashion* (St. Martin's Press, 2019).

29. Kansas Historical Society, "Aaron Douglas," accessed February 9, 2023, https://www.kshs.org/kansapedia/aaron-douglas/12039.

30. Michael J. Lansing, "An American Daughter in Africa: Land of My Fathers: Era Bell Thompson's Midwestern Vision of the African Diaspora," *Middle West Review* 1, no. 2 (2015): 1–28.

31. Malcolm X, *The Autobiography of Malcolm X* (Bantam Press, 1998).

32. Harry Haywood, *Black Bolshevik: Autobiography of an Afro-American Communist* (University of Minnesota Press, 1978).

33. Kevin Smokler, "'As Though It Is Everywhere': An Interview with Hanif Abdurraqib," *Belt Magazine*, March 17, 2021.

34. Lisa A. Long, "A New Midwesternism in Toni Morrison's 'The Bluest Eye'," *Twentieth Century Literature* 59, no. 1 (2013): 104–25, 106.

35. Burger, "The Black Autobiographer's Response," 46.

36. Ronald Primeau, "Slave Narrative Turning Midwestern: Deadwood Dick Rides into Difficulties," in *MidAmerica I: The Yearbook of the Society for the Study of Midwestern Literature,* ed. David D. Anderson (Midwestern Press, 1974), 23.

37. Richard Wright, "How 'Bigger' was Born," in *Native Son* (Harper Perennial, 1940), 515–16.

38. Roxanne Gay, "Black in Middle America," *Brevity* 53 (September 12, 2016). https://brevitymag.com/nonfiction/black-in-middle-america/.

39. Danez Smith, "summer, somewhere," *Poetry Foundation*, accessed February 9, 2023, www.poetryfoundation.org/poetrymagazine/poems/58645/from-summer -somewhere.

40. Hanif Abdurraqib, "The Generosity of Toni Morisson," *BuzzFeed News*, August 7, 2019.

41. Emma Frankart Henterly, "The World According to Saeed Jones," *Columbus Monthly*, November 11, 2020.

42. Rita Dove, *Thomas and Belulah* (Carnegie Mellon University Press, 1986).

43. Gwendolyn Brooks, *Bronzeville Boys and Girls* (HarperCollins, 1956).

44. Long, "A New Midwesternism," 104.

45. Dick Gregory, *Nigger: An Autobiography*, reprint (Plume, 2019); Richard Pryor, *Pryor Convictions and Other Life Sentences* (Pantheon Books, 1995); Amber Ruffin and Lacey Lamar, *You'll Never Believe What Happened to Lacey* (Grand Central Publishing, 2021).

46. Wesley Yin, "Timeline: It Took Over 100 Years from the African American Museum to Become a Reality," *Washington Post*, September 21, 2016.

47. *The Homesteader,* directed by Oscar Micheaux (Micheaux Film, 1919); *A Time for Burning*, directed by Barbara Connell and Bill Jersey (Quest Productions, 1966); *Crossroad Stories*, directed by Alyse Tucker Bounds (Ryan Furr Creative, 2014).

48. Joseph Stromberg, "Lost and Found Again: Photos of African-Americans on the Plains," *Smithsonian Magazine*, February 2013.

49. Ross Russell, *Bird Lives! The High Life and Hard Times of Charlie (Yardbird) Parker* (DaCapo Press, 1973), 31–32.

50. Andrea Swensson, *Got to Be Something Here: The Rise of the Minneapolis Sound* (University of Minnesota Press, 2017), 1; Kirsten Delegard and Michael J. Lansing, "Prince and the Making of the Minneapolis Mystique," *Middle West Review* 5, no. 1 (2018): 1–24.

51. Scot Brown, "A Land of Funk: Dayton, Ohio," in *The Funk Era and Beyond*, ed. T. Bolden (Palgrave Macmillan, 2008).

52. Portia Maultsby, "Dayton Street Funk: The Layering of Multiple Identities," in *The Ashgate Research Companion to Popular Musicology*, ed. Derek B. Scott (Routledge, 2009), 262.

53. Maultsby, "Dayton Street Funk," 270.

54. Tony Bolden, "Groove Theory: A Vamp of the Epistemology of Funk," *American Studies* 52, no. 4 (2013), 10; Tony Bolden, "Theorizing the Funk: An Introduction," in *The Funk Era and Beyond*, ed. Tony Bolden (Palgrave Macmillan, 2008), 15. Bolden builds

his argument using Henry Louis Gate's theory, which is the source quoted here. Henry Louis Gates, *The Signifying Monkey: A Theory of African American Literary Criticism* (Oxford University Press, 1989), 47.

55. Roy Kay, "Minneapolis, Prince, and the Minneapolis Sound," *boundary* 49, no. 2 (2022): 213.

56. Black Midwest Initiative, "Mission," *The Black Midwest*, April 4, 2023, https://www.theblackmidwest.com/mission-vision-values.

E. JAMES WEST

# 4

# FROM FRONTIER TO HEARTLAND

The Black Press and the Middle West

In the summer of 1885, a new Black periodical appeared on the streets of the Twin Cities in Minnesota. Edited by Frederick Douglass Parker, the *Western Appeal* was issued every Friday with the aim of "advancing the condition of the Negro."[1] This ambition was in keeping with the broader reputation of the Black press (a term I use here to encompass Black-owned newspapers, magazines, and press agencies) as a "defender of the race."[2] Like other Black Midwestern print enterprises such as the *Western Post*, founded in Hastings, Nebraska, in 1876, and the Western Negro Press Association, founded in Kansas City, Missouri in 1896, the *Western Appeal*'s title reflected its initial identification with the American frontier.[3] When the *Western Appeal* was launched, the Dakota, Wyoming, and Montana territories all remained unincorporated. However, within just a few years, North Dakota (1889), South Dakota (1889), Montana (1889), Washington (1889), Idaho (1890), and Wyoming (1890) had all been granted statehood. The *Western Appeal*'s proximity to the frontier was becoming increasingly distant.

The paper rebranded itself as the *Appeal*, a move that historian David Vassar Taylor suggests was prompted by executive changes and efforts to become "a national Afro-American newspaper."[4] However, I argue that this renaming was just as closely linked to shifting conceptualizations of both the American frontier and the *Appeal*'s regional influence. By 1890, the *Appeal* had added columns on Des Moines, St. Louis, and a host of other Midwestern cities.[5] John Quincy Adams, the paper's new editor, explicitly sought "to make the *Appeal* a Chicago paper."[6] In his pursuit of this goal, Adams opened a Chicago bureau, headed by his brother Cyrus Adams, and began publishing a Chicago edition. By the turn of the twentieth century, the *Appeal* had begun to distinguish between the "West"—the location with which it had first sought association—and the "Middle West"—a concept and a space that was in the process of creation.

This chapter explores the development of the Black Midwestern press and its positionality within Midwestern history and African American studies. It is guided by two key concerns. First, how have Midwestern historians understood and interrogated the role of Black people (generally) and the Black press (specifically) in the region's development? Second, how have scholars of Black history (generally) and the Black press (specifically) reflected on and written about the relationship between Black Midwestern periodicals and the region they inhabited? In the period since the publication of Henry Lewis Suggs's landmark 1996 collection *The Black Press in the Middle West*, parallel waves of scholarship have helped to reshape the fields of Midwestern history and African American studies. Focusing on the Chicago *Defender* and the Omaha *Star*, this chapter explores the productive possibilities of placing these bodies of scholarship in closer conversation. Just as the editorial focus of the *Appeal* and other Black Midwestern publications moved from the frontier to the heartland, I argue for the need to recenter the Black Midwestern press within Midwestern history and African American studies. In doing so, I emphasize the role of the Black press in making the Midwest "the Black media capital of America and the world."[7]

Since the formation of *Freedom's Journal* in 1827, Black periodicals have advocated for Black interests and provided an outlet for Black people to articulate their concerns. Historically, the struggle for civil rights has shaped this voice, with Black journalists and editors seeing it as their duty "to vindicate our brethren, when oppressed."[8] More broadly, Black periodicals have served as key organs for community formation, documentation, and racial uplift. Led by outlets such as *Freedom's Journal* and *The North Star*, the first wave of antebellum Black newspapers was concentrated in the Northeast and closely linked to the abolitionist cause. Following the end of the Civil War, a second wave of Black periodicals, headed by newspapers such as the *Colored Citizen*, sprung up across the American South. In both North and South, Black periodicals were largely created for, and sustained by, Black urban communities: from vibrant free Black enclaves in antebellum northern cities such as New York, Boston, and Philadelphia, to Southern cities such as Atlanta, Georgia and Birmingham, Alabama, where emancipated African Americans coalesced during and following Reconstruction.[9]

By contrast, Black migration into the Midwest lagged behind. In the 1860 census, the Black population of Illinois was 7,628. In neighboring Wisconsin, the Black population numbered just 1,171—less than two-tenths of 1 percent of the state's total population.[10] Mae Najiyyah Duncan claims that one of the region's first Black newspapers, the Cincinnati-based *Disenfranchised American*, began publication in the early 1840s.[11] Yet, for the most part, the low numbers and wide dispersal of Black Midwesterners made it difficult to sustain antebellum Black print enterprises. Consequently, the first wave of significant Black Midwestern periodicals, headed by publications such as the Chicago-based *Conservator* (1878) and the *Indianapolis Leader* (1879), did not emerge until the last quarter of the nineteenth century. In his landmark 1891 work on *The Afro-American Press and Its Editors*, I. Garland Penn identified more than 150 Black periodicals nationwide, of which just 15 percent were located in the Midwest. For Penn and many of his contemporaries, the Black press in the Midwest remained little more than an afterthought—a peripheral press for a peripheral people.[12]

This would quickly change, as the onset of the Great Migration, an outflow of Black Southerners that occurred in two major waves and encompassed much of the twentieth century, transformed the Midwest. In 1900 there were fewer than 500,000 Black residents spread across the region. By 1970, this number had grown to more than 4.5 million. The majority of Black migrants settled in Chicago, Detroit, Cleveland, and other Great Lakes cities.[13] Between 1900 and 1970, the Black population of Illinois rose from 85,000 to nearly one and a half million. In Michigan over the same period, the Black population leapt from 16,000 to nearly one million. A parallel, albeit much smaller, migration saw Black Southerners settle in the Upper Midwest and Great Plains states, predominantly in urban centers such as Minneapolis, Minnesota and Omaha, Nebraska.[14]

As the number of Black Midwesterners increased, so too did the size and stature of the publications that served them. Accordingly, by the time that the next major work of Black press scholarship, Frederick Detweiler's *The Negro Press in the United States*, appeared in 1922, the region's Black periodicals had assumed a significantly larger role. As Detweiler notes, by 1920, four of the nation's six most populous cities were located in the Midwest, and all of them—Chicago, Detroit, Cleveland, and St. Louis—were "centers of Negro journalism."[15] Perhaps no single publication better reflects this growth than the Chicago *Defender*, which was founded by Georgia native Robert Abbott in 1905. By the beginning of the 1920s, the *Defender* had been transformed from a decidedly amateur operation into the nation's most widely read Black periodical.[16] Two and a half decades later, Vishnu Oak, a professor at Wilberforce University in Ohio, counted some fifty Black periodicals based in the Midwest, close to double the percentage of Black Midwestern publications represented in Garland's 1891 survey.[17] No longer an afterthought for Black press scholars, the Black Midwestern press featured prominently in subsequent survey texts such as Roland Wolseley's *The Black Press, USA* (1971). Finally, the publication of Henry Lewis Suggs's *The Black Press in the Middle West* (1996) provided readers with the first in-depth and comparative analysis of the region's Black periodicals.[18]

Close to three decades after its original release, there is still much to admire about Suggs's work. Each chapter of the collection focuses on a specific state, examining the impact of individual publications and their coverage of issues such as "the family, education, migration, racial solidarity, entrepreneurship, and self-help."[19] Reviewers praised the text as a vital guide "to a rich and often neglected" history, and it remains an invaluable source of information.[20] However, the text is limited by several structural issues, not least uneven access to archival material across the region. For many contributors, Suggs complained, the "quest for needles in haystacks" led to dead ends "in archival collections administered by white curators who dismissed and ignored the black press."[21] It is also important to acknowledge developments in the fields of Midwestern history and African American studies that have occurred since the publication of *The Black Press in the Middle West*—developments that have raised important questions, and challenges, for both.

Responding to Jon K. Lauck's provocative description of the Midwest as a "lost region," a raft of new scholarship has reiterated "why the Midwest matters to the broader course of American history."[22] One welcome part of efforts to revive Midwestern history has been an increased focus on peoples and communities that have suffered from neglect and inattention within the field itself, including the experiences of its Black residents.[23] Given that many European

American settlers made little secret of "their plans for an intentionally white republic," it is unsurprising that early Black pioneers often met hostility.[24] At the same time, the emerging Midwest promised a (relatively) safe harbor from the horrors of slavery and was seen as a land of opportunity by Black homesteaders and industrial workers alike. Much recent scholarship in Midwestern history has sought to better address this dual legacy of racial oppression and possibility; to catalog "the Midwest's many failings, but also to recognize signs of progress."[25]

The years since the publication of *The Black Press in the Middle West* have also witnessed a growing attentiveness to both locality and regionality among scholars of the Black experience in the United States. Much of this work has been driven by scholarship on the modern Black freedom struggle, character-ized and—to a degree—catalyzed by John Dittmer's enormously influential 1994 study *Local People*.[26] From Milwaukee, Wisconsin, to Wichita, Kansas, a new generation of scholars has transformed our understanding of Black Midwest-ern activism at the local level.[27] Efforts to explore the ways in which the Black Midwestern experience was unique (or not) from Black life in other areas of the country have also contributed to the emergence of "Black Midwestern studies" and the birth of projects such as the Black Midwest Initiative—founded in 2017 with the aim of promoting "academic scholarship and popular writing about both the historic and contemporaneous experiences of black Midwesterners."[28] The Black press has become an increasingly central part of such work, aided by the digital revolution that has made Black Midwestern periodicals more accessible than ever before. Through the use of resources such as Proquest Historical Newspapers and the Library of Congress's "Chronicling America" project, present-day scholars have found the "quest for needles in haystacks" significantly easier than it was for Suggs and his contemporaries.[29]

Given that scholarly attentiveness to Black Midwestern communities, and the publications that served them, has tended to follow the flow of Black migrants themselves, it is unsurprising that much of this energy has focused on Chicago. This is hardly a new development: as part of his report on the city's 1919 race riots, journalist Carl Sandburg described the existence of a Black "newspaper row" on Chicago's South Side; a mighty "propaganda machine . . . that every week reaches hundreds of thousands of people of the colored race."[30] By the time that St. Clair Drake and Horace Cayton published *Black Metropolis* (1945), their landmark study of Black life in Chicago, the Windy City had become the region's undisputed center for Black journalism.[31] This position was cemented further by the impact of Johnson Publishing Company and the popularity of its flagship publication *Ebony*. First published in 1945, *Ebony* quickly became the nation's most popular Black periodical and "helped to make Chicago the black publishing capital of the world."[32]

Chicago's stranglehold over scholarship on the Black Midwest has, in many ways, only strengthened during the years since the publication of *The Black Press in the Middle West*, with work by Davarian Baldwin, Adam Green, Darlene Clarke Hine, John McCluskey, Marcia Chatelain, and others continuing to expand our understanding of Black Chicago and its periodicals.[33] Alongside the magazines of Johnson Publishing Company, the *Defender* has attracted the lion's share of attention, owing in large part to its perceived importance in driving Black migration to the city and its reputation as the "dean" of Chicago's Black press. In *Chicago's New Negroes*, Baldwin credits the *Defender* for impacting Black Chicagoans in ways that were "both material and far-reaching."[34] Similarly, in *South Side Girls*, Chatelain charts the experiences of Black girls and women who arrived in Chicago "hoping that . . . the *Defender*'s stories of the 'promised land' were indeed true."[35] For scholars such as Hilary Mac Austin, the newspaper's appeal was predicated on its ability to link local and regional identities with larger concerns, reiterating how Black Chicagoans—and Black Midwesterners—were "part of a larger community."[36]

Perhaps the most significant recent work on the *Defender* is Ethan Michaeli's 2016 study of the same name.[37] Michaeli, a former employee of the newspaper, authors a sprawling and exhaustively researched epic tracing the *Defender*'s development from a humble community organ into the nation's most powerful Black periodical. In the process, he weaves together key moments in the *Defender*'s history—such as its role in the Great Migration, or its efforts to publicize the racist murder of Chicago teenager Emmett Till in 1955—to create a cohesive and compelling narrative. Michaeli's work is indicative of new scholarship that seeks to more explicitly place Chicago's Black periodicals and publishing enterprises at the center of broader debates about race, education, civil rights, and community politics in the Windy City—a body of work that includes Robert Weems' *The Merchant Prince of Black Chicago* (2020), Gerald Horne's *The Rise and Fall of the Associated Negro Press* (2017), and E. James West's *Ebony Magazine and Lerone Bennett Jr.* (2022) and *A House for the Struggle* (2022).[38]

Through his detailed account of the *Defender*'s development and impact, Michaeli is also able to more closely interrogate the paper's relationship to place and its connections to the Midwest. This is important, given that relatively few scholars of Black Chicago would primarily identify themselves as regional historians. Accordingly, their analyses of Black life have largely skirted broader debates around regionality or the historical and geographic boundaries of the Midwest. In turn, their discussions of Chicago's Black periodicals have focused primarily on their role in documenting the long Black freedom struggle. By comparison, the ways in which Black periodicals and their editors understood and engaged with the idea of the "Midwest," and negotiated their own identification (or not) as "Midwestern," have received relatively short thrift.

In much of the existing scholarship on Black Chicago, the *Defender*'s rise is practically synonymous with the onset of the Great Migration. From this perspective, the *Defender* wholeheartedly embraced Chicago's reputation as a "promised land" for Black Southerners. Yet as Michaeli notes, the *Defender*'s migration boosterism—at least initially—was far from assured. During the early years of World War I, as demand for Black labor in northern cities continued to grow, the newspaper actually shied away from supporting mass migration. Instead, the *Defender* suggested that the lives of Black Southerners could be improved through charity and greater intervention by the federal government. Linking this ambivalence back to the classism and racism experienced by publisher Robert Abbott in Chicago following his move from rural Georgia, Michaeli helps to complicate the notion that Black migrants uniformly embraced their new identity as "Midwesterners" or uncritically championed the region's potential as a "promised land" for Black migrants.[39]

Through his attentiveness to Abbott's origins, as well as the origins of other early *Defender* contributors, Michaeli tugs on an important thread regarding regionality and the newspaper's own geographic identity. Many (although by no means all) nineteenth-century Black newspapers located in the Northeast or the South were edited by people from those regions. One notable example was Samuel Cornish, who was born in Delaware and relocated to Philadelphia and then New York, where he edited publications such as *Freedom's Journal* and *The Rights of All*. Black abolitionists Charles Bennett Ray, Philip Alexander Bell, and James McCune Smith, who at different points all edited the New York–based *Colored American*, were all born on the East Coast and lived and worked there for the majority of their lives. Another paper of the same name, one of the first Black newspapers to be printed in Georgia, was founded in 1866 by John Shuften, who was born in the state.[40] By contrast, very few of the *Defender*'s early contributors were Midwestern by birth. In addition to Abbott, who hailed from Georgia, early contributors included sportswriter Frank "Fay" Young, who was born in eastern Pennsylvania and raised in Massachusetts, cartoonist

L. N. Hoggatt, a Mississippi native, and society editor Julius Avendorph, who hailed from Alabama.[41]

What does it mean to describe Abbott and other early *Defender* contributors as Midwestern, given that they were born and raised outside of the region? In some ways, this experience helped them to better understand and articulate the collective experiences of Black migrants to the Midwest. Yet in other ways, and for some journalists more than others, it underpinned an ambivalence toward Chicago (in particular) and the Midwest (in general). Of course, by the early decades of the twentieth century, the creation of new periodicals by Black migrants that sought to reach both local and national audiences was hardly exclusive to the Midwest. The editors of two of the *Defender*'s most prominent competitors, the Pittsburgh *Courier* and the Harlem-based *Negro World*, hailed respectively from North Carolina and Jamaica. Nevertheless, these competing tensions—between wanting to be a part of the Midwest and wanting to be apart from it—are key to understanding some of the region's most prominent Black periodicals. This is perhaps most true of *Ebony*, a magazine "rooted in Black Chicago institutions and topics" but reliant on a geographically diverse staff whose "varied experiences and social orientation equipped it to represent postwar black life in uniquely ambitious ways."[42] This approach paired proudly Midwestern staffers such as Era Bell Thompson, who was raised in Iowa and North Dakota, with writers such as Allan Morrison, a zealous New Yorker "who believed [that] civilization stopped at the Hudson River."[43]

If a renewed focus on Chicago's Black press provides fresh perspectives on Black life and print culture in the Windy City, then other work helps to build on the foundations laid down in *The Black Press in the Middle West* by expanding our gaze beyond Chicago's "Black Metropolis" to examine Black communities and Black periodicals in other Midwestern locales. A useful example of such work is *Black Print with a White Carnation*, Amy Helen Forss's 2013 biography of Mildred Brown, a pioneering Black female journalist and longtime publisher of the Omaha *Star*, which remains Nebraska's largest Black newspaper.[44] Like so many other Black Midwestern publishers and editors, Brown was born and raised in the South. However, Brown took a more circuitous route than most throughout the region, first settling in Chicago with her first husband before relocating to Iowa, where she began her career in journalism with the *Silent Messenger* in Sioux City. By the time that Brown moved to Omaha, Nebraska, in early 1937, she had experienced a range of different Midwestern cities, impressing upon her the region's demographic and cultural diversity.[45]

*Black Print with a White Carnation* is important for a number of reasons, not least because it goes some way toward correcting an enduring scholarly fascination with Black male publishers and journalists such as Robert Abbott and John H. Johnson. The *Star* is one of the relatively few newspapers in the United States that was founded by a Black woman. Forss champions this point, detailing Brown's role as "the black matriarch of Omaha's Near North Side" and her efforts to present "an appearance of mannered impeccability as a means to refute racial and gender stereotypes."[46] In this regard, *Black Print with a White Carnation* forms part of an ongoing effort by Black press scholars to recover the work of pioneering Black female journalists and publishers such as Alice Dunnigan and Ethel Payne, and to more fully document the gender politics of the Black press on both a local and national level.[47]

Forss's work is also a timely reminder that, while Chicago still looms large in the scholarly imagination, there is much that remains to be said about other Black Midwestern communities and the periodicals that served them. This includes Detroit, with scholars such as Julius Thompson, Herb Boyd, and Beth Tompkin Bates documenting its transformation into a majority-Black city and an important hub for Black print enterprises such as the Michigan *Chronicle* and Dudley Randall's Broadside Press.[48] Cleveland, home to the *Call and Post*, and Indianapolis, which spawned Black publications such as the *Recorder* and the *Leader*, have also attracted significant scholarly attention over recent decades.[49] That Ethan Michaeli was able to author an extensive history of the *Defender*, one of the country's most popular Black periodicals based in one of the nation's most widely studied Black communities, should not be surprising. That Forss was able to do something similar, albeit on a smaller and less ambitious scale, should provide optimism that similar work on Black periodicals across the region will emerge in the near future.

From a different perspective, both Michaeli and Forss's work offer exciting examples of how increased archival access and newspaper digitization has fostered new opportunities for in-depth work on the Black Midwestern press. The scope of Michaeli's study would have been impossible without access to the extensive Abbott family papers, housed at Chicago Public Library, or digitized and indexed copies of the *Defender* itself. Similarly, Forss's ability to root her study of the Omaha *Star* within the city, state, and region where it was printed is indebted to her archival work, with the author utilizing material from sites such as the Des Moines Historical Society, Minnesota Historical Society Archives, and Wisconsin State Historical Society. There is also, perhaps, something to be said here about the importance of an author's own regional identity and their attentiveness to more localized acts of historical recovery. Forss attended Peru State College and the University of Nebraska. She has taught at Metropolitan Community College, located in Omaha, for more than two decades. Her book was published by the University of Nebraska Press. It is a project whose attentiveness to locality and to the Midwest as a region is shaped not only by its subject matter but by the experiences of its author. As universities across the region continue to hemorrhage history faculty, this is a point worth reiterating.[50]

Placed in conversation, Michaeli and Forss help to highlight the complexities of race and region, and the relationship between Black journalists, Black periodicals, and the Midwest. Their work emphasizes both the diversity of Black Midwestern periodicals and the shared experiences of many Black publishers and their publications. Publications such as the *Defender* and the *Star* were born from and—at least initially—responded to distinctly local issues. To a lesser (in the case of the *Star*) and greater (in the case of the *Defender*) extent, their coverage spread beyond the local to address regional and national concerns. Mildred Brown and Robert Abbott were indelibly tied to Omaha, Nebraska, and Chicago, Illinois—Midwestern cities that were geographically and culturally distinct from one another. At the same time, they were bound together by their shared experiences as Black Southern migrants to the region. Their individual accomplishments, and the impact of their publications, are a reminder of the Midwest's importance as a center—perhaps *the* center—of African American life and Black journalism in the modern United States.

## NOTES

1. "Western Appeal," *Western Appeal*, June 13, 1885, 1.

2. This framing of the Black press's social and political significance was vigorously promoted by Black journalists and has been well documented by scholars. See William Jordan, *Black Newspapers and America's War for Democracy, 1914–1920* (University of North Carolina Press, 2001), 1; Fred Carroll, *Race News: Black Journalists and the Fight for Racial Justice* (University of Illinois Press, 2017).

3. D. G. Paz, "The Black Press and the Issues of Race, Politics, and Culture on the Great Plains of Nebraska, 1865–1985," in *The Black Press in the Middle West*, ed. Henry Lewis Suggs (Greenwood Press, 1996), 215.

4. David Vassar Taylor, "John Adams and the *Western Appeal*" (PhD diss., University of Nebraska, 1971), 24.

5. Henry Lewis Suggs, "Democracy on Trial," in *The Black Press in the Middle West*, 168.

6. "Take Notice," *Western Appeal*, February 25, 1888, 1.

7. "History and Headlines," *Chicago Crusader*, accessed January 21, 2024, https://chicagocrusader.com/history-and-headlines.

8. "To Our Patrons," *Freedom's Journal*, March 16, 1827, 1.

9. Frankie Hutton, *The Early Black Press in America, 1827 to 1860* (Greenwood Press, 1993); Armistead Scott Pride and Clint C. Wilson, *A History of the Black Press* (Howard University Press, 1997), 65.

10. 1860 Census: Population of the United States, *United States Census Bureau*, accessed April 11, 2023, https://www.census.gov/library/publications/1864/dec/1860a .html.

11. Mae Najiyyah Duncan, *A Survey of Cincinnati's Black Press & Its Editors 1844–2010* (Xlibris, 2011), 3.

12. I. Garland Penn, *The Afro-American Press and Its Editors* (Wiley, 1891).

13. Isabel Wilkerson, *The Warmth of Other Suns: The Epic Story of America's Great Migration* (Knopf, 2010); Steven Reich, ed., *The Great Black Migration* (Greenwood, 2014).

14. Campbell Gibson and Kay Jung, "Historical Census Statistics on Population Totals by Race, 1790 to 1990," Working Paper No. 56 (U.S. Census Bureau, September 2002).

15. Frederick G. Detweiler, *The Negro Press in the United States* (University of Chicago Press, 1922), 2.

16. Ethan Michaeli, *The Defender: How the Legendary Black Newspaper Changed America* (Houghton Mifflin Harcourt, 2016).

17. Vishnu Oak, *The Negro Newspaper* (Antioch Press, 1948), appendix II.

18. Roland Wolseley, *The Black Press, USA* (Iowa State University Press, 1971).

19. Suggs, "Introduction," in *The Black Press in the Middle West*, 1.

20. Walter Freidman, "The Black Press in the Middle West," *Business History Review* 71, no. 1 (1997): 125–26.

21. A. Gilbert Belles, "The Black Press in the Middle West," *Illinois Historical Journal* 90, no. 1 (1997): 70.

22. Jon K. Lauck, *The Lost Region: Toward a Revival of Midwestern History* (University of Iowa Press, 2013), 7.

23. Michael Steiner, "The Birth of the Midwest and the Rise of Regional Theory," in *Finding a New Midwestern History*, ed. Jon K. Lauck, Gleaves Whitney, and Joseph Hogan (University of Nebraska Press, 2018), 4.

24. Jeffrey Helgeson, "Politics in the Promised Land," in Lauck et al., *Finding a New Midwestern History*, 112.

25. Jon K. Lauck, *The Good Country: A History of the American Midwest, 1880–1900* (University of Oklahoma Press, 2022), 121.

26. John Dittmer, *Local People: The Struggle for Civil Rights in Mississippi* (University of Illinois Press, 1994).

27. For examples of recent scholarship on Black activism in the Midwest, see Patrick Jones, *The Selma of the North: Civil Rights Insurgency in Milwaukee* (Harvard University Press, 2009); Kerry Pimblott, *Faith in Black Power: Religion, Race, and Resistance in*

*Cairo, Illinois* (University Press of Kentucky, 2017); and Nishani Frazier, *Harambee City: The Congress of Racial Equality in Cleveland and the Rise of Black Power Populism* (University of Arkansas Press, 2017).

28. "About Us," *Black Midwest Initiative*, accessed April 11, 2023, https://www.theblackmidwest.com/about-us.

29. Belles, "The Black Press," 70.

30. Carl Sandburg, *The Chicago Race Riots* (Harcourt, Brace and Howe, 1919), 51.

31. St. Clair Drake and Horace Cayton, *Black Metropolis* (University of Chicago Press, 2015), 12.

32. Walker, "The Promised Land," 12.

33. For recent scholarship on Black Chicago, see Davarian Baldwin, *Chicago's New Negroes: Modernity, the Great Migration, and Black Urban Life* (University of North Carolina Press, 2007); Marcia Chatelain, *South Side Girls: Growing Up in the Great Migration* (Duke University Press, 2015); Adam Green, *Selling the Race: Culture, Community, and Black Chicago, 1940–1955* (University of Chicago Press, 2007); and Darlene Clark Hine and John McCluskey Jr., eds., *The Black Chicago Renaissance* (University of Illinois Press, 2012).

34. Baldwin, *Chicago's New Negroes*, 14–15.

35. Chatelain, *South Side Girls*, 2.

36. Hilary Mac Austin, "The *Defender* Brings You the World," in Hine and McCluskey Jr., *The Black Chicago Renaissance*, 57.

37. Michaeli, *The Defender.*

38. Robert Weems, *The Merchant Prince of Black Chicago: Anthony Overton and the Building of a Financial Empire* (University of Illinois Press, 2020); E. James West, *Ebony Magazine and Lerone Bennett Jr.: Popular Black History in Postwar America* (University of Illinois Press, 2020); West, *A House for the Struggle: The Black Press and the Built Environment in Chicago* (University of Illinois Press, 2022); Gerald Horne, *The Rise and Fall of the Associated Negro Press* (University of Illinois Press, 2017).

39. Michaeli, *The Defender*, 63–65.

40. Penn, *The Afro-American Press*, 219.

41. Michaeli, *The Defender*, 23, 29, 37.

42. Green, *Selling the Race*, 15.

43. John H. Johnson and Lerone Bennett Jr., *Succeeding Against the Odds* (Amistad, 1989), 164.

44. Amy Helene Forss, *Black Print with a White Carnation: Mildred Brown and the Omaha Star Newspaper, 1938–1989* (University of Nebraska Press, 2013).

45. Forss, *Black Print*, 37–41.

46. Fred Carroll, "Black Print with a White Carnation," *American Journalism* 31, no. 3 (2014): 406–408.

47. Kim Gallon, *Pleasure in the News: African American Readership and Sexuality in the Black Press* (University of Illinois Press, 2020); D'Weston Haywood, *Let Us Make Men: The Twentieth-Century Black Press and a Manly Vision for Racial Advancement* (University of North Carolina Press, 2018); James McGrath Morris, *Eyes on the Struggle:*

*Ethel Payne, First Lady of the Black Press* (HarperCollins, 2017); Carole McCabe Booker, *Alone Atop the Hill: The Autobiography of Alice Dunnigan* (University Press of Georgia, 2015).

48. Julius E. Thompson, *Dudley Randall, Broadside Press, and the Black Arts Movement in Detroit, 1960–1995* (McFarland, 2005); Herb Boyd, *Black Detroit: A People's History of Self-Determination* (Amistad, 2017); Beth Tompkins Bates, *The Making of Black Detroit in the Age of Henry Ford* (University of North Carolina Press, 2012).

49. Frazier, *Harambee City*; David Williams, *African Americans in Indianapolis* (Indiana University Press, 2022).

50. Lauck, "The Ongoing History Crisis," vii (see introduction, n. 8).

OLIVIA M. HAGEDORN AND ERIK S. MCDUFFIE

5

# THE LIFE AND DIASPORIC JOURNEYS OF CHICAGO ORGANIZER AND GLOBETROTTER CHRISTINE JOHNSON

Christine Johnson was determined. She was president of the African-American Heritage Association (AAHA), a Chicago-based organization committed to advancing global Black freedom through public history. In the spring of 1960, the AAHA called on Black Chicagoans to stop working for five minutes in honor of African Freedom Day. The April 15 celebration was created in 1958 at the First Congress of Independent African States convened in Accra, Ghana.[1]

A teacher and world traveler, Christine Johnson understood the importance of working with Black people across the political spectrum.[2] Working alongside local labor leader and Communist Party leader Ishmael Flory, Johnson urged Black Chicagoans to honor the stoppage and situate their economic struggles within the larger framework of global racial capitalism. These protests, she wrote, were at their most basic level a "protest against 'racism'—the fig-leaf of super-exploitation, colonialism, imperialism, and modern war."[3] News of the

AAHA campaign was reported in the *Chicago Defender*, the largest Black-owned newspaper in the world.[4]

Christine Johnson remained in the public eye in the years that followed through her leadership in the AAHA and Nation of Islam; friendships with Kwame Nkrumah, the US Black nationalist Malcolm X, and Black cultural luminaries like Margaret Burroughs; groundbreaking educational work; and international travels.[5] Yet despite her remarkable achievements, Christine Johnson largely has been erased from prevailing historical narratives of Black Chicago, the US Midwest, Black internationalism, and the African Diaspora.[6]

This chapter offers a new angle on the history of Black people in the Midwest and the African Diaspora by tracing the life, activism, and overseas travels of Christine Johnson. Her life reveals the history of the "diasporic Midwest."[7] This framing resists notions of Midwestern provinciality; extends the study of the African Diaspora beyond the Atlantic Seaboard; and positions the Midwest as a germinal center of Black international thought, movement formation, and political action. Johnson's work and global travels also elucidate the importance of "diasporic cultural feminism" to the region. Diasporic cultural feminism describes the politics and subject position of Black women cultural workers like Johnson, whose transnational lives and Black feminist practice expanded the global reach of the Midwest. Combined, the diasporic Midwest and diasporic cultural feminism frameworks foreground how local, regional, and global forces converged to make Chicago an epicenter of Black women's international activism.

Christine Johnson's life provides a lens for appreciating the Midwest as a region indelibly shaped by global Black thought and protest. Her life transcends the community study framework that continues to dominate the field of Black Midwestern studies.[8] While these studies have demonstrated the national significance of Black Midwestern cities to African American political, social, and cultural life, they have downplayed the transnational and gendered valances of Black life, culture, and protest in the region. This framing implies that the Black Midwest formed apart from the broader African Diaspora and that Black women played no part in its development as a region. Christine Johnson's writings, travels, and activism therefore stand as important counterpoints to common misperceptions of the twentieth-century Midwest as a white, heteropatriarchal, provincial flyover country—"a place where one leaves" never to return for better opportunities and a new life.[9] Her life reminds us that the Black Midwest is deeply emmeshed in the currents of the African Diaspora, and her activism has helped sustain the region's diasporic connections for decades. Indeed, Johnson's life locates Chicago as a site of generative potential, a space where African American women forged cutting-edge transnational movements and advocated transformative social change locally and globally.[10]

Telling Christine Johnson's story is a difficult task. Her life demonstrates the challenges of recovering the histories of Black Midwestern women who left few records and whose legacies have been minimized or denigrated.[11] Johnson's personal papers and belongings are lost, and much of what we know about her life comes from the men whose lives she influenced.[12] This erasure reminds us that archives continue to be sites of impossibility for Black women. Given this reality, telling Christine Johnson's life story—and the life stories of Black Midwestern women generally—requires that historians "[trespass] the boundaries of the archive" and reflect on what Lisa Lowe describes as the "what could have been."[13] This means using the few primary sources we do have—including journalism, writings, and correspondence—alongside those produced by Johnson's peers and secondary scholars to imagine her possible experiences and reckon with the contested nature of Black Midwestern history.

## EARLY YEARS

Coming of age in the Jim Crow era and migrating to Chicago left an indelible mark on Johnson's life and shaped the trajectory of her activism. One of five children, Mary Christine Claybourne was born in 1909 outside of Versailles, Kentucky. Her father, Brock, was a farm laborer. Her mother, Mattie, labored as a domestic worker.[14] Mattie worked out of necessity to keep her family afloat.[15] Recalling her mother's courage in the *ABC's of African History*, Christine Johnson commended Mattie's "courage, struggles, and success in providing for and keeping together a family of five children." Such "was the saga of this fearless Black woman in the American colony."[16] Framing her mother's efforts as a form of resistance, Johnson gestured toward her early but enduring belief that Black women were central to the struggle for self-determination.

After graduating from the all-Black Chambers Avenue High School in 1927, Johnson then enrolled as a nursing student at Meharry Medical College in Nashville, Tennessee. Founded in 1876, Meharry was a historically Black institution with an international student body that included Malawi's first president, Dr. Hastings Kamuzu Banda. Meharry opened her eyes to Black diasporic communities in the United States and introduced her to global liberation movements.[17] Johnson subsequently studied at the Universal School of Handicrafts and Occupational Therapy in New York City. The city was home to an eclectic mix of communists, labor organizers, and Black left feminists who were committed to Black liberation, women's rights, decolonization, socialism, peace, and international solidarity.[18] It was in Harlem where Johnson first met and forged a lasting friendship with Kwame Nkrumah, Ghana's first president.[19]

Christine Johnson left Harlem in the 1940s and settled in Chicago, where she married Earl Johnson.[20] She joined a wave of Black migrants who moved to the city as part of the First Great Migration. Between 1910 and 1945, nearly 300,000 migrants descended on Chicago, which saw its Black population balloon from 44,103 in 1910 to over 337,000 in 1945.[21] Migrants transformed Chicago into a bustling epicenter of African American culture, art, and politics. The *Chicago Defender* and the Associated Negro Press placed the Midwestern metropolis at the center of a global Black publishing network.[22] Meanwhile, Black nationalist organizations like Marcus Garvey's Universal Negro Improvement Association, Mittie Maude Gordon's Peace Movement of Ethiopia, and the Nation of Islam flourished. These organizations stoked New Negro radicalism and bolstered transnational outlooks among Black Chicagoans.[23]

These forces hastened the Black Chicago Renaissance. Beginning in the 1930s and stretching into the 1950s, the Chicago Renaissance comprised a dynamic period of Black cultural and artistic expression. Writers, artists, educators, and performers such as Gwendolyn Brooks, Richard Wright, Margaret Burroughs, and Elizabeth Catlett, among others, used their art to explore questions of freedom, identity, belonging, and dignity. This expression had a distinctly working-class and internationalist perspective, and Black women's productions often evinced a Black feminist worldview.[24] A diasporic cultural feminist, Christine Johnson surely drew inspiration from the cultural fluorescence that greeted her.

Nevertheless, racial violence, segregation, and discrimination persisted in Chicago. Anti-Black violence confined most African Americans to the "Black Belt," a two-mile-long corridor on the South Side. Records do not reveal where Christine Johnson lived as a newly arrived migrant, but she likely joined thousands of other Black residents who lived in decrepit one-room apartments known as kitchenettes. Escaping kitchenette living was nearly impossible in the face of housing discrimination and terrorism. The most heinous violence occurred during the Chicago "Riot" of 1919, when white residents invaded Black neighborhoods and terrorized residents for over a week.[25] Certainly, the violence of 1919 would have lingered in the mind of Christine Johnson as she navigated life as a Black woman in Chicago.

## EARLY ACTIVISM

Christine Johnson blossomed as a grassroots Black internationalist in the 1950s and early 1960s. Her work during these years reveals the creative ways Black Midwestern women engaged internationalist politics at the local level while asserting their voices on an international stage.

In 1948, Johnson accepted a position as a substitute teacher for the Chicago Public School (CPS), and in 1955, she took a permanent position as an elementary school teacher on the city's southwest side.[26] Working for the CPS fueled Johnson's politicization. It was one of the most segregated and discriminatory school systems in the nation. As Elizabeth Todd-Breland writes, "CPS [officials] systematically assigned Black children to poorer-quality schools that were overcrowded and inequitably and inadequately funded."[27]

Johnson's frustrations with the CPS, combined with her interest in Black history, led her to cofound the African-American Heritage Association in 1958 with Ishmael Flory. Together, Johnson and Flory tapped into Chicago's "infrastructure of possibility" and grew the AAHA into one of the Midwest's most prominent Black public history organizations.[28] The AAHA's very name illustrated Johnson's understanding of the diasporic dimensions of Black history. She was ahead of the curve in proudly identifying Black Americans as "African Americans" at a moment when most Black people referred to themselves as "Negroes."

Johnson and Flory used public history to "wipe away inaccuracies, distortions, misrepresentations, and falsifications about peoples of African descent."[29] AAHA programs celebrated Negro History Week, Emancipation Day, DuSable Week, and Africa Freedom Day. The group also pushed for the civic recognition of Haitian fur trader Jean Baptiste Pointe du Sable as the city's first settler. Finally, the AAHA published pamphlets, hosted political forums, taught Black history classes, and sponsored talks by prominent Black scholars and activists.[30]

AAHA programs emphasized how racial capitalism, white supremacy, and imperialism operated simultaneously at local, national, and international registers. Christine Johnson understood that racial formations operated across geographic boundaries with devasting consequences for people of color globally, and she stood against Western hypocrisy. Johnson lambasted Western hypocrisy in a 1959 letter to US Secretary of State Christian Herter. Johnson wrote, "The American press hysterically reports on the internal struggles of Laos, with the information that the State Department is preparing to call upon the [United

Nations] to send in fact-finding observers." Yet the State Department refused to support a similar mission in South Africa, where a "government of minority whites have subverted the rights and the land of 9 million . . . Black people. What manner of moral posture Americans must present to the world, when we pretend to be steamed up about . . . so-called captive peoples, while saying nothing about human beings struggling for freedom and dignity in South Africa?"[31]

Johnson articulated similar critiques outside of the AAHA. Incensed by the inequities she faced at the CPS, Johnson accepted a position as principal of the University of Islam, an independent school affiliated with the Nation of Islam (NOI). Founded in Detroit in 1930 by Wallace D. Fard, the Nation was the largest Black nationalist organization in the United States. Elijah Muhammad succeeded Fard in 1934 and with moved NOI's headquarters to Chicago the aid of his wife, Clara. The pair grew the organization into a powerful beacon of Black pride and economic self-sufficiency. At its height, the NOI claimed anywhere between 10,000 and 100,000 members, fifty temples across twenty-two states, and hundreds of small commercial enterprises.[32] The most recognizable NOI minister, of course, was Malcolm X. Born in Omaha, Nebraska, to Garveyite parents, Malcolm X joined the NOI from prison. He rose quickly within the NOI's ranks after earning parole in 1952, and he gained international celebrity as minister of Temple No. 7 in Harlem.[33]

Johnson joined the NOI in the late 1950s. She credited Elijah Muhammad for giving her "an incentive to rededicate myself to the service of my people and a new belief in them."[34] If Elijah Muhammad's appeals to racial pride drew Johnson to the NOI, so too did the NOI's "promise of patriarchy." As Ula Y. Taylor has shown, the NOI's promise of supportive husbands and financial independence appealed to many Black women. Heralding Black women as worthy of protection, the NOI confronted the devaluation of Black womanhood head-on and "provided a space for women who had been disrespected, abused, and who had struggled to find a 'home' in racial America."[35] This promise certainly appealed to Christine Johnson, who watched her mother struggle as the family's sole provider.

Johnson quickly emerged as the organization's foremost authority on education. She oversaw the education of more than 350 students at the Chicago University of Islam (UOI) campus at 5333 South Greenwood Avenue.[36] As she had with the AAHA, Johnson used education and history to challenge racist myths about Black inferiority and draw connections between the experiences of African Americans living in Chicago and those of African-descended peoples worldwide. In the process, Johnson transformed the UOI into an arena for the celebration of global Blackness. "We need teachers who understand themselves as Black men and women, working to free themselves from the forces of the Devil and who can pass this knowledge to our children and our nation," Johnson wrote in a 1961 editorial for the Nation's newspaper, *Muhammad Speaks*. Such educators, she concluded, would "help us find our rightful place in . . . the world on the basis of a solid and prideful knowledge of the history of Africa and the relation of people of African descent to the world and its development."[37]

Johnson's appeal aligned with Elijah Muhammad's teachings about self-reliance and racial separatism. However, her editorial challenged NOI doctrine on Africa and the African Diaspora. Muhammad was "as anti-African as he was anti-white," Malcolm X proclaimed in 1965 after his 1964 exit from the NOI.[38] In fact, the NOI's genealogical myth identified Mecca as the origin of humanity and African Americans' ancestral homeland. Johnson's words therefore constituted an important challenge to NOI doctrine and reflected her personal commitment to engaging global Islam, Black internationalism, and the African Diaspora through education. The UOI curriculum reflected this commitment. Students learned Arabic as part of their studies, and instructors took UOI students on field trips to study the Chicago Art Institute's exhibition of African art and sculpture.[39] These trips, along with a diverse international faculty, further cemented the UOI's status as a site of global engagement.[40]

Meanwhile, Johnson created space for women's activism within the male-dominated NOI. Johnson believed that the "regenerated so-called Negro woman" was critical to the struggle for Black liberation. NOI women could play an "equally vital role" in the construction of a new Black nation if they flexed their feminine authority as wives, mothers, and educators to stimulate race pride, build international solidarities, and "furnish an atmosphere of mutual cooperation and helpfulness." Only then, she concluded, would NOI women "change the winter of our discontent into [a] glorious summer of racial solidarity."[41] Identifying motherhood as the location from which Nation women's authority sprang, Johnson upheld the patriarchal teachings of NOI doctrine and seemed to confirm Elijah Muhammad's message that motherhood was Allah's blessing. Yet claiming "natural" authority as a woman and an educator meant that Johnson could "trump patriarchy" and espouse pan-Africanist politics in open defiance to Elijah Muhammad. "Trumping patriarchy" arguably helped Johnson retain her prominent leadership position.[42]

Johnson's relationship with Elijah Muhammad and the NOI eventually soured. She resented Muhammad's interference at the UOI, and she expressed frustration with the cult of personality surrounding him.[43] Her attachment to the NOI waned further after Malcolm X's 1965 assassination. While many NOI members denounced Malcolm, Johnson celebrated him. In 1966, she gave a eulogy at a memorial service sponsored by the civil rights organization ACT! and the Educational Fund for the Children of Malcolm (X) Shabazz.[44] She also professed her support in writing. Two of her poems appeared in the 1967 anthology *For Malcolm: Poems on the Life and Death of Malcolm X*.[45] Johnson's actions likely infuriated Elijah Muhammad, and her words constituted an effective declaration of independence from the Nation.[46]

## CULTURAL POLITICS AND TRAVEL IN THE AGE OF BLACK POWER

Johnson's split from the NOI created new opportunities for her to advance diasporic cultural feminism as the Black Power Movement gained momentum in the mid-1960s. Now a respected veteran and cultural figure, Johnson relished the opportunity to support younger Black Power activists, including African American communist professor and political prisoner Angela Davis. Davis faced death for her alleged role in a courtroom revolt on August 7, 1970, in Marin County, California.[47] Recognizing how Davis's case symbolized injustice faced by Black women globally, Johnson founded Chicago's Angela Davis Defense Committee. This brought Johnson into collaboration with the Black Panther Party, Communist Party, and Southern Christian Leadership Conference; Davis's family; and the global amnesty movement. Indeed, Johnson's efforts cemented Chicago's status as a focal point in the worldwide struggle to free Davis.[48]

Meanwhile, Johnson established Black institutions focused on the survival and wellbeing of local Black communities. In 1970, she founded the Day Care Center for Severely and Profoundly Mentally Handicapped Children. The center was the first of its kind in the country to serve Black urban communities.[49] Johnson's advocacy on behalf of Angela Davis and ongoing educational work focused on Black children evinced her special concern for the dignity and respect of Black women and children.

This concern animated her decision to author two textbooks for African American children: *Muhammad's Children* and *ABC's of African History*. *Muhammad's Children: A First Grade Reader* was groundbreaking. Published in 1963, the 130-page book used lessons in phonics and grammar and biographical sketches to enhance Black children's "self-love," counter Eurocentrism, and

promote nation-building for the NOI. Information about Africa appeared prominently, and while the book contained a biographical sketch of Elijah Muhammad, it also featured non-Muslim Black people like Mary McCleod Bethune,
W. E. B. Du Bois, and Frederick Douglass.[50] While Johnson's textbook might
seem mainstream by today's standards, her 1963 text anticipated the liberatory
pedagogy of the Black Panther Party and promoted African American–centered
education before these ideals became popular.

*ABC's of African History* illustrated Johnson's tenacity following her break
from the Nation of Islam. Published in 1971, the book used biographical sketches
and pictures of famous people of African descent to celebrate the contributions of
African-descended people to world history since the dawn of humanity. Marcus
Garvey and Malcolm X appeared prominently in the book. Johnson's sketch of
Malcolm X stressed his self-transformation, global travels, and uncompromising
commitment to the liberation of oppressed people everywhere. This work kept
his legacy alive and made him relevant to Black youth.[51]

Meanwhile, Christine Johnson organized on multiple fronts domestically
and internationally. As historians Keisha Blain and Tiffany Gill argue, "travel
provided the primary vehicle for advancing the cause of black internationalism" for countless Black women who came "into physical contact with a diverse
group of men and women who helped to refine, and even redefine, their ideas."[52]
This certainly was the case for Christine Johnson, who traveled abroad alone.

Ghana was an important destination. Ghana emerged as the beacon of global
Black freedom after gaining its independence from the United Kingdom on
March 6, 1957.[53] Johnson visited Ghana several times, but one of her most important visits occurred in June 1962, when she attended the Accra Assembly: The
World Without the Bomb. Delegates from Africa, Latin America, Europe, and
the United States gathered for the week-long conference and rallied against
"nuclear imperialism," or efforts by Western powers to maintain colonialism
in Africa through promoting Cold War politics and weapons testing.[54] The
conference raised Johnson's international profile and placed her at the center
of the global peace movement.[55]

Johnson's attendance at the conference illustrates how Black women cultural workers in Chicago reshaped dominant practices of respectability.[56]
Johnson traveled alone, and newspaper coverage made no mention of her
husband, Earl. Newspapers depicted Johnson as a seasoned traveler and Black
internationalist—as a guest and respected confidant of Pan-African luminaries
such as Kwame Nkrumah. Traveling alone and interacting with anticolonial

leaders on a world stage was certainly a transgressive move in the context of the Cold War, when women were expected to "embrace domesticity in service to the nation."[57]

Johnson's travels reveal the limitations of her internationalist worldview, though. Her unshakable support for Kwame Nkrumah is a case in point. Johnson remained a staunch ally of her friend after a military coup toppled him in February 1966. Nkrumah subsequently relocated to Conakry, the capital of Guinea, where President Sékou Touré appointed him co-president.[58] Like countless Black radicals around the world, Johnson believed that Nkrumah was unjustly overthrown by a US-backed military coup carrying out the dirty work of Western nations.[59] In a show of support, she visited Nkrumah in Guinea in 1969.[60]

Johnson's loyalty prompted her to dismiss the complex political realities and authoritarian tendencies in Ghana and Guinea. There is no question that US government officials viewed the Ghanaian president as a threat to American global interests and that US operatives were active in Accra. But these developments do not explain fully the causes of Nkrumah's overthrow. As Kevin Gaines observes, Nkrumah's "acquiescence to widespread corruption and his intolerance of dissent undermined . . . popular support."[61] Similarly, Sékou Touré's rule of Guinea grew increasingly autocratic by the late 1960s.[62] Johnson ignored these realities when she dismissed Nkrumah's critics as dupes of American imperialism.[63]

Johnson's conclusions about Ghana and Guinea speak to how Black internationalists overlook what Benjamin Talton calls the "political messiness" of Black rulers who embrace "the political posture of Pan-Africanism while advancing authoritarian domestic policies."[64] Johnson's diasporic cultural feminism enabled her to travel the world and to connect African American freedom to global struggles. Yet her global vision was unable to account fully for the paradoxes of Black politics and life.

## FINAL YEARS AND CONCLUSIONS

Christine Johnson had always lived a private life, but her presence in Chicago's activist circles waned considerably in the 1980s. A handful of her letters appeared in local newspapers.[65] She also published two books, *Goluba-African Masks* (1983) and *Ghana Under Nkrumah* (1994).[66] The last years of her life are otherwise shrouded in mystery. We have no way of knowing why Christine Johnson chose to retreat from public life. One thing is certain, though: her death on March 16, 1999, marked the end of a fascinating life that defies simple categorization.[67]

Johnson's life provides a genealogy for uncovering the predecessors of contemporary Black movements, most notably Black Lives Matter/Movement for Black Lives (BLM/M4BL). As the activist-intellectual and longtime Chicago resident Barbara Ransby has observed, "Black feminist politics have been the ideological bedrock of Black Lives Matter and the Movement for Black Lives. Black women have been prominent in leadership and as spokespersons and have insisted on being recognized as such." Chicago emerged as a hotspot for BLM/M4BL and Black feminist organizing against police brutality and racism. Few if any activists who took to Chicago's streets in the summer of 2020 knew about Christine Johnson and her work. Still, this new generation of Black activists stood on her shoulders. Johnson's diasporic cultural feminism anticipated BLM's intersectional and transnational understanding of justice. Moreover, her eschewing of the politics of respectability, fervent calls for Black self-love, accountability, and self-care, and belief in the importance of intergenerational solidarity are in line with the demands of many young Black feminists today.[68] Young people have much to learn from Johnson's triumphs and mistakes while making the diasporic Midwest.

## NOTES

1. "Plan Work Halt on 'Africa' Day," *Chicago Defender* (hereafter *CD*), April 9, 1960, 3.

2. Deborah Gray White, *Too Heavy a Load: Black Women in Defense of Themselves* (W. W. Norton, 1999).

3. AAHA to ANP, March 26, 1960, box 210, folder 1, Claude Barnett Papers, Series 2, Chicago Historical Society (hereafter CHS), Chicago, IL; "Plan Work Halt on 'Africa' Day," *CD*, March 31, 1960.

4. Myiti Sengstacke Rice, "Robert Sengstacke Abbott, 1868–1940," in *Building the Black Metropolis: African American Entrepreneurship in Chicago*, ed. Robert E. Weems Jr. and Jason P. Chambers (University of Illinois Press, 2017), 44–47, 51, 57.

5. Olivia M. Hagedorn, "'Call Me African': Black Women and Diasporic Cultural Feminism in Chicago, 1930–1980" (PhD diss., University of Illinois at Urbana-Champaign, 2022).

6. Michael West, Waldo Martin, and Fanon Che Wilkins describe Black internationalism as "the ideal of universal emancipation, unbounded by national, imperial, continental, or oceanic boundaries—or even by racial ones." Michael West, Waldo Martin, and Fanon Che Wilkins, eds., *Toussaint to Tupac: The Black International Since the Age of Revolution* (University of North Carolina Press, 2009), xi.

7. For more on the diasporic Midwest, see Erik S. McDuffie, *The Second Battle for Africa: Garveyism, the U.S. Heartland, and Global Black Freedom* (Duke University Press, 2024); Olivia M. Hagedorn, "'Chicago's Renaissance Woman': The Life, Activism,

and Diasporic Cultural Feminism of Dr. Margaret Taylor Goss Burroughs," *African and Black Diaspora: An International Journal* 13, no. 3 (2020): 296–313; Courtney Pierre Joseph, "Diasporic Ambassadors: Black Women, Pageants, and Building across the African Diaspora in the Late Twentieth Century," *African and Black Diaspora: An International Journal* 14, no. 1 (2022): 41–51; Courtney Pierre Joseph, "Ou Ayisyen? The Making of a Haitian Diasporic Community in Chicago, 1933–2010" (PhD diss., University of Illinois at Urbana-Champaign, 2017).

8. Drake and Cayton, *Black Metropolis* (see chapter 4, n. 31); Bill V. Mullen, *Popular Fronts: Chicago and African-American Cultural Politics, 1935–1946* (University of Illinois Press, 1999, 2015); Anne Meis Knupfer, *The Chicago Black Renaissance and Black Women's Activism* (University of Illinois Press, 2006); Green, *Selling the Race* (see chapter 4, n. 33); Baldwin, *Chicago's New Negroes* (see chapter 4, n. 33); James Grossman, *Land of Hope: Chicago, Black Southerners, and the Great Migration* (University of Chicago Press, 2011); Hine and McCluskey Jr., *The Black Chicago Renaissance* (see chapter 4, n. 33); Christopher Robert Reed, *The Rise of Chicago's Black Metropolis, 1920–1929* (University of Illinois Press, 2014).

9. Quoted in Hogan et al., *The Sower and the Seer*, xiii (see introduction, n. 26). See also Hoganson, *The Heartland* (see chapter 1, n. 1); Anne Trubek, ed., *Voices from the Rust Belt* (Picador, 2018); Faranak Miraftab, *Global Heartlands: Displaced Labor, Transnational Lives, and Local Place Making* (Indiana University Press, 2016); Martin F. Manalansan IV, Chantal Nadeau, Richard T. Rodríguez, and Siobhan B. Somerville, "Queering the Middle: Race, Region, and a Queer Midwest," *GLQ: A Journal of Lesbian and Gay Studies* 20, no. 1–2 (2014): 1–12.

10. For recent scholarship on the global significance of the twentieth-century Black Midwest, see Terrion L. Williamson, ed., *Black in the Middle: An Anthology of the Black Midwest* (Belt Publishing, 2020); Keisha N. Blain, *Set the World on Fire: Black Nationalist Women and the Global Struggle for Freedom* (University of Pennsylvania, 2016); Ashley M. Howard, "Then the Burnings Began: Omaha's Urban Revolts and the Meaning of Political Violence," *Nebraska History* (Summer 2017): 82–97; Scott Kurashige, *The Fifty-Year Rebellion: How the U.S. Political Crisis Began in Detroit* (University of California Press, 2017); Joseph Hogan, "Malcolm X in Michigan," *Middle West Review* 3, no. 2 (2017): 137–42; Ford, *A Brick and a Bible* (see chapter 3, n. 17).

11. Erik S. McDuffie, "The Diasporic Journeys of Louise Little: Grassroots Garveyism, the Midwest, and Community Feminism," *Women, Gender, and Families of Color* 4, no. 2 (2016): 165.

12. Hagedorn, "'Call Me African,'" 27; Robert T. Starks, interviewed by Larry Crowe, December 15, 2009, session 1, tape 6, story 3, HistoryMakers Digital Archive, Chicago, IL.

13. Saidiya Hartman, "Venus in Two Acts," *Small Axe* 26 (June 2008): 2, 9–12; Lisa Lowe, "The Intimacies of Four Continents," in *Haunted by Empire: Geographies of Intimacy in North American History*, ed. Ann Laura Stoler (Duke University Press, 2006), 208.

14. United States Census, 1910, Kentucky, Scott County, Powder House, ED 91, NARA microfilm publication T624; United States Census, 1920, Kentucky, Scott Country,

Powder House, ED 151, NARA microfilm publication T625 (National Archives and Records Administration, n.d.).

15. George C. Wright, *Racial Violence in Kentucky, 1865–1940: Lynchings, Mob Rule and "Legal Lynching"* (Louisiana State University Press, 1990).

16. Christine Johnson, *ABC's of African History* (Vantage Press, 1971), iv.

17. Allison O'Connor, "Meharry Medical College," January 11, 2010, https://www.Blackpast.org/african-american-history/meharry-medical-college-1876.

18. Dayo Gore, *Radicalism at the Crossroads: African American Women Activists in the Cold War* (New York University Press, 2011); Erik S. McDuffie, *Sojourning for Freedom: Black Women, American Communism, and the Making of Black Left Feminism* (Duke University Press, 2011).

19. Reiland Rabaka defines pan-Africanism as "*a simultaneously intellectual, cultural, social, political, economic and artistic project that calls for the unification of and liberation of all people of African ancestry, both on the continent and in the African Diaspora*" (emphasis in the original). Reiland Rabaka, "Introduction: On the Intellectual Elasticity and Political Plurality of Pan-Africanism," in *Routledge Handbook of Pan-Africanism*, ed. Reiland Rabaka (Routledge 2020), 8.

20. We know little about Earl Johnson except that he worked as a real estate broker and pool hall owner. Christine Johnson funeral program, Patricia Liddell Researchers' Archives, Vivian G. Harsh Research Collection of Afro-American History and Literature, Chicago Public Library, Chicago, IL.

21. Drake and Cayton, *Black Metropolis*, 8.

22. Horne, *Associated Negro Press* (see chapter 4, n. 38).

23. Baldwin, *Chicago's New Negroes*.

24. Mullen, *Popular Fronts*; Hine and McCluskey Jr., *The Black Chicago Renaissance*; Knupfer, *Chicago's Black Renaissance*.

25. William M. Tuttle, *Race Riot: Chicago in the Red Summer of 1919* (Atheneum, 1970), 10.

26. "University of Islam Adds to Faculty," *Muhammad Speaks* (hereafter *MS*), October–November 1961, 9.

27. Elizabeth Todd-Breland, *A Political Education: Black Politics and Education Reform in Chicago Since the 1960s* (University of North Carolina Press, 2018), 2–3, 26–27.

28. Baldwin uses the phrase "infrastructure of Black possibility" to describe the generative potential of Chicago's South Side. Baldwin, *Chicago's New Negroes*, 23.

29. AAHA Constitution, ca. 1959, box 9, folder 22, Records of the Africana Library, Northwestern University Archives, Evanston, IL.

30. AAHA, "Coexistence, Colonialism, and Peace" poster advertisement, 1959; W.E.B. Du Bois to Ishmael Flory, April 18, 1960, both in W.E.B. Du Bois Papers, Special Collections and University Archives, University of Massachusetts Amherst, Amherst, MA.

31. Christine Johnson to Christian Herter, September 10, 1959, box 209, folder 9, Barnett Papers, Series 2, CHM.

32. Ula Y. Taylor, *The Promise of Patriarchy: Women and the Nation of Islam* (North Carolina University Press, 2017), 74; Edward E. Curtis, IV, *Black Muslim Religion in the Nation of Islam: A Short History* (Oxford University Press, 2009), 4. For more on Elijah Muhammad, see Claude Andrew Clegg III, *The Life and Times of Elijah Muhammad* (University of North Carolina Press, 2014).

33. McDuffie, "The Diasporic Journeys of Louise Little," 146–48, 158–60.

34. Christine Johnson, *Muhammad's Children* (Nation of Islam, 1963), 10.

35. Taylor, *Promise of Patriarchy*, 5.

36. Ibrahim M. Shalaby, "The Role of the School in Cultural Renewal and Identity Development in the Nation of Islam in America" (PhD diss., University of Arizona, 1967), 46; Essien-Udom, *Black Nationalism: A Search for Identity in America* (University of Chicago Press, 1962), 231–35.

37. Christine Johnson, "Educate Your Own Children Now," *MS*, December 1961, 15.

38. Malcolm X, "The Black Muslim Movement: An Assessment," in *February 1965: The Final Speeches*, ed. Steve Clark (Pathfinder Press, 1992), 205; Taylor, *Promise of Patriarchy*, 147.

39. Photograph, *MS*, January 1962, 6.

40. "University of Islam Graduates, Tomorrow's Leaders," April 1962, 13; "University of Islam PTA Sponsors Brilliant Musical Program at School, April 1962, 12; "Ghanian Greets Muhammad, Sees African Unity," May 8, 1964, 6, all in *MS*.

41. Christine Johnson, "Describes Importance of a Regenerated 'So-called Negro Woman,'" *MS*, February 1962.

42. Taylor, *Promise of Patriarchy*, 122, 179.

43. Clemmont E. Vontress, "Threat, Blessing, or Both? The Black Muslim Schools," *The Phi Delta Kappan* 47, no. 2 (1965): 87.

44. "Malcolm X Memorial Set," *CD*, February 19, 1966, 1.

45. Christine Johnson, "When You Died," in *For Malcolm X: Poems on the Life and Death of Malcolm X*, ed. Randall Dudley and Margaret Burroughs (Broadside Press, 1967), 71–72.

46. Christine Johnson to Kwame Nkrumah, May 21, 1969, box 5, folder 5, Kwame Nkrumah Papers (hereafter KNP), Moorland-Spingarn Research Center, Howard University, Washington, DC.

47. Frank Barat, ed., *Freedom Is a Constant Struggle: Ferguson, Palestine, and the Foundations for a Movement* (Haymarket Books, 2016), vii.

48. "Launch Local Free Angela Move [sic]," October 20, 1970; "Free Angela Meeting Set," December 29, 1970, *CD*.

49. "KOCO Opens Day Care Center," *CD*, October 27, 1970.

50. Johnson, *Muhammad's Children*, 88–89.

51. Johnson, *ABC's*.

52. Keisha N. Blain and Tiffany M. Gill, "Introduction: Black Women and the Complexities of Internationalism," in *To Turn the Whole World Over: Black Women and Internationalism*, ed. Blain and Gill (University of Illinois Press, 2019), 5.

53. Jeffrey S. Ahlman, *Living with Nkruhamism: Nation, State, and Pan-Africanism in Ghana* (Ohio University Press, 2017), 3.

54. Frances W. Herring, *World Without the Bomb: Story of the Accra Assembly* (Women for Peace, 1962), 35; Jean Allman, "Nuclear Imperialism and the Pan-African Struggle for Peace and Freedom, Ghana, 1961–1962," *Souls: A Critical Journal of Black Politics, Culture, and Society* 10, no. 2 (2008): 83–102.

55. "Attended Ban Bomb Confab," *Amsterdam News*, July 28, 1962.

56. Historian Evelyn Brooks Higginbotham uses "politics of respectability" to describe a strategy for racial uplift in the early twentieth century that "equated public behavior with individual self-respect and . . . the advancement of African Americas as a group." Evelyn Brooks Higginbotham, *Righteous Discontent: The Women's Movement in the Black Baptist Church, 1880–1920* (Harvard University Press, 1993), 14. See also Victoria W. Wolcott, *Remaking Respectability: African American Women in Interwar Detroit* (University of North Carolina Press, 2001); E. Frances White, *Dark Continent of Our Bodies: Black Feminism and the Politics of Respectability* (Temple University Press, 2001).

57. Elaine Tyler May, *Homeward Bound: American Families in the Cold War Era* (Basic Books, 1988, 2008), 98.

58. Kevin K. Gaines, *American Africans in Ghana: Black Expatriates and the Civil Rights Era* (University of North Carolina Press, 2006).

59. Christine Johnson, "Letter to the Editors of *Freedomways* on the Ghana Coup," *Freedomways* 6, no. 2 (1966): 152–58.

60. Christine Johnson to Kwame Nkrumah, March 24, 1969; Johnson to Nkrumah, April 18, 1971, box 5, folder 5, KNP.

61. Quoted in Gaines, *American Africans in Ghana*, 243.

62. Peniel E. Joseph, *Stokely: A Life* (Basic Civitas, 2014), 277.

63. Quoted in Kwame Nkrumah to Christine Johnson, August 12, 1969; Johnson to Nkrumah, April 18, 1971, box 5, folder 5, KNP.

64. Monique Bedasse, Kim D. Butler, Carlos Fernandes, Dennis Laumann, Tejasvi Nagaraja, Benjamin Talton, and Kira Thurman, "*AHR Conversation:* Black Internationalism," *American Historical Review* 125, no. 5 (2020): 1716.

65. Christine Johnson, "Commends Mayor's OK on Burroughs," March 29, 1984; "A Praise for Marva Collins," March 20, 1982; "Activists/Authors Share Experiences," May 18, 1982, all in *CD*.

66. Christine Johnson, *Goluba-African Mask* (Reed and Associates, 1983); Christine X. Johnson, *Ghana under Nkrumah* (Printed by the author, 1994).

67. Starks interview.

68. Ransby, *Making All Black Lives Matter*, 2–3. Mariame Kaba, *We Do This 'Til We Free Us: Abolitionist Organizing and Transforming Justice* (Haymarket Books, 2021); Mikki Kendall, *Hood Feminism: Notes from the Women That a Movement Forgot* (Viking, 2020).

### 6

# FROM LA PIETRA TO THE PRAIRIE

Writing the New Midwestern History
into the Transnational Narrative

While the revival of Midwest regional studies is a recent phenomenon, the roots of transnational history may be found several decades ago, especially during the 1990s, which first witnessed what may be termed the "transnational" turn in historical research and writing. In *The Limits of Transnationalism*, historian Nancy Green explains how the transnational "moment" reflected the "epistemological trends of the late twentieth century," linking its first noticeable attention to Ian Tyrrel's 1991 article "American Exceptionalism in an Age of International History."[1] By the end of the 1990s, transnational history had become influential enough that the Organization of American Historians (OAH) hosted a four-year study by over seventy historians at the Villa La Pietra in Italy. In its concluding report written by Thomas Bender, historians offered several recommendations for incorporating transnational scholarship and themes into undergraduate and graduate education, as well as postdoctoral training and faculty development. Among those themes were:

1. The nation-state is neither self-contained nor undifferentiated;
2. Studies of nations and historical phenomena must be resituated in larger contexts;
3. Historical inquiry needs to be aware of historical processes beyond the nation-state;
4. Globalizing historical inquiry requires comparative approaches and widening of social analysis;
5. While national history remains essential, it is recommended to resituate it in a larger framework sensitive to diverse relationship and structures, and;
6. Transnational inquiry is not a call for a "new" history to replace other lines of inquiry but an opportunity to create a more inclusive scholarship and pedagogy.

The report also offered both a caveat and an objective. First, it cautioned against using transnational studies to "produce a form of historiographical imperialism or an ideological justification for globalization and American hegemony."[2] Second, it called for a "variety of local conversations and varied strategies" for addressing its recommendations, before proceeding to outline objectives for pedagogy and faculty development.[3]

The revival of Midwestern studies might appear contradictory to the goals of La Pietra, offering a narrower regional lens into the past as well as struggling to reclaim legitimacy itself as an area of historiographical study. In *The Lost Region: Toward a Revival of Midwestern History*, Jon K. Lauck argues that by the 1950s, scholarly interest in the Midwest and its history waned. He states, "[T]he old cohesion of the Prairie Historians had dissolved, and American historians focused their energies elsewhere. When the postwar academic boom fizzled and economic pressures began to squeeze history departments beginning in the 1970s, the combined effect of new research agendas, declining budgets, and the retirement of an older generation of historians resulted in fewer professors, courses, and books focused on midwestern history."[4] There were attempts in the late twentieth century to reverse the region's declining scholarly reputation. In 1989, James R. Shortridge, professor of cultural geography at the University of Kansas, published an intriguing study of the Midwest, emphasizing a "humanist" approach to the understanding of place, specifically how the meaning, identity, and space of the Midwest changed over time.[5] A year later Andrew R. L. Cayton and Peter S. Onuf published *The Midwest and the Nation*, followed over a decade later by Cayton and Susan E. Gray's essay collection *The Identity of the American Midwest*.[6] The former work sought to encourage more systematic thinking by historians in relation to the region, focusing on the Old Northwest of the nineteenth century.

The real boon to Midwestern historical and regional studies occurred in the 2010s and witnessed not only revitalized scholarship but a new publication in *Middle West Review* and the founding of the Midwest History Association in 2014. Five years earlier, David S. Brown resurrected regional scholarship in *Beyond the Frontier: The Midwestern Voice in American Historical Writing*, examining the works and influences of such luminating figures as Charles Beard, William Appleman Williams, and Christopher Lasch. Noting the especially impactful legacy of the University of Wisconsin's history department, Brown explains how education in Madison came "in a distinctly 'American' dialect. Suspicious of Eastern power, many interior historians embraced a frankly provincial and populistic vision of the past" that revealed both positive and negative personal and regional values.[7] Continuing this re-evaluation of the impact of Midwestern historical writing, Jon K. Lauck's *Toward a Revival of Midwestern History* not only explores the travails of the field from the 1930s through 1990s but also a type of coverage myopia of the Midwest by contemporary national media outlets. Commenting on the earlier work, Lauck states, "Brown begins his discussion, as any discussion of midwestern history must, with Frederick Jackson Turner . . . [who] argued that midwestern settlers advanced American democratic practices on the frontier and begat a tradition of historical writing about and from the Midwest."[8] A moving force in recent Midwestern studies, Lauck has provided opportunities for a variety of voices to shape and reshape the field in such collections as *Finding a New Midwestern History* and *The Making of the Midwest: Essays on the Formation of Midwestern Identity, 1787–1900*.[9] The first of these collections affords a broad spectrum of analysis emphasizing the Midwest as a region, its people, iconography, landscapes, voices, and regional experience, while the latter more specifically focuses on Midwestern history from the Old Northwest to the fin de siècle. The pivotal analytical question, thus, becomes: does such scholarship reflect the Midwestern provincialism Brown suggests, or are there opportunities to translate this regional approach into the transnational framework?

A cursory glance at three different works on transnational themes in history suggests the traditional marginality of the Midwest. Following the *La Pietra Report*, Thomas Bender and several project participants published *Rethinking*

*American History in a Global Age.*[10] The work offers an instructive template on the then state of transnational historiography and its potential applicability to the discipline—a type of "how-to" manual for the La Pietra project. Understandably general in nature, the work nevertheless neglects the Midwest in relation to other regions in the nation. From a regional perspective the various authors only touch upon the North, South, and West, while the Atlantic and Pacific worlds receive more intensive discussions. For the Midwest only a brief reference to the role of the Ohio Valley in the formation of national consciousness appears. Four years later, Bender followed up the collection of essays with a popular narrative transnational history of the United States. *A Nation Among Nations: America's Place in World History* opens provocatively by declaring that it "proposes and then elaborates a new framing of U.S. history. It rejects the territorial space of the nation as the sufficient context for a national history."[11] No sense of American regional history appears in this work; however, ten states are specifically mentioned in the index with the Midwest only represented by Missouri, reflecting the author's emphasis on locality dependent on the British colonies and westward expansion. Interestingly, Bender spends as much time discussing the Mississippi River and Ohio Valley as the Atlantic and Pacific Oceans combined, providing needed geographic centrality to his narrative.[12] As part of its Explorations in World History series, in 2007, McGraw-Hill published Carl Guarneri's *America in the World: United States History in Global Context.* The series editors aver that the book, which functions either as a curriculum guide or textbook, "represents a coming together of two currents of historical thinking. One is a growing effort to 'internationalize' the teaching of U.S. history, while the second seeks to find an appropriate place for the United States within the larger story of world history."[13] This work's geographic focus is disproportionately skewed to the Atlantic World as opposed to the Pacific with no mention of the Mississippi or Ohio River Valleys nor the Gulf of Mexico. In addition, of the twelve states mentioned only two are from the Midwest and are only included because of the role of slavery in Missouri and Kansas. The author's discussion of the Louisiana Purchase concentrates on the Caribbean and New Orleans, and he fails to discuss the Old Northwest. It is understandable that broadly conceived reorientations of US history in a transnational framework might either purposefully or incidentally neglect the role of region or locality in that intricate tapestry of national development in a global context; therefore, might we look to a history from the "bottom up," where regional studies provide perspectives to write into the larger narratives?

The borders among local, regional, and transnational history are more porous than impenetrable and may be evidenced as early as the European exploration and colonization of North America. As discussed previously, scholars often credit Frederick Jackson Turner with the formation of Midwestern regional identity and history. Turner's 1893 paper "The Significance of the Frontier in American History" was, at least in part, a reaction to his mentor Herbert Baxter Adams's "germ theory," and both interpretations sought to situate the local in the global. For Adams, the white settlement of North America was principally a product of the Atlantic World: most specifically, the transfer of Anglo-Saxon heritage to the newly discovered continent; in contrast, Turner understood the immigration of Europeans to be in temporally and geographically differentiated segments that constantly changed due to the successive stages of frontier encounters.[14] Thus, for Turner, the frontier process beginning with first encounters along the Atlantic Seaboard progressively moved westward, leaving in its wake settled locales where historical processes and cultural interaction fostered larger regional identities. Michael C. Steiner comments, "The Midwest became the central room in this worthy house and the model for Turner's larger frontier regional theory."[15] Turner's later work on American sections and the New West intensifies this regional focus,[16] and Steiner incidentally suggests that this analytical development possessed a broader perspective than locality or region. He writes, "Turner wisely asserted that 'the world needs now more than ever the vigorous development of highly organized provincial life to serve as a check upon mob psychology on a national scale, and to furnish that variety which is essential to vital growth and originality.'"[17] This statement relates directly to the *La Pietra Report*'s call for resituating history in larger contexts and widening social analysis, although by moving from the local to regional to global rather than merely national to transnational.[18]

■  ■  ■

As historians followed Turner, discovering, repudiating, and rediscovering the role of locality and region in narratives of the nation, one may look for ways in which either intentionally or not these scholars offered perspectives that link the Midwest to a larger transnational perspective. Jon K. Lauck's newest publication *The Good Country* emphasizes comparative historical analysis and suggests that from a global perspective the Midwest developed a distinctive democratic character.[19] In the selective review of literature to follow, I argue that there are three areas of traditional Midwest historiography in which one may find transnational themes. Admittedly, the specific works that follow are merely a handful of fine studies that scholars may find on such topics, and my own research interests bias the selection to the Old Northwest, particularly Illinois, but their inclusion is meant to be illustrative of what has been done that relates the Midwest to the transnational and what may still be done.

Undoubtedly, the best topic in which to begin examining the transnational nature of Midwest studies is that of the colonial period, especially first encounters and ongoing relationships among indigenous peoples, the French and British, and native-born North American colonists. For Turner, the Atlantic Frontier bequeathed the "Indian Trader's Frontier." He writes, "All along the coast from Maine to Georgia the Indian trade opened up the river courses. Steadily the trader passed westward, utilizing the older lines of French trade. The Ohio, the Great Lakes, the Mississippi, the Missouri, and the Platte, the lines of western advance, were ascended by traders," differentiating the Atlantic Seaboard English agricultural colonization from the Trans-Appalachian French fur commodity colonization.[20] More recent scholarship, reflecting borderland theory, indigenous studies, and New Western writing, have recast the Turnerian view of the frontier and its people into a more complex and socially multi-varied place and process. Richard White's pathbreaking *The Middle Ground: Indians, Empires, and Republics in the Great Lakes Region, 1650–1815* provides a template from which to write regional history into the transnational. While the work's geographic scope on the *Pays d'en Haut* extends beyond the Midwest into Canada, it offers a nuanced discussion of indigenous and French relationships and how those fostered cultural transformation, which changed over the course of time due to a variety of factors in which imperial warfare, especially that with the English, proved significant. David Andrew Nichols returned to this subject in *Peoples of the Inland Sea: Native Americans and Newcomers in the Great Lakes Region, 1600–1870*, where the author builds on White's earlier work to discuss cultural exchange and accommodation, indigenous communities and resilience to foreign encroachment, and national and imperial politics related to colonization and expansion. A third useful work in this regard, moving beyond the indigenous peoples and French, is Brett Rushforth's *Bonds of Alliance: Indigenous & Slaveries in New France*, where the author argues that previous scholarship had neglected the role of slavery in the *Pays d'en Haut* that also reflected ethno-racial negotiations and the role of conflict and violence in those relationships. While few in number, the introduction of hundreds of African slaves in New France and slaveholders' attempts to replicate Caribbean slave institutions in the North broaden the global framework of the colonial Midwest.[21]

Closely related to these studies are those focused on boundaries—both political and geographic—that historically have defined the Midwest. Under the guidance of Walter Nugent and Malcolm Rohrbough, Indiana University Press published a series of works on the Trans-Appalachian frontier. Works such as James Davis's *Frontier Illinois* and Mark Wyman's *The Wisconsin Frontier* examined the critical processes of cultural interchange, accommodation, and conflict from colonization and imperial warfare through United States expansion and white settlement of the Trans-Appalachian region, with early politics and institution-building conditioned by remaining tensions with Britain through the War of 1812, continuing negotiations and subsequent displacement of indigenous peoples, and the political processes of territorial governance in a region bordered by British Canada to the north and the Spanish (later French) Louisiana Territory to the south and west.[22] More recently, Bethel Saler's *The Settler's Empire: Colonialism and State Formation in America's Old Northwest* provides a broader and more nuanced perspective on this early national period. While concerned with how the development of the Northwest Territory fundamentally shaped early national identity, particularly in resolving the apparent contradictions between a republican ethos and westward "empire"-building, the author relates how regional and national politics affected not only white settlers but also indigenous peoples, French foreign nationals, and European immigrants.[23] In addition to political boundaries, geographic ones helped make the Midwest. While books on the region's waterways abound, especially the principal river systems—the Mississippi, Missouri, and Ohio—and their connections to exploration, commerce, colonization, and empire-building, studies of the Great Lakes, with Canada to the region's north and accessibility to Atlantic Ocean trade to the east, offer opportunities for transnational focus.[24] Daniel Gifford's recent work *The Last Voyage of the Whaling Bark* Progress: *New Bedford, Chicago and the Twilight of an Industry* conjoins the global whaling industry with the preindustrial economic history of the United States and the rising cultural ascendancy of the Midwest as attested by the 1893 World's Columbian Exposition, where the *Progress* became a much-viewed museum piece for international audiences. Historian Theodore Karamanski's indefatigable research into maritime history has produced several works, including *Schooner Passage: Sailing Ships and the Lake Michigan Frontier*, *Maritime Chicago*, and *Navigating the Inland Seas: Great Lakes Navigation Aids in American History*.[25] Finally, journalist Dan Read provides a fascinating and important read on the history of the Great Lakes from an interdisciplinary perspective. His 2017 *The Death and Life of the Great Lakes* not only charts the course of lacustrine geography and cultures but the more global implications of commerce, infrastructure development, industrial pollution, and invasive foreign species for the Upper Midwest's principal waterways.[26]

Boundaries often become borders, and the very human story of immigration across national borders is critical to both transnational scholarship and the historical identity of the Midwest. With the turn to the New Social History in the 1960s and 1970s, immigration and ethnic studies proliferated, and historians interested in the Midwest played an essential role in this scholarship. The University of Nebraska's Frederick Luebke published numerous works on immigrants in the Great Plains, including the seminal *Immigrants and Politics: The Germans of Nebraska, 1880–1900.*[27] The late Jon Gjerde studied both the American Midwest and West but was especially interested in ethnohistory, as evidenced by works such as *From Peasants to Farmers: The Migration from Balestrand, Norway, to the Upper Middle West* and *The Minds of the West: Ethnocultural Evolution in the Rural Middle West, 1830–1917.*[28] Midwestern immigration histories, however, were not merely rural based. Kathleen Neils Conzen's *Immigrant Milwaukee, 1836–1860: Accommodation and Community in a Frontier City* located transnational experiences in a frontier urban environment, while Rudolph J. Vecoli's studies of Italians in Chicago significantly redefined the field when challenging Oscar Handlin's "uprooted" thesis and eventually led to the creation of the Immigration Research History Center at the University of Minnesota, one of the principal scholarly institutions for immigration studies in the world.[29] Moving beyond European immigrants, the University of Illinois Press launched the series Latinos in Chicago and the Midwest that includes such titles as *Pots of Promise: Mexicans and Pottery at Hull House, 1920–1940, Latina Lives in Milwaukee,* and *Defending Their Own in the Cold: The Cultural Turns of U.S. Puerto Ricans.*[30] Numerous other ethnic groups in the Midwest continue to be studied, including the Hmong, Chinese, Syrian, Filipino, and others, enriching the contributions of Midwestern studies to transnational historiography.

■   ■   ■

As attested by the aforementioned survey of selected texts, there has been a long tradition of Midwestern historical and regional studies that relate to the recent trend in transnational historiography, whether intentionally or not.

This tendency reveals that scholars focusing on the local or regional have not "missed the forest for the trees" but have provided essential narratives that may contribute the personal and intimately human faces and voices to more national and global historical perspectives. The fields surveyed above merely represent a surface skimming of the potential areas of inquiry linking Midwestern studies to the world.

I would like to suggest four areas of transnational interest in particular that merit investigation from scholars of the Midwest. One related to immigration history is that of missionary work both from foreign missionaries to the Midwest and from the Midwest to abroad. Deborah E. Kantner's *Chicago Católico*, while not specifically on missionary work, nonetheless reveals the evolving ethnic nature of Midwestern Christianity as older urban European communities witnessed the influx of Latino immigration. Studies of agriculture and agribusiness offer a variety of tools for integrating the regional with the global, particularly in labor migration, technological development, corporate planning, and international trade. Companies, such as Deere and Company, International Harvester, DeKalb Genetics, and Monsanto historically transcended regional boundaries to become major players in global agribusiness. And the Midwest has contributed globally beyond agricultural science and technology. Such institutions as Argonne National Laboratory, Fermi National Accelerator Laboratory, and Purdue University School of Aeronautics and Astronautics have placed the region at the center of international physics and space studies. Finally, the application of aesthetics to technology with global implications are best represented by towering figures such as Frank Lloyd Wright, Eero Saarinen, Mies van der Rohe, and other Midwestern architects whose work transcended regional and national boundaries throughout the twentieth century.[31] These and other areas of scholarly inquiry offer opportunities for those interested in Midwestern regional studies to find applicability to transnational perspectives.

Interestingly, as I finished this chapter, the recent issue of *Middle West Review* arrived in the mail. Fortuitously, all four articles in the issue linked the local and regional with the global. John Mack Faragher's article on the emigration of the Faragher brothers from the Isle of Man to Wisconsin before migrating to Minnesota and South Dakota continues the theme of European immigration to the Midwest, while Cormac Broeg's study of Midwestern German influences on antebellum politics is reminiscent of Frederick Luebke's early work in Nebraska, although with national implications related to the ascendancy of Abraham Lincoln in Illinois. Nathan Ellstrand's examination of the role of Chicago churches in the Sanctuary Movement of the 1980s moves beyond immigration history to examine the influences of foreign policy and global politics in the Cold War on localities. Finally, Mark Friedberger's article on the impact of race, ethnicity, and class community relations in a Midwest suburb incorporates analysis of the effects of the AIDS epidemic and COVID-19 pandemic, bringing global health concerns to community studies.[32] Ironically, these articles appear in the same issue that includes a sobering editorial on the "ongoing history crisis," which threatens not only the livelihoods of history professionals but the influence of the discipline itself on civic education and culture. In connecting the personal histories of the local and regional with the broader frameworks of national and transnational history, citizens, scholars, and policymakers alike will realize our discipline's unique ability to provide "a wider vision" leading to "a firmer knowledge of the histories of other peoples, nations, and transnational regions of the world" as the *La Pietra Report* aspired and the reinvigoration of Midwest regional history promises.[33]

## NOTES

1. Nancy Green, *The Limits of Transnationalism* (University of Chicago Press, 2019), 40. See Ian Tyrrell, "American Exceptionalism in an Age of International History," *American Historical Review* 96, no. 4 (1991): 1031–55. Hoganson, *The Heartland* (see chapter 1, n. 1) offers a discerning analysis of the complexities of negotiating local, regional, national, and global history from the Midwestern perspective.

2. Thomas Bender, *La Pietra Report: Project of Internationalizing the Study of American History—A Report to the Profession* (OAH, 2000), 7.

3. Bender, *La Pietra Report*, 5–9. For fuller scholarly discussions of transnational historiography, see, for example, "The Nation and Beyond: Transnational Perspectives on United States History—a Special Issue," *Journal of American History* (1999); C. A. Bayly, Sven Beckert, Matthew Connelly, Isabel Hofmeyr, Wendy Kozol, and Patricia Seed, "*AHR* Conversation: On Transnational History," *American Historical Review* 111, no. 5 (2006): 1440–64; "Special Issue: Immigration, Incorporation, Integration, and Transnationalism: Interdisciplinary and International Perspectives," *Journal of American Ethnic History* (Winter–Spring 2006).

4. Lauck, *The Lost Region*, 72 (see chapter 4, n. 22).

5. James R. Shortridge, *The Middle West: Its Meaning in American Culture* (University of Kansas Press, 1989), xiii–xiv.

6. Andrew R. L. Cayton and Peter S. Onuf, *The Midwest and the Nation: Rethinking the History of an American Region* (Indiana University Press, 1990); Andrew R. L. Cayton and Susan E. Gray, *The Identity of the American Midwest: Essays on Regional History* (Indiana University Press, 2001).

7. David S. Brown, *Beyond the Frontier: The Midwestern Voice in American Historical Writing* (University of Chicago Press, 2009), xxi.

8. Quoted in Lauck, *The Lost Region*, 31; see also 1–9.

9. See Lauck et al., *Finding a New Midwestern History* (see introduction, n. 4), and Lauck, *The Making of the Midwest* (see introduction, n. 3). In addition, Lauck, *The Interior Borderlands* (see introduction, n. 24) refocuses study of the region from historical to include geography and culture in addressing what regional identity represents, especially in discussing the relationships between the states of the Old Northwest and the trans-Mississippi states.

10. Thomas Bender, ed., *Rethinking American History in a Global Age* (University of California Press, 2002).

11. Thomas Bender, *A Nation Among Nations: America's Place in World History* (Hill and Wang, 2006), ix.

12. See Bender, *A Nation among Nations*, 349–68.

13. Carl Guarneri, *America in the World: United States History in Global Context* (McGraw-Hill, 2007), xi.

14. See, for example, Frederick Jackson Turner, "The Significance of the Frontier in American History," 1893, Chicago, American Historical Association, accessed December 7, 2022, https://www.historians.org/about-aha-and-membership/aha-history-and-archives/historical-archives/the-significance-of-the-frontier-in-american-history-(1893); Raymond J. Cunningham, "The German Historical World of Herbert Baxter Adams: 1874–1876," *The Journal of American History* 68, no. 2 (1981): 261–75

15. Steiner, "Birth of the Midwest," 15 (see chapter 4, n. 23). An interesting perspective on Turner and the Midwest and the unsustainability of regional and sectional history as the scholarly discipline developed in the twentieth century. See John E. Miller, "Frederick Jackson Turner and the Dream of Regional History," *Middle West Review* 1, no. 1 (2014): 1–8. See also Frederick Jackson Turner, *The American Nation; A History, Volume XIV—Rise of the New West, 1819–1829* (1906), Project Gutenberg, accessed December 7, 2022, https://gutenberg.org/cache/epub/3826/pg3826.html and "The Significance of Sections in American History," *Wisconsin Magazine of History* (March 1925): 255–80.

16. In his 1925 "The Significance of Sections in American History," Frederick Jackson Turner argues: "[A]rising from the facts of physical geography and the regional settlement of different peoples and types of society on the Atlantic coast there was a sectionalism from the beginning . . . involved and modified by the fact that these societies were expanding into the interior, following the frontier." In Frederick Jackson Turner, *History, Frontier, and Section: Three Essays* (University of New Mexico Press, 1993), 93.

17. Steiner, "Birth of the Midwest," 16.

18. Bender, *La Pietra Report*, 5–9.

19. Lauck, *The Good Country*, 3–14 (see chapter 4, n. 25).

20. Turner, "Significance of the Frontier."

21. See Richard White, *The Middle Ground: Indians, Empires, and Republics in the Great Lakes Region, 1650–1815* (Cambridge University Press, 1991); David Andrew

Nichols, *Peoples of the Inland Sea: Native Americans and Newcomers in the Great Lakes Region, 1600–1870* (Ohio University Press, 2018); Brett Rushforth, *Bonds of Alliance: Indigenous & Slaveries in New France* (University of North Carolina Press, 2012).

22. See James E. Davis, *Frontier Illinois* (Indiana University Press, 1998); Mark Wyman, *The Wisconsin Frontier* (Indiana University Press, 1998); Andrew L. Cayton, *Frontier Indiana* (Indiana University Press, 1996); and R. Douglas Hart, *The Ohio Frontier: Crucible of the Old Northwest, 1720–1830* (Bloomington Indiana University Press, 1996). The series also included works on frontier Kentucky and Tennessee. See also the earlier work, Malcolm Rohrbough, *The Trans-Appalachian Frontier: Peoples, Societies, and Institutions, 1775–1850* (Oxford University Press, 1978).

23. Saler, *The Settler's Empire* (see chapter 2, n. 27).

24. See, for example, Paul Schneider, *Old Man River: The Mississippi River in North American History* (Henry Holt, 2013); James L. Theler, *Twelve Millennia: Archaeology of the Upper Mississippi River Valley* (University of Iowa, 2003); Daniel Patterson, ed., *Missouri River Journals of John James Audubon* (University of Nebraska, 2016); Michael E. Dickey, *The People of the River's Mouth: In Search of the Missouria Indians* (University of Missouri Press, 2011); John Ed Pearce, *The Ohio River* (University of Kentucky Press, 1989); and R. E. Banta, *The Ohio* (University Press of Kentucky, 1998).

25. Theodore Karamanski, *Schooner Passage: Sailing Ships and the Lake Michigan Frontier* (Wayne State University Press, 2000); Theodore Karamanski and Deane Tank, *Maritime Chicago* (Arcadia Press, 2001); Theodore Karamanski, *Navigating the Inland Seas: Great Lakes Navigation Aids in American History* (University of Wisconsin, 2020). See also Theodore Karamanski and Eileen M. McMahon, *North Woods River: The St. Croix Valley in Upper Midwest History* (University of Wisconsin Press, 2009).

26. Dan Read, *The Death and Life of the Great Lakes* (W. W. Norton, 2017).

27. See Frederick Leubke, *Immigrants and Politics: The Germans of Nebraska, 1880–1900* (University of Nebraska Press, 1969).

28. See Jon Gjerde, *From Peasants to Farmers: The Migration from Balestrand, Norway, to the Upper Middle West* (Cambridge University Press, 1989) and *The Minds of the West* (see chap, 1, n. 5).

29. See Kathleen Neils Conzen, *Immigrant Milwaukee, 1836–1860: Accommodation and Community in a Frontier City* (Harvard University Press, 1976). For Rudolph J. Vecoli, see, for example, *The People of New Jersey* (Von Nostrand, 1965) and *Italian Immigrants in Rural and Small Town America* (The Association, 1989). His revisionist critique of Handlin's *The Uprooted* appeared as "*Contadini* in Chicago: A Critique of *The Uprooted*," *Journal of American History* 51, no. 3 (1964): 404–17. For the Immigration History Research Center, see https://cla.umn.edu/ihrc.

30. See Cheryl R. Ganz and Margaret Strobel, eds., *Pots of Promise: Mexicans and Pottery at Hull House, 1920–1940* (University of Illinois Press, 2004); Theresa Delgadillo, *Latina Lives in Milwaukee* (University of Illinois Press, 2015); and Marc Zimmerman, *Defending Their Own in the Cold: The Cultural Turns of U.S. Puerto Ricans* (University of Illinois Press, 2011). For a complete list of volumes in the series, see https://www.press.uillinois.edu/books/find_books.php?type=series&search=LCM.

31. Deborah E. Kantner, *Chicago Católico: Making Catholic Parishes Mexican* (University of Illinois Press, 2020). See also, for example, Neil Dahlstrom, *Tractor Wars: John Deere, Henry Ford, International Harvester, and the Birth of Modern Agriculture* (Matt Holt, 2022); Gabriel Apechlaner, *Corporate Crops: Biotechnology, Agriculture, and the Struggle for Control* (University of Texas Press, 2012); Lillian Hoddeson, Adrienne W. Kolb, and Catherine Westfall, *Fermilab: Physics, the Frontier, and Megascience* (University of Chicago, 2011); Alexander Eisenschmidt and Jonathan Mekinda, eds., *Chicagoisms: The City as Catalyst for Architectural Speculation* (University of Chicago Press, 2011).

32. See the Fall 2022 issue of the *Middle West Review*, for John Mack Faragher, "'Ho! My Boys, This Is the Place!' The Manx in the Midwest and the Emigration of the Faragher Brothers," 1–24; Nathan Ellstrand, "Politicized Refuge: Chicago and the Transformation of the Sanctuary Movement," 25–48; Cormac Broeg, "How the Germans Beat Bates: Gustav Koerner, Carl Schurz, and the Republican National Convention of 1860," 49–74; Mark Friedberger, "Community-Building and Diversity in a Midwest Suburb: The Case of Oak Park, Illinois," 75–98; and Lauck, "The Ongoing History Crisis," vii–xi (see introduction, n. 8).

33. Bender, *La Pietra Report*, 8.

EMILIANO AGUILAR

**7**

# LATINIZATION OF THE MIDWEST

## Documenting and Interrogating Latina/o Experiences across the US Heartland

Writing for *National Geographic*, Daisy Hernández likens the familiarity of the Midwest with their Latin American upbringing, arguing that the two are more connected than one might believe. Latin America and the Midwest contain typical regional dynamics that make the two regions feel similar. Hernández claims, "Maybe it is this tension—the departures, the returns, the decision to stay, a constant reference to migration—that also makes the Midwest familiar to me."[1] However, I would add that it is not just this tension of mobility or permanency that makes the two seem similar. From *panaderias* and *taquerias* to churches and rekindled downtown spaces, Latinas/os have demarcated their presence across the Midwest since the late nineteenth century.[2] Their long history within the region is written across the built environment of the Midwest and continues to add to the heterogeneity of a space often seen as homogeneous.

The restructuring of quintessential Midwestern towns to invoke their migrant communities became increasingly notable as the Midwestern Latina/o continued to grow. In the first decade of the twenty-first century, the Latina/o population increased by more than 73 percent across eight Midwestern states.[3] During this period, the national level of Latinas/os grew by 43 percent, while in the Midwestern states, it grew by 49 percent, with an estimated five million in the region today.[4] Overwhelmingly, the Latina/o population in the region is of ethnic Mexican descent. However, nationally and within the Midwest, this is drastically changing. The Latino Policy and Politics Institute at the University of California Los Angeles claimed that this demographic fueled growth in the South and the Midwest. For instance, the total population in Indiana increased by 11 percent, but the Latina/o population change was 133 percent. Not only was it the highest growth, with an increase of 280,680 individuals, but the Salvadoran community alone increased by 767 percent.[5] This pattern is seen across the region, with predominantly Central American communities, such as Guatemalans (Minnesota, Iowa, and Michigan) or Hondurans (Wisconsin), fueling this growth. This data offers a vital opportunity to document these often-understudied heritage groups—an opportunity some institutions are beginning to seize.

Although now gaining renewed attention from scholars, the study of Latina/o communities began over five decades ago. In the 1970s, scholars documented the experiences of the primarily ethnic Mexicans that settled across the Midwest in the late nineteenth and early twentieth centuries. Bereft of the historical and institutional support of ethnic Mexicans in the Southwest, these individuals and families forged a place in various areas as relative newcomers to the region. Although this cohort of scholars produced foundational research about an ethnic Mexican Midwest, both rural and urban geographies, the subfield gained slow traction in the broader field of Latina/o history. Overall, Latina/o history, as Lilia Fernández argues, became rooted in geographic essentialism, still overwhelmingly focused on the Southwest, journeying beyond the region and occasionally dissecting experiences in states like New York and Florida.[6] Despite these varying levels of attention and engagement, the strong migration patterns of Latinas/os, particularly those of Central American descent, leave the study of this demographic a rich field for historians, policymakers, and educators within the Midwest and beyond.

This chapter will provide readers unfamiliar with Latina/o history with a good primer on the rich historiography of Midwestern communities. Additionally, the chapter will serve as a vital piece for the new cohort of emerging scholars left without a resource that compiles this scholarship. This new generation of scholars represents the progress made within the past ten years of the Midwestern history revival, which offers opportunities for its continued growth. Ensuring they possess the adequate resources to engage in this field is crucial. Additionally, Midwestern history scholars will benefit from understanding the decades of scholarship that have placed Latina/o communities as vital to the region's development, both as relative newcomers and entrenched communities with over a century of history. For Midwestern history to continue to progress during its revival, we must understand and incorporate the rich scholarship that is often a separate thread into the fold. This chapter offers the first step toward doing so.

I will first present a brief overview of the Latina/o Midwest scholarship. Central to the revival of the field of Midwestern history is the growing scholarship that seeks to reconceptualize our understanding of the region. Recent edited volumes and monographs have documented the presence of Latina/o communities and interrogated their experiences within the region and with their fellow Midwesterners. However, as the editors of the seminal *The Latina/o Midwest Reader* argue, "The Latina/o Midwest is thus a region of distinct but overlapping Latinidades, rural and urban, established and emergent, which have been forged over the past one and a half centuries through labor migration, urbanization, placemaking, and cultural production."[7] Heeding their call, the field has to embrace the nuances of the Midwest, as well as the Latina/o community that remade iconic small towns and bustling metropolitan regions alike. The vast diversity of the Midwest, in terms of demographics, population density, and environmental space, is reflected in the various experiences scholars have detailed.

However, this community is often absent in conceptualizations of Midwestern history and Latina/o history. The instrumental edited volume *Finding a New Midwestern History* contains no entry about Latinas/os. Several chapters note the vital goal of not viewing the region as a homogeneous space, instead acknowledging the enduring presence of indigenous communities and the hopeful opportunity it represents for African American communities. Many Midwestern studies acknowledge some of the chief catalysts that brought Latinas/os to the region, such as monographs about agriculture, railroads, meatpacking, stockyards, and manufacturing. However, few interrogate the vibrant field of scholarship concerning Latinas/os.[8] While we are witnessing a revival in Midwestern history, we must recognize what history we are writing and whose stories we share. This recognition is imperative in presenting the region for what it is, a multitude of diverse stories and experiences that are constantly changing due to the continued migration of communities into the Midwest, particularly the Latina/o demographic.

Through presenting this rich, fifty-year scholarship, the chapter offers insights into the intersections of the fields of Midwestern history and the Latina/o Midwest. How does including Latina/o histories complement and complicate our understanding of the Midwest? What differences exist in the trajectory of Latina/o history in the Midwest instead of typically studied regions, such as the Southwest, Florida, and New York? What is the role of Chicago in these studies about Latina/o migration throughout the Midwest to areas that recent scholars study, such as Wisconsin, Michigan, and Indiana? As Lilia Fernández claims, "Due to its demographic significance and diversity, the Midwest lends itself readily to doing comparative, interethnic histories of Chicanos/as and other Latinos/as."[9] Echoing Fernandez, while not exceptional, the Midwest offers an opportunity for Latina/o history to break from geographic essentialism and the nationalism that has defined the field. By incorporating Latina/o history into our understanding of Midwestern history, we can present the field for what it truly is: a complicated piece of the national mosaic—one intertwined beyond the confines of the region.

## A MIDWESTERN REVIVAL

In 2013, a call for revitalizing Midwestern history led to the creation of the Midwest History Association (MHA). In his monograph about the field of Midwest history, Jon K. Lauck bleakly assessed that "the field of midwestern history is now comatose."[10] He argued that Midwestern history had been kept alive by local historical societies and remained marginalized in the history of the United States. Since the local historical societies isolated islands of knowledge production firmly rooted in a single space, they were left unincorporated into broader narratives. His critique helped to prompt the resurgence of Midwestern history, centered around the organization of the MHA in 2014. The MHA's annual meeting in Grand Rapids allowed scholars to reconceptualize how Midwest history can offer insights into the national narrative that often focuses on the coastal regions and large metropolitan centers. The tenth-anniversary milestone reinvigorated conversations concerning the state of the field, featuring vital moments of consensus and disagreement about the historiography of the subfield.[11] Some scholars have noted that the field "has returned from beyond the grave with new insights to impart."[12] I echo the criticism that this mentality prioritized some academic work at the expense of others.[13] The organization's anniversary offered an opportunity for the field to revalue whose histories are preserved and incorporated and where the work thrives and needs further attention—both in terms of region and communities but also institutionally.

However, this new scholarship is not without its limitations. In a revival narrative, the field sacrificed the Midwest's diversity to create a homogeneous, almost romanticized region. Within the edited volume *Finding a New Midwestern History*, the lived experiences of many groups remain incomplete.[14] The work includes chapters on the Midwest's indigenous, European immigrant, and African American communities. While not the purpose of this chapter, the rich range of studies about African American communities in cities like Chicago and Detroit alone showcases the field's vitality. However, communities of Latina/o heritage are neglected. This community would fit in conversations like "The Iconic Midwest," which included work on small Midwestern towns, agricultural communities, and sports. Notably, in recognizing the growth of Midwestern scholarship, we should recognize the essential need to integrate the decades of scholarship pertaining to ethnic Mexicans and Puerto Ricans, as well as encourage new studies of the dozens of Latin American heritage groups.

## SOCIAL SCIENTISTS AND EARLY FIELDWORK

The earliest studies about the Midwest's Spanish-speaking communities came in the 1920s and 1930s. Economists, sociologists, and other social scientists compiled hyper-local case studies and broader regional and national accounts about Mexican communities. University of Southern California sociologist Emory S. Bogardus encouraged his students to study minority communities in the United States, particularly ethnic Mexicans. Many of these studies, primarily on the Southwest with some Midwest case studies, appeared in the journal he edited, *Sociology and Social Research*.[15] Some students published outside this journal, such as Anita E. Jones's "Mexican Colonies in Chicago."[16] Others, like social worker Agnes Fenton, published their accounts through the Young Women's Christian Association.[17] Additionally, Mexican anthropologist Manuel Gamio conducted extensive fieldwork and interviews during his tenure with the Social Science Research Council. Gamio's vast scholarship provided a foundation for subsequent national studies on Mexican communities.[18] Regardless of the venue, these early studies are instrumental starting points for scholars to document the history of Latina/o communities in the Midwest while simultaneously underscoring that these are not newcomers of the past few decades; instead, they continue a rich tradition of placemaking.

An influential component of this early research stemmed from the models applied by social scientists to understand the Mexican community, often with racial biases. In his 1930 study of Flint, Michigan, sociologist William Albig detailed the negative attitudes held by European immigrants about ethnic Mexicans.[19] Ruth Camblon argued that the indigenous heritage of Chicago's Mexican community led them to "lacks [lack] physical resistance. His [the Mexican migrant] inherited lack of health habits or scientific health standards, combined with his migratory life make him peculiarly susceptible to disease."[20] In Omaha, geographer Earl Sullenger advocated for institutional support to assimilate and correct perceived cultural deficiencies, noting ethnic Mexican traits like "passive" and "mentally lazy" attitudes in the community.[21]

However, arguably one of the most significant contributions to the study of Midwestern Mexican communities is the work of Paul S. Taylor. From 1927 to 1934, Taylor conducted fieldwork and research to write the instrumental, multivolume study, *Mexican Labor in the United States*, published by the University of California. This fieldwork included interviews with over a thousand people in three years, from Mexican laborers to businessmen to supervisors. The places studied included Chicago and the neighboring Calumet Region in Indiana, Michigan, Illinois, and Nebraska. Additionally, Taylor utilized newspapers in the areas of study, documents from private and municipal agencies, and obtained workplace data. Research from these articles provided the foundation for Taylor's numerous academic publications, such as *Southwestern Historical Quarterly*, the *American Journal of Sociology*, the *Journal of Political Economy*, and the *Journal of the American Statistical Association*.

Taylor's study, spanning eleven monographs, found renewed attention in the 1960s with the burgeoning field of Chicano history. In 1968, reprints of ten monographs became a common source for this new field of historical research. Reflecting on the legacy of Taylor's work, Abraham Hoffman recognized the exceptional and unrepeatable nature of the research. Through his fieldwork, Taylor obtained company data from various industrial plants and railroads, a task that Hoffman claimed: "might well prove an impossible task" for contemporary researchers.[22] Taylor's success in synthesizing extensive fieldwork and information from corporate archives was emblematic of early scholarship about primarily ethnic Mexican communities across the United States.

However, the Great Depression and subsequent Repatriation Movement of ethnic Mexicans across the country altered the positive gains made by Taylor's study. Dennis N. Valdés linked this to the disruption caused by the economic crisis, which an entire generation of scholars "attributed to the extremely difficult conditions attending to the urban life of Mexican folk."[23] Well into the 1960s, this generation of scholarship about Midwestern Mexican immigrants emphasized the community as a problem. Edward Bauer claimed that "unless Mexicans are able to move out of the colony and establish themselves in the larger community the process of assimilation will be much slower than has been the case in ethnic groups of European origin."[24] While discussing the integration of Mexicans in Detroit, sociologist Norman D. Humphrey claimed that the successful route would rely on "the acquisition of relatively superficial layers of American culture and the shedding of equally shallow Mexican elements."[25] Reflecting on the idea of mobility and a willingness to reject permanency, Mark Reisler claimed that "only his [Mexican] effort to preserve his native identity and his hope of returning to the homeland alleviated the despair of the culture of poverty."[26]

## A MIDWESTERN RESPONSE TO THE CHICANO MOVEMENT

In the 1960s and 1970s, students protested educational inequality throughout the Southwest and demanded that their education reflect their heritage. The field of Chicana/o studies offered some of the earliest attempts to document these Midwestern experiences. This first wave of scholarship coincided with the Civil Rights Era and produced a variety of scholarship seeking to understand present marginalization in a long history of discrimination against ethnic Mexican communities.[27] However, this production of scholarship did not solely focus on the Southwest; a range of scholarship about the Midwest was released from the late 1960s to mid-1970s. This scholarship included a special issue of *Aztlán*, the first dissertations about Chicanos in the Midwest, and several working papers, most notably Julian Samora and Richard Lamanna's "Mexican-Americans in a Midwest Metropolis: A Study of East Chicago, Indiana."[28] Situated within the context of the Chicano Movement and the call for the history of Chicano, these early efforts proved instrumental in documenting the history of these communities. As numerous Latina/o studies scholars detailed, the field owed its roots to a generation of academics wanting to document the history of their Latina/o communities.[29]

In 1967, Julian Samora and Richard Lamanna published "Mexican-Americans in a Midwest Metropolis: A Study of East Chicago, Indiana." This working paper presented foundational information for a manuscript in progress from Samora that he never finished, tentatively entitled "Chicanos of East Chicago." The working paper became one of the first studies to juxtapose a Midwest experience against the Southwest. Samora and subsequent scholars noted that, unlike the Southwest, the Midwest offered a region where ethnic Mexicans were relative newcomers. As migrants to the region in the late nineteenth and early twentieth centuries, they were bereft of the institutional and societal support that existed in the Southwest, such as Spanish-language newspapers, religious institutions, and sociopolitical groups like mutual-aid societies. Instead, Latinas/os in the Midwest forged their support network or transplanted Southwest institutions, such as the League of United Latin American Citizens (LULAC). Samora and Lamanna's study was well received by academics, undergraduates and graduate students, activists, and various Latina/o-focused nonprofits across the United States.[30] These requests and a plethora of letters of praise highlight the receptibility of this Midwestern scholarship beyond the region.

Aside from the numerous letters of support and requests for further information Samora received, the study helped spur considerable inquiry in the field. In the 1970s, historians began to explore the history of ethnic Mexicans and Puerto Ricans in the Midwest. In 1973, the *Pacific Historical Review* published an issue on Chicana/o history, including an essay on the repatriation of Mexicans in the Midwest during the Great Depression.[31] A few years later, in 1976, *Aztlán* published a special issue on "Chicanos in the Midwest."[32] This special issue coincided with the defense of the groundbreaking PhD dissertation by Louise Año Nuevo Kerr, which proved instrumental in documenting and arguing for the importance of Midwestern ethnic Mexican communities.[33] Incidentally, Samora's influence in the field extended beyond his study, as students at the University of Notre Dame authored two-thirds of the essays in the special issue for *Aztlán*. This special issue represented both a vital moment in the nascent years of Chicana/o studies and an acceptance of the field in understanding the community outside of the Southwest as well.

However, this generation of scholarship contained several limitations. First, few of these studies extended their chronology beyond the 1930s. Since much of the Midwestern historical literature emphasized or outright rejected the last immigrant analogy, many studies focused on the urban experience. Second, some students noted that their history professors proved uninterested in this work. Ciro Sepulveda, whose dissertation focused on Depression-era ethnic Mexicans in East Chicago, Indiana, claims that his professors at Notre Dame "faked interest." According to Sepulveda, the field's interest "lay in the large cities, the presidency, the Congress, the economic categories at the bedrock of the real and the meaningful decisions that shaped and formed the history of the nation."[34] This institutional neglect of the topic reinforced a disconnect between the subfield of Latina/o history and its connection to US history in general. Like the experiences of early scholars of Latina/o communities at large, the Midwestern cohort had to do double work to sell their institutions on Chicana/o history and Midwestern communities.

## RECENT TRENDS AND STATE OF THE FIELD TODAY

In the 1990s, scholars noted a significant change in the demographics of the Midwestern states. In 1990, the ten regional states contained approximately 2.1 million foreign-born residents. According to one study, "Chicago is to the Midwest in immigration matters what Los Angeles is to California—the home of most of the Midwest's Hispanics and immigrants."[35] Truly, Chicago represented an essential and problematic focal point for the field.[36] The University of Illinois Press's critical series, Latinos in Chicago and the Midwest, incorporated the city as a sort of entry point into the region and the study of its Latina/o residents. While some may have considered the last three decades as a plateau for understanding Midwest history at large, they have proved a productive period to address the increasingly large Latina/o community. From the publication of memoirs to the increased production of articles in state history journals, this period has produced a receptive audience for understanding the Latinization of the Midwest.

Early monographs attempted to understand the region—in urban and rural environments—in relation to other immigrant groups. As historian Dennis N. Valdés claims, "The early Midwesterners were overwhelmingly immigrants who lived and worked among their European predecessors and, more recently-arrived African Americans. With roots mostly in the interior of Mexico, they did not share a collective memory of United States conquest or the concomitant loss of ancestral lands."[37] Many of these early settlers arrived to work in agriculture, such as in the sugar beet fields of the Great Lakes Region.[38] Given the immense importance of agriculture to the Midwest's economy, the undersold contributions of Latina/o labor might represent the most significant omission or missed opportunity in bridging Latina/o history and Midwest history.

Additionally, these works desired to form regional narratives, such as finding common characteristics in the sugar beet industries across the northern Great Lakes region or in urban environments across the Midwest or an attempt at a synthesis for the entire area.[39]

Arguably, the most productive space for the support of Latina/o Midwest history has been state historical journals. Echoing Theodore J. Karamanski's optimistic assessment of the field, considerable praise and recognition should be devoted to the small local institutions that "mount exhibits, collect material culture, and preserve the records of their communities."[40] While this chapter does not have the space to highlight the numerous articles in the state journals, these offer a vital starting point for future work in the field. Additionally, the increasing interest of state university presses in publishing memoirs from Latina/o communities provides digestible and engaging sources for our classrooms, too.

Even within the last decade, the mainstream fields have slowly begun to come to terms with the Midwest. In their contribution to a 2016 edited volume, Lilia Fernández claims: "This ethnically diverse Latino/a demographic did not fit easily into bicoastal paradigms of conquest, migration, or racialization, or identity formation. The Midwest begged to be studied on its own terms and in all its particularities."[41] Fernández argues that there were four necessary steps to maintain a viable and relevant Chicano/a history scholarship. These steps included looking for moments of cross-ethnic interactions, extending the field's boundaries to look for inter-Latina/o encounters, and moving beyond the typical sites of inquiry.[42] The scholarship of this generation is still relatively geocentric; however, for the Midwest, this has meant a considerable amount of attention toward Chicago. As Ashley Howard reminds us, when understanding race and the Midwest, we cannot allow parts to stand for the whole experience.[43] Work such as that of Delia Fernández-Jones and Sergio Gonzalez has illuminated the experiences of Latinas/os in Grand Rapids, Michigan, and twentieth-century Wisconsin, moving our attention away from Chicago while still acknowledging its prime role as a gateway.[44]

As the Midwestern Latina/o communities grow, plenty of potential work remains. Midwestern history and the study of Latinas/os needs to acknowledge the gaps and opportunities for further study, such as locations beyond Chicago, like Kristy Nabhan-Warren's reminder of the countless small towns that dot the region.[45] Since 2000, the Midwest has increasingly become home to Central American communities. Their stories of placemaking in these new regions offer an opportunity to learn more about the groups maintaining the Midwest.

While many scholars may hope to discuss a declension narrative in Rust Belt cities and rural peripheries, Latinas/os have remained or become a significant presence in these areas—quite literally remaking these spaces.[46] They join an over-century-old Latina/o Midwest history, often neglected in our narratives. As we reflect on a decade of Midwestern history, it is imperative that we do not fall into the trap of binary history. Latin American and Caribbean-descent communities are strong (and growing) in the Midwest. Our histories of the region should both acknowledge their presence and recognize that in writing the region, we must recognize its heterogeneous space.

## NOTES

1. Daisy Hernández, "How the Midwest Is Latin American," *National Geographic*, June 2022, 16.

2. Note on terminology: I largely rely on the Latina/o to reference the pan-ethnic label used in the United States to describe those of Latin American and Caribbean descent. The chapter also references Chicano, which refers to someone of Mexican descent born in the United States. This chosen identity was reclaimed during the Chicano Civil Rights Movement to express solidarity across cultural, ethnic, and community ties, often rejecting assimilation.

3. United States Census Bureau, "2010 Census" (U.S. Census Bureau, 2010).

4. Karen R. Humes, Nicholas A. Jones, and Roberto R. Ramirez, "Overview of Race and Hispanic Origin: 2010," U.S. Department of Commerce, Economics and Statistics Administration (U.S. Census Bureau, 2011).

5. Jie Zong, "A Mosaic, Not a Monolith: A Profile of the U.S. Latino Population, 2000–2020," Latino Policy & Politics Institute, University of California, October 26, 2022.

6. Lilia Fernandez, "Moving Beyond Aztlán: Disrupting Nationalism and Geographic Essentialism in Chicano/a History," in *A Promising Problem: The New Chicana/o History*, ed. Carlos K. Blanton (University of Texas Press, 2016).

7. Omar Valerio-Jiménez, Santiago Vaquera-Vásquez, and Claire F. Fox, *The Latina/o Midwest Reader* (University of Illinois Press, 2017), 18.

8. While not exhaustive, some texts that document this history include Dennis Nodín Valdés, *Al Norte: Agricultural Workers in the Great Lakes Region, 1917–1970* (University of Texas Press, 1991); Dionicio Nodín Valdés, *Barrios Norteños: St. Paul and Midwestern Mexican Communities in the Twentieth Century* (University of Texas Press, 2000); Zaragosa Vargas, *Proletarians of the North: A History of Mexican Industrial Workers in Detroit and the Midwest, 1917–1933* (University of California Press, 1993); Richard Santillán, "Rosita the Riveter: Midwest Mexican American Women During World War II, 1941–45," in *Perspectives in Mexican American Studies: Mexicans in the Midwest*, ed. Juan R. García (University of Arizona Press, 1996); García, *Mexicans in the*

*Midwest* (see chapter 1, n. 10); Gina M. Pérez, *The Near Northwest Side Story: Migration, Displacement, and Puerto Rican Families* (University of California Press, 2004); Gabriela F. Arredondo, *Mexican Chicago: Race, Identity, and Nation, 1916–39* (University of Illinois Press, 2008); Fernández, *Brown in the Windy City* (see chapter 1, n. 9); Michael Innis-Jiménez, *Steel Barrio: The Great Migration to South Chicago, 1915–1940* (New York University Press, 2013); and Valerio-Jiménez et al., *The Latina/o Midwest Reader.*

9. Fernández, "Moving Beyond Aztlán," 64.

10. Lauck, *The Lost Region*, 73 (see chapter 4, n. 22).

11. See *Middle West Review* 10, no. 2 (2024).

12. Amy Laurel Fluker, "A Ghost Among Regions": Considering a Spectral History of the Midwest, *Middle West Review* 10, no. 2 (2024): 69.

13. Andrew Klumpp, "Not A Revival. A Convention," *Middle West Review* 10, no. 2 (2024): 117.

14. Lauck et al., *Finding a New Midwestern History* (see introduction, n. 4).

15. See Abraham Hoffman, "An Unusual Moment: Paul S. Taylor's Mexican Labor in the United States Monograph Series," *Pacific Historical Review* 45, no. 2 (1976): 256.

16. Anita E. Jones, "Mexican Colonies in Chicago," *Social Service Review* 2 (1928): 579–97.

17. Agnes M. Fenton, "The Mexicans of the City of Milwaukee, Wisconsin" (Y.W.C.A. International Institute, 1930).

18. For context on Gamio's research see Robert Redfield, "The Antecedents of Mexican Immigration to the United States," *American Journal of Sociology* 35 (1929): 433–38. A brief selection of Gamio's scholarship includes Manuel Gamio, *Mexican Immigration to the United States: A Record of Human Migration and Adjustment* (University of Chicago Press, 1930); Gamio, *The Mexican Immigrant: His Life Story* (University of Chicago Press, 1931) reissued as Gamio, *The Life Story of the Mexican Immigrant* (Dover Books, 1971). This reissue included an introduction by Paul S. Taylor and edited interviews with seventy-six Mexican immigrants.

19. William Albig, "Opinions Concerning Unskilled Mexican Immigrants," *Sociology and Social Research* 15, no. 1 (1930): 62–72.

20. Ruth S. Camblon, "Mexicans in Chicago," *The Family* 7, no. 7 (1926): 211.

21. Earl T. Sullenger, "The Mexican Problem of Omaha," *Journal of Applied Sociology* 8 (1924): 289–93.

22. Hoffman, "An Unusual Moment," 270.

23. Dennis N. Valdés, "Region, Nation, and World-System: Perspectives on Midwestern Chicana/o History," in *Voices of a New Chicana/o History*, ed. Refugio I. Rochín and Dennis N. Valdés (Michigan State University Press, 2000), 122.

24. Edward Bauer, "Delinquency Among Mexican Boys in South Chicago" (master's thesis, University of Chicago, 1938), 55.

25. Norman D. Humphrey, "The Housing and Household Practices of Detroit Mexicans," *Social Forces* 24, no. 4 (1946): 437.

26. Mark Reisler, "The Mexican Immigrant in the Chicago Area during the 1920s," *Journal of the Illinois State Historical Society* 66 (1973): 158.

27. For the early years of Chicana/o studies see Rodolfo Acuña, *The Making of Chicana/o Studies: In the Trenches of Academe* (Rutgers University Press, 2011).

28. Julian Samora and Richard A. Lamanna, "Mexican-Americans in a Midwest Metropolis: A Study of East Chicago," Mexican-American Study Project (University of California, Los Angeles, July 1967).

29. Vicki L. Ruiz, "Nuestra América: Latino History as United States History," *The Journal of American History* 93, no. 3 (2006): 655–72; George J. Sánchez, "Y tú qué? (Y2K): Latino History in the New Millennium," in *Latinos! Remaking America*, ed. Marcelo Suarez-Orozco and Mariela Paez (University of California Press, 2022).

30. See "Requests for 'Mexican Americans in a Midwest Metropolis, 1969–1970" and "Requests for 'Mexican Americans in a Midwest Metropolis, 1971–1974," in Julian Samora Papers, Box 139, Folder 12–13, Benson Latin American Collection, University of Texas at Austin.

31. *Pacific Historical Review* 42, no. 3 (1973). For the Reparation Movement in the Midwest, see the article in this journal by Neil Betten and Raymond A. Mohl, "From Discrimination to Repatriation: Mexican Life in Gary, Indiana during the Great Depression."

32. *Aztlan*, no. 2 (Summer 1976). This issue included articles from some of the founding scholars of ethnic Mexicans, whom they referred to as Chicanos, in the Midwest. These scholars included Gilbert Cardenas, Francisco Arturo Rosales, Nicolás Kanellos, Juan R. Garcia, and Ciro Sepulveda.

33. Louise Año Nuevo Kerr, "The Chicano Experience in Chicago, 1920–1970" (PhD diss., University of Illinois at Chicago, 1976).

34. Ciro Sepulveda, "On Respect and Teaching," in *Moving Beyond Borders: Julian Samora and the Establishment of Latino Studies*, ed. Alberto López Pulido, Barbara Driscoll de Alvarado, and Carmen Samora (University of Illinois Press, 2009), 199.

35. Phillip Martin, Edward Taylor, and Michael Fix, "Immigration and the Changing Face of Rural America: Focus on the Midwestern States," Occasional Paper No. 21, Latino Studies Series (Michigan State University, 1996), 3.

36. For Chicago, see Kerr, "The Chicano Experience in Chicago, 1920–1970"; Felix Padilla, *Latino Ethnic Consciousness: The Case of Mexican Americans and Puerto Ricans in Chicago* (University of Notre Dame Press, 1985); Pérez, *The Near Northwest Side Story*; Arredondo, *Mexican Chicago*; Fernández, *Brown in the Windy City*; and Innis-Jiménez, *Steel Barrio*.

37. Valdés, "Region, Nation, and World System," 116.

38. Valdés, *Al Norte* and García, *Mexicans in the Midwest*.

39. See Valdés, *Al Norte*; Valdés, *Barrios Norteños*; and García, *Mexicans in the Midwest*.

40. Theodore J. Karamanski, "Midwest History: Will The Past Be Prologue?" *Middle West Review* 10, no. 2 (2024): 93.

41. Lilia Fernández, "Moving Beyond Aztlán: Disrupting Nationalism and Geographic Essentialism in Chicana/o History," in *A Promising Problem: The New Chicana/o History*, ed. Carlos Kevin Blanton (University of Texas Press, 2016), 72.

42. Fernández, "Moving Beyond Aztlán," 76.

43. Howard, "Race and Iowa History," 380 (see chapter 3, n. 3).

44. Delia Fernández-Jones, *Making the MexiRican City: Migration, Placemaking, and Activism in Grand Rapids, Michigan* (University of Illinois Press, 2023); Sergio González, *Strangers No Longer: Latino Belonging and Faith in 20th Century Wisconsin* (University of Illinois Press, 2024).

45. Nabhan-Warren, *Meatpacking America* (see chapter 1, n. 11).

46. Latina/o urban historians have reminded us that Latina/o immigration has quite literally revitalized urban space. See Andrew Sandoval-Strausz, *Barrio America: How Latino Immigrants Saved the American City* (Basic Books, 2019) and Mike Amezcua, *Making Mexican Chicago: From Postwar Settlement to the Age of Gentrification* (University of Chicago Press, 2022).

SARA EGGE

8

# THE ELASTIC REGION

Unraveling Gender in the Midwest

In the 1910 federal census, the enumerator for Ward 13, a neighborhood in Chicago, Illinois, listed forty-six-year-old Mary B. Shannon as the head of household.[1] She rented an apartment with two nonbiological children, two-year-old John J. O'Connor and one-year-old Joseph Boyle.[2] Shannon, a widow, resided on Warren Avenue, a long road that ran perpendicular to Garfield Park, a 184-acre urban park located about five miles west of Chicago's downtown. The park's west side had served several purposes, first as the site of seasonal events, including an agricultural fair, annual circus, and the show grounds for Buffalo Bill's "Wild West Shows," and second as the Garfield Park racetrack.[3] By 1892, the racetrack had gained a "bad reputation" as a place for gambling, and police shut it down after a raid turned into a deadly gunfight.[4] Four years later, the park board opened a bicycle track on the park's south side, which the *Chicago Tribune* dubbed the "finest cycle track in Chicago."[5] While the census included no information about the parentage of either O'Connor or Boyle, it did specify that Shannon's mother was American, born in Tennessee, and her father was Irish. Shannon and the two boys—whose last names indicated Irish heritage as well—probably felt at home in the Garfield Park neighborhood because most residents living there in 1910 were either Irish or German.[6]

There is no evidence to explain exactly why Shannon was living with the two young boys. Scattered records leave distinct gaps that reveal little about her life. Perhaps a distant kinship connection brought the toddlers to Shannon's Chicago home. Maybe an Irish community association or Irish networks within Chicago's Catholic archdiocese helped identify Shannon as a caregiver.[7] It is possible that the boys arrived in Chicago via a baby train operated by a Catholic agency like the New York Foundling Hospital, part of a faith-based social welfare system that placed children born in Eastern cities with Midwestern foster parents.[8] The duration and nature of her guardianship are also unknown; the lack of parental information for both O'Connor and Boyle make them difficult to trace among extant archival sources. John O'Connor fits the profile of a man who worked as a parking and filling station attendant and who enlisted in the Coast Guard Artillery Corps of the National Guard in September 1940.[9] Joseph Boyle may be one of the young insurance agents listed in the 1928 Chicago City Directory.[10]

While primary sources offer few specific details about the lives of Shannon, O'Connor, and Boyle, even this small glimpse into their household confirms the centrality of gender to the analysis of the Midwest. Gender, as expression, performance, notion, and system, organized life in the region.[11] It anchored relationships, shaped generational connections, and informed a dizzying array of family, community, and state structures. As a category of inquiry, it offers critical interventions in Midwestern historiographies about family structures, urban planning, labor, technology, agricultural production, political culture, and economic development, among other topics. Gender analyses also reveal a region that was neither frontier, middle ground, nor borderland; the Midwest existed as and continues to be a place without edges. Likewise, gender confirms that the people who forged a Midwestern identity created one that defied easy categorizations. There was no typical Midwesterner; encounters among diverse peoples in this vast interior generated a kaleidoscope of possible identities. The implicit, yet open, acceptance of this gender fluidity defines the Midwest. While people often ascribed to normative gender ideals, Midwesterners approached gender with an elasticity that produced contradictory expressions and behaviors, one that applied not only to others but also to themselves. Midwesterners were the ultimate shapeshifters.[12]

Framing the Midwest by using gender analysis brings precision to ambiguity and uncovers novel insights. What the region's history lacks is not attention; scholars have studied its urban hubs and rural "heartlands" since people began to characterize the nation's interior as a distinct "middle" place. Midwestern history has suffered because region-making itself was a contested process carried out during the late nineteenth and early twentieth centuries by regional boosters, academics, observers, and artists who judged Midwestern significance through specific identities.[13] Historians often relied upon these accounts to portray "The Midwest" as the cradle of democracy and capitalistic growth, where people with shared ethnic, racial, and religious backgrounds embraced an enlightened vision of individual liberty and progress.[14] Such a limited focus not only privileged an elite perspective at the expense of countless other voices but also told a one-dimensional narrative.[15] Using a gendered framework helps to uncover the silences. It demands precision and specificity, which is why this story features a widow and two young children living in Chicago. Perhaps more importantly, it reveals a region in which people deviated from norms and disrupted hierarchies radically and frequently. In this way, gender provides the Midwest with an approach that accounts for the contested intersections that can overlap, compete with, or even contradict each other in unexpected ways.

While Chicago's urban landscape might have seemed similar to that of cities in the East, its chronological development and particular combination of urban and rural elements cemented Chicago as "the premier Midwestern metropolis" by 1890.[16] As historian Jon Teaford explains, Midwestern cities were "creations of the nineteenth century" that reflected the "economic and technological conditions of that century."[17] Midwestern cities emerged along navigable rivers, and water power served as a key energy source for early entrepreneurs. By mid-century, railroads began to connect the region's cities to each other and to their rural hinterlands, which created a "thick web of rail lines" by the late nineteenth century[18] Cities like Chicago, St. Louis, Minneapolis, Omaha, and Grand Rapids operated as hubs of distribution and processing of the region's mineral, forest, and agricultural resources. Populations soared as steel factories, flour mills, stockyards, and furniture manufacturers demanded more workers.[19]

The East Garfield Park neighborhood where Shannon, O'Connor, and Boyle resided showcased the specific characteristics of Midwestern metropolises that Teaford described. On its eastern side was the site of the Bull's Head cattle yard, the first stockyards in Chicago. In its southwest corner stood the massive catalog factory for Sears, Roebuck, & Company. The Chicago and Northwestern railroad formed its northern boundary.[20] While these industrial and economic features were notable, a gendered framework illuminates how nineteenth-century boosters understood this development. Using imperialist metaphors, they forecasted the hegemonic takeover of Midwestern metropolises from Eastern cities. These promoters envisioned urban sites like Chicago as the anchors of a great commercial empire, one connected by water and rail to a countryside that served as a tributary designed only to support urban centers with their resources. They imagined a region in which controlled flows of resources created hierarchies in which Midwestern cities acted as fathers to dependent rural hinterlands.[21]

Gendered analyses also incorporate the ethnic, religious, educational, and civic elements of the Midwest that scholars often ignore but that attest to the complexity of the Midwestern experience. Urban neighborhoods like Chicago's East Garfield not only contained economic or agricultural elements; they also held the features of a vibrant organizational culture driven by gendered ideals of mutuality, sociability, and care for younger generations. First, Midwesterners enjoyed active religious lives expressed as congregations of believers. Surrounding Shannon's home were several churches, with denominations including Presbyterian, Catholic, Congregational, Baptist, Universalist, Methodist, and Episcopal that offered religious and missional services. Second, the Midwest prioritized education. As the *Chicago Tribune* noted, Shannon's neighborhood contained theological seminaries, medical schools, public high schools, "a large number of grammar schools and parochial schools and convents."[22] Those parochial schools, including the German American Academy and the German School of the Holy Trinity, favored the German and Irish Catholics who resided there and who sought to perpetuate their ethnic and religious identities.[23] While professional schools practiced gender segregation, the existence of Northwestern University Women's Medical School promised Midwestern women the opportunity for medical training. Such a "lively, spirited" student body gave the neighborhood an educational character.[24] Finally, gender inclusivity animated the Midwestern civic impulse to found community-focused organizations. Locals—both men and women—raised funds, served on boards, or worked for a slew of charitable public institutions, including the Salvation Army, whose headquarters were on West Madison Street, the County Hospital, which offered free medical care, and the Martha Washington Home, which gave a place for recovery to "women inebriates."[25] These civic-facing, charity-granting institutions were anchors of their communities. One of the most famous, Hull House, a social settlement founded by Jane Addams and Ellen Gates Starr in

1889, stood just under five miles away and offered clubs, daycare facilities, an employment office, cultural events, and a meeting space for trade unions.[26]

While urban landscapes like the East Garfield neighborhood showcased a vibrant institutional culture, there were some instances when a matter seemed to fall outside acceptable Midwestern propriety. Abortion was an issue serious enough that secrecy shrouded its appearance in the historical record, but historians have stitched together compelling narratives about it from fragmentary evidence. A kaleidoscope of factors, including religious beliefs, presumptions of family support, access to medical care, state enforcement of existing abortion laws, and the community's willingness to care for the children of unwed mothers, all shaped the ways in which abortions occurred. In the late nineteenth-century rural Midwest, ethnic identity, class status, and community attitudes toward "deviant" behaviors meant that poor, unwed, and immigrant women were more likely to seek abortions. Conversely, in urban areas, local healthcare professionals were more available to perform abortions or provide birth control.[27] Joan Jensen notes that Catholic Midwesterners often held strong views against abortion, which may indicate why O'Connor and Boyle, the two presumably orphaned boys, resided with the widowed Mary Shannon.[28]

The East Garfield household of Shannon, O'Connor, and Boyle reveals how taboo subjects like abortion helped to define the various ways in which Midwesterners structured their families. Many families strayed far from patriarchal norms, religious dictates, or agrarian myths, constituting themselves instead out of so-called deviant behaviors.[29] Midwestern kinship was complicated. As Tamara Gaskell Miller notes about early Ohio, household composition varied remarkably as people intermingled, divorced, remarried, or moved.[30] Most Midwesterners tacitly understood this reality as they both created formal welfare structures and practiced informal neighborliness to assist vulnerable populations. While these practices were not distinct to the region, they were essential to Midwestern identity formation because precarity was an experience common to many residents. The fragility was the result of awe-inspiring geographic vastness, uneven infrastructure development, agricultural booms and busts, indigenous and settler conflicts, jarring political and economic shifts, domestic violence, and clashes over racial and ethnic identities.[31] Navigating these issues required Midwesterners to amplify the importance of local connections. For example, as Megan Birk explains about poor farms, public funds supported these ubiquitous county-level institutions without a test or labor requirement. In other words, necessity, not worthiness, was the standard by which communities supported their poorest residents. Birk also explains that poor farms most helped those without kinship or neighborly networks, housing largely non-able-bodied, single, and elderly white men by the early twentieth century.[32] In this way, poor farms did for unattached elderly people what Shannon offered for the two nonbiological children in her care. Many Midwesterners prized a community-centered ethos, one that encouraged civic attention to initiatives that promised to uplift, provide care for, or aid people with or without families. Feminine tropes of hospitality, friendliness, partnership, cooperation, and mutuality became synonymous with the Midwest.[33]

Women and men were influential in forming the political and civic spirit of the Midwest because norm-bending behaviors, along with the necessity of infrastructure development, fostered an associational culture that drove community-building efforts. As the East Garfield neighborhood demonstrated, constructing libraries, schools, opera houses, parks, and other public spaces brought people together to pursue strategies that required broad coalitions of individuals with time, energy, and money. Many women had these qualities, which often put them at the forefront of civic initiatives. Therefore, gender directly shaped Midwestern placemaking.[34] While most community-focused organizations practiced gender segregation by forming women's affiliates, auxiliaries, or clubs, women nevertheless took advantage of whatever leverage they had to foster partnership and collaborations with their male counterparts. Through those networks, women honed their political organizing abilities. For example, Jenny Barker Devine argues that Iowa's female township-level Farm Bureau clubs, auxiliaries to the male-dominated Farm Bureau Federation, offered political authority by connecting partisan politics to domesticity, a process that politicized homemaking roles. When these farm women surveyed rural mail delivery routes, studied school food options, or assembled first aid kits, they did so to improve the health and welfare of their neighbors and families, which earned them public reputations as competent civic leaders.[35]

Racial, ethnic, class, and religious identities intersected with gender to fragment Midwestern placemaking work. In the case of Mary Shannon, her Irish Catholic background undoubtedly influenced the stance she took on civic and political matters, like the institutional care for orphans. In other places, like Minnesota and North Dakota, Scandinavian women took up the suffrage cause alongside their native-born counterparts in the Minnesota Woman Suffrage Association, arguing that they supported female enfranchisement because of an ethnic heritage steeped in liberty and equality.[36] While some women united because they shared an ethnic, religious, or class identity, others experienced white supremacy, antisemitism, or other oppressive exclusionary policies, which created divisions. Segregationist policies among federated women's clubs prompted African American women in Illinois to champion racial and gender equality through colored women's clubs. As Wanda Hendricks asserts, their exclusion from the all-white board of the 1893 Chicago World's Columbian Exposition prompted a regional effort to organize "race women" to combat both racism and sexism.[37] Indiana's women also took up political work for temperance, suffrage, and other reforms through groups like the Council of Jewish Women and Branch Number 7, an Indianapolis-based affiliate of the Equal Suffrage Association created specifically for Black advocates.[38]

Men practiced homosocial organization by forming fraternal or civic associations like their female counterparts, but heteropatriarchal norms facilitated their dominance in political and economic life. For much of Midwestern history, men took political office, formed third parties, headed corporations, and led unions.[39] Scholarship on these topics rarely engages with gender analysis, and when it does, it often aligns with existing frameworks that value individualism over mutuality. For example, during the nineteenth and early twentieth centuries, politics erupted outside the two-party system, in groups like the Grange, Populists, Knights of Labor, and Farmers' Alliance. In this reading, anti-corruption agrarian antagonism fueled a progressive political transformation, one that scholars have characterized as moderate, not revolutionary. They saw measured reforms that maintained economic hierarchies and political hegemonies to privilege the few against any potentially drastic upheavals that favored the masses.[40] But this argument overlooks the radical deviance of Midwestern socialists and labor activists. Early twentieth-century examples like Eugene Debs and Henry Demarest Lloyd showcase how agricultural and industrial developments fostered blistering anti-corporate attacks from male socialists.[41] People who were not native-born, white, elite, or male also took up radical labor causes. Chicago-based anarchist and Black revolutionary Lucy Parsons spoke, wrote, and agitated extensively about labor issues before helping to found the Industrial Workers of the World.[42]

Midwestern states offered divergent reactions to post–World War II political and economic issues, which made discord and conflict, not conformity, an essential characteristic of the region. For farmers, gender served as a principal organizer of labor, but farming was fickle and gender roles weak, which created a flexible work system. Exigency thwarted adherence to any gender division of labor, as rural women drove tractors, put up fences, and castrated livestock without blushing.[43] Men saw the physical demands of farming change with mechanization, and some grew uncomfortable when "push-button farming" removed the powerful physicality that defined their sense of masculinity.[44] For industrial laborers, organizers perceived the Midwest as a labor stronghold, but renewed political assaults sought to undermine union efforts. Indiana passed a right-to-work law in 1957, but Ohio voters rejected a similar right-to-work measure the following year. Wisconsin followed in 1959 with the nation's first limited public-sector bargaining law. As Marc Dixon explains, while rallying public support amid persistent business and political opposition made labor unity difficult, Midwestern unions pursued labor rights where they could.[45] Labor organizing was one of many topics that exposed the conflicts at the heart of the Midwestern experience. For some scholars, state-supported agricultural and industrial growth anchors the narrative of the Midwestern experience, which assumes masculine notions of individual enterprises seeking patriarchal rationality and controlled progress within spatialized hierarchies. For others, centering radical politics and anti-capitalist agitation reveals a Midwestern critique of systemic inequities, one that deviates from normativity.

Some of the scholars who examined marginalized Midwesterners did not necessarily intend to offer an explicit critique of conformity, but their studies nevertheless challenged assumptions about the region, recasting indigeneity or queerness as essential Midwestern qualities. For example, according to James LaGrand, Chicago emerged as "an Indian metropolis" in the thirty years after World War II.[46] As its indigenous population ballooned, the city fostered compelling new ideas about identity, especially a shared pan–Native American one.[47] Chicago's designation as indigenous ought to extend to the entire region; native peoples profoundly shaped the Midwest in every era and place. Kristen Hoganson explains how the Kickapoo people living in what became central Illinois navigated anti-indigenous violence by moving extensively to avoid conflict, often to the consternation of white American settlers who immediately wrote them out of local pioneer histories.[48] Incomplete scholarly narratives built out of these prejudiced sources wrongly argued that native peoples like the Kickapoo left the region because they could not conform to masculinist settler designs for land ownership, agricultural production, and civic life. Unraveling these twisted tales exposes instead generations of indigenous ingenuity, resourcefulness, and resilience. White settler expressions of masculinity failed to account for how agility and creativity nurtured toughness as native peoples reimagined communities and fostered relationships across the region and in spite of oppression.[49] Among the many contributions made by indigenous people to Midwestern identity, perhaps the most compelling stem from challenges to white, settler-colonial gender cultures. As Lisa Tatonetti makes clear, by practicing gender expansiveness through the body as an archive of knowledge, native peoples rebuffed narrow visions of white masculinity, countering with masculinities and queer identities that offered advocacy, kinship, and care.[50] Claims about the Midwest's gender normativity fall apart when confronted by the vibrant history of non-cis-gender Midwesterners.

As they did in the rest of the Midwest, queer people in Chicago dramatically shaped this urban space. A few miles northeast of Shannon's residence in the East Garfield neighborhood, German immigrant Henry Gerber founded the Society for Human Rights in 1924. His German family chose Chicago because of its large German population, a preference that mirrored the ethnic familiarity Shannon also enjoyed as a person of Irish descent.[51] The Society was the first documented LGBTQ-rights organization in the United States, and Gerber served as its secretary. In the group's charter, Gerber condemned "public prejudices against" LGBTQ people "abused and hindered in the legal pursuit of happiness which is guaranteed them by the Declaration of Independence."[52] He published and distributed the Society's newsletter, *Friendship and Freedom*, from his Chicago home, which violated the Comstock Act. While police raided Gerber's residence in 1925, shutting down the Society, scholars note that Gerber influenced generations of queer people to use the press to advance the cause of civil rights.[53] By the 1950s, queer activists in Chicago also found support by joining Black civil rights leaders to force change through growing liberal political channels. As Timothy Stewart-Winter explains, by the 1980s, gay advocates began to win local political office, and they worked specially to curb police abuse.[54]

Perhaps most compelling is the tangled nature of gender in the Midwest as it developed out of these contradictions. Examining Midwestern masculinity has shown how many residents championed a heteronormativity that venerated individuality, shrewdness, and discipline while also simultaneously celebrating anti-capitalist and anti-elitist radicals for supporting farmers, laborers, and other underdogs. The same region that prized railroad tycoon James J. Hill, oil magnate John D. Rockefeller, car manufacturer Henry Ford, and milling mogul Charles Pillsbury also nurtured anarchist Albert Parsons, who helped organize the 1886 Haymarket Square protest in Chicago, Eugene Debs, a powerfully influential socialist, labor activist, and presidential candidate, William Jennings Bryan, an antagonistic Populist and political force for over three decades, and Gus Hall, born Arvo Kustaa Halberg, the last chair of the Communist Party in the United States.[55] While such divergence in a region as vast and varied as the Midwest was unsurprising, it was the proximity of these conflicting visions of masculinity that was striking. Midwesterners often expressed admiration for men like Rockefeller, Parsons, and Bryan in the same breath.[56] In other words, those often recognized as the most masculine were both the cutthroat elites with economic and political dominance and the hardnosed resisters who fought against them. Midwestern masculinity functioned as juxtaposition and often at the intersection of capitalism, protest, and power.

In this region without borders, Midwesterners understood and expressed gender in countless ways. Most striking was that it was elastic, bending norms and defying assumed roles, and contradictory, often with no explanation needed. While many residents ascribed to patriarchal expectations and heteronormative structures, they also shapeshifted outside of whatever bounds seemingly placed by those same constructions. Midwestern women were civic leaders, queer Midwesterners created coalitions to combat inequities, and masculinities splintered as people admired cunning Midwestern politicians or business leaders and the rugged resisters who fought them. What defines the Midwest was the ease with which Midwesterners lived out these contradictory gender identities and the notable lack of overt angst from their neighbors, friends, or family members who lived with them. To be clear, homophobia, sexism, and gender discrimination shaped the region in detrimental ways for many vulnerable people. Evidence from civic institutions, poor farms, labor unions, suffrage associations, Farm Bureau clubs, the East Garfield neighborhood, and the household of Mary Shannon, John O'Connor, and Joseph Boyle, however, illuminates how the pliability of gender in the Midwest elevated friendship, cooperation, partnership, and mutuality.

## NOTES

1. Mary B. Shannon, Ward 13, Chicago, Cook County, Illinois, Thirteenth Census of the United States, Roll T624_255, page 6A (Ancestry.com, 2006).

2. While it is possible that O'Connor and Boyle were Shannon's biological children, it is unlikely considering her age, her unmarried status, and the fact that the US census enumerator listed the boys as "roomers" in her household. Assigning the designation to the two young children seems to indicate an orphaned status.

3. "Chicago at a Glance—Eleventh, Twelfth, and Thirteenth Wards, Places and Things of Historic and Present Interest Located by Wards," *Chicago Tribune*, June 3, 1900.

4. "Chicago at a Glance."

5. "Chicago at a Glance."

6. Mary B. Shannon, Ward 13, Chicago, Cook County, Illinois, Thirteenth Census of the United States, Roll T624_255, page 6A (Ancestry.com, 2006).

7. David Noel Doyle, "The Irish in Chicago," *Irish Historical Studies* 26, no. 103 (1989): 293–99.

8. Dianne Creagh, "The Baby Trains: Catholic Foster Care and Western Migration, 1873–1929," *Journal of Social History* 46, no. 1 (2012): 197–218.

9. "U.S. World War II Army Enlistment Records, 1938–1946," Reel 74, Box Number 03533, Record Group 64, National Archives at College Park (Ancestry.com, 2005).

10. Chicago City Directory, 1928, "U.S. City Directories, 1822–1995" (Ancestry.com, 2011).

11. Mary Neth, "Seeing the Midwest with Peripheral Vision: Identities, Narratives, and Region," in *The Identity of the American Midwest: Essays on Regional History*, ed. Andrew R. L. Cayton and Susan E. Gray (Indiana University Press, 2001).

12. Pekka Hämäläinen, *Lakota America: A New History of Indigenous Power* (Yale University Press, 2019), 1–10. Scholars Britt Halvorson and Joshua O. Reno argue that the "cultural work of place-making" that imagines the Midwest as "heartland" has rendered the region as bland, plain, or homogenous, serving as a screen from which people have assumed normativity about whiteness and sought to pursue national and global projects such as nativism, imperialism, and white supremacy. Characterizing the Midwest through the lenses of pastoralism, insularity, virtue, or hard-working white laborers leads to claims that the Midwest was ordinary and average. Those claims are one-dimensional and fail to account for the diverse and divergent ways that Midwesterners from myriad identity groups constituted their identities and contributed to the region. Britt Halvorson and Joshua O. Reno, *Imagining the Heartland: White Supremacy and the American Midwest* (University of California Press, 2022), 11.

13. Lauck et al., *Finding a New Midwestern History* (see introduction, n. 4). While there are headings for a few individual women in the book's index, there is no heading for "gender" or "women."

14. Shortridge, *The Middle West* (see chapter 6, n. 5); Terry A. Barnhart, "An Emerging Voice: The Origins of Regional Identity and Mission in the Old Northwest," in Lauck, *The Making of the Midwest* (see introduction, n. 3); Marcia Noe, "The Innocent Midwest and the New Midwestern Pastoral," in Lauck, *The Making of the Midwest*; Cayton and Onuf, *The Midwest and the Nation* (see chapter 6, n. 6).

15. Andrew R. L. Cayton and Susan E. Gray, "The Story of the Midwest: An Introduction," in Cayton and Gray, *The Identity of the American Midwest*; Klumpp, "Not a Revival" (see chapter 7, n. 11).

16. Jon Teaford, "The Development of Midwestern Cities," in *Finding a New Midwestern History*, ed. Jon K. Lauck, Gleaves Whitney, and Joseph Hogan (University of Nebraska Press, 2018), 213.

17. Teaford, "Development of Midwestern Cities," 211, 212–13.

18. Teaford, "Development of Midwestern Cities," 215.

19. Teaford, "Development of Midwestern Cities," 216–19.

20. "Chicago at a Glance."

21. Cronon, *Nature's Metropolis*, 41–54 (see chapter 1, n. 7). About Ohio, authors Andrew R. L. Cayton and Stuart D. Hobbs posit that it existed at "the center of a great empire," arguing that states in the Midwest "developed at a critical moment in the history of the world and of North America." It was a "full-fledged experiment in republican government, in the power of the market, in democratic social organization, and in the necessity of organized competition in politics, religion, labor, and commerce." See Andrew R. L. Cayton and Stuart D. Hobbs, eds., *The Center of a Great Empire: The Ohio Country in the Early Republic* (Ohio University Press, 2005), 4–6.

22. "Chicago at a Glance."

23. "Chicago at a Glance."

24. "Chicago at a Glance." For more on the Midwest's co-educational history in land-grant colleges, see Andrea G. Radke-Moss, *Bright Epoch: Women & Coeducation in the American West* (University of Nebraska Press, 2008); Lauck, *The Good Country*, 154–90 (see chapter 4, n. 25).

25. Lauck, *The Good Country*, 154–90.

26. Jane Addams, *Twenty Years at Hull-House: With Autobiographical Notes* (Dover Publications, 1910).

27. Laura Kaplan, *The Story of Jane: The Legendary Underground Feminist Abortion Service* (University of Chicago Press, 1997); Leslie Reagan, *When Abortion Was a Crime: Women, Medicine, and Law in the United States, 1867–1973* (University of California Press, 1998).

28. Joan M. Jensen, "The Death of Rosa: Sexuality in Rural America," *Agricultural History* 67, no. 4 (1993): 1–12; Joan M. Jensen, *Calling This Place Home: Women on the Wisconsin Frontier* (Minnesota Historical Society Press, 2006); Rachel Kleinschmidt, "'What to do with our Girls': Prescriptive Literature and the Girl Problem in the Rural Midwest, 1865–1900" (PhD diss., Iowa State University, 2013). In the Eleventh, Twelfth, and Thirteenth Wards, the three neighborhoods closest to the East Garfield Park neighborhood, there were two institutions for orphans, the Masonic Orphans' Home and the Foundlings' Home. See "Chicago at a Glance."

29. Lisa Payne Ossian argues persuasively that temperance women were neither engineers of a failed moralistic experiment nor "conservative and complicit in their own oppression." Instead, they were "strong, sensible women" who dealt with real circumstances of drunkenness and violence. See Lisa Payne Ossian, "The 'I Too' Temperance Movement: A Reevaluation of Midwestern Women's Political Action at the Turn of the Last Century," in Lauck, *The Making of the Midwest*, 215–29; Gabriel Rosenberg, *The 4-H Harvest: Sexuality and the State in Rural America* (University of Pennsylvania Press, 2016).

30. Tamara Gaskell Miller, "'My Whole Enjoyment & Almost My Existence Depends Upon My Friends': Family and Kinship in Early Ohio," in Cayton and Hobbs, *The Center of a Great Empire*.

31. While Deborah Fink charted abuse, neglect, and struggle in Nebraska and Iowa, Sharon Wood examined how well-to-do women in Davenport, Iowa, sought to provide relief to a growing number of prostitutes and working-class women. That they clung desperately to traditional gender values amid an ever-growing number of prostitutes merely validated the fragility of those ideals. Pamela Riney-Kehrberg also studied how humiliation shaped how farm wives approached food insecurity during the 1980s farm crisis. See Deborah Fink, *Open Country, Iowa: Rural Women, Tradition, and Change* (SUNY Press, 1986); Deborah Fink, *Agrarian Women: Wives and Mothers in Rural Nebraska, 1880–1940* (University of North Carolina Press, 1992); Sharon Wood, *The Freedom of the Streets: Work, Citizenship, and Sexuality in a Gilded Age City* (University of North Carolina, 2005); and Pamela Riney-Kehrberg, "A Special and Terrible Irony: Hunger on Iowa's Farms during the Agricultural Crisis of the 1980s," *The Annals of Iowa* 78, no. 4 (2019): 361–90.

32. Megan Birk. *The Fundamental Institution: Poverty, Social Welfare, and Agriculture in American Poor Farms* (University of Illinois Press, 2022); Megan Birk, *Fostering on the Farm: Child Placement in the Rural Midwest* (University of Illinois Press, 2015).

33. Mary Neth, *Preserving the Family Farm: Women, Community, and the Foundations of Agribusiness in the Midwest, 1900–1940* (Johns Hopkins University Press, 1998).

34. Sara Egge, "The Emergence of Midwestern Political Culture in Northwest Iowa," in Lauck, *The Making of the Midwest*, 199–213; Egge, *Woman Suffrage* (see chapter 1, n. 15).

35. Jenny Barker Devine, "'The Secret to a Successful Farm Organization': Township Farm Bureau Women's Clubs in Iowa, 1945–1970," *The Annals of Iowa* 69, no. 4 (2010): 418–48; Jenny Barker Devine, "Hop to the Top with the Iowa Chop': The Iowa Porkettes and Cultivating Agrarian Feminisms in the Midwest, 1964–1992," *Agricultural History* 83, no. 4 (2009): 477–502; Devine, *On Behalf of the Family Farm* (see chapter 1, n. 15). For more on the organizational culture of the Farm Bureau, see Berlage, *Farmers Helping Farmers* (see chapter 1, n. 15).

36. Barbara Stuhler, *Gentle Warriors: Clara Ueland and the Minnesota Struggle for Woman Suffrage* (Minnesota Historical Society, 1995); Barbara Stuhler, "Organizing the Vote: The Minnesota's Woman Suffrage Movement," in *The North Star State: A Minnesota History Reader*, ed. Anne J. Aby (Minnesota Historical Society 2002); Anna Marie Peterson, "Adding 'a Little Suffrage Spice to the Melting Pot': Minnesota's Scandinavian Woman Suffrage Association," *Minnesota History* 62, no. 8 (2011–12): 288–97; Anna Peterson, "Making Women's Suffrage Support an Ethnic Duty: Norwegian American Identity Constructions and the Women's Suffrage Movement, 1880–1925," *Journal of American Ethnic History* 30, no. 4 (2011): 5–23.

37. Wanda Hendricks, *Gender, Race and Politics in the Midwest: Black Club Women in Illinois* (Indiana University Press, 1998).

38. Anita Morgan, *"We Must Be Fearless": The Woman Suffrage Movement in Indiana* (Indiana Historical Society Press, 2020).

39. Edward O. Frantz, "When the Midwest Controlled the Presidency, 1860–1930," in Lauck, *The Making of the Midwest*.

40. Nye, *Midwestern Progressive Politics*, 3–32. The Fall 2021 issue of the *Middle West Review* features a roundtable discussion of six articles on Nye's work. See *Middle West Review* 8, no. 1 (2021): 133–68.

41. Ray Ginger, *The Bending Cross: A Biography of Eugene Victor Debs* (Haymarket Books, 2007); Richard Digby-Junger, *The Journalist as Reformer: Henry Demarest Lloyd and Wealth Against Commonwealth* (Greenwood Press, 1996).

42. Daniel Nelson, *Farm and Factory: Workers in the Midwest, 1880–1990* (Indiana University Press, 1995); Carolyn Ashbaugh, *Lucy Parsons: American Revolutionary* (Haymarket Books, 2011); Jacqueline Jones, *Goddess of Anarchy: The Life and Times of Lucy Parsons, American Radical* (Basic Books, 2017).

43. Women welcomed technology in various spaces of the farm household. See Katherine Jellison, "Let Your Corn Stalks Buy a Maytag: Prescriptive Literature and Domestic Consumerism in Rural Iowa," *The Palimpsest* 69, no. 3 (1988): 132–39; Katherine Jellison, *Entitled to Power: Farm Women and Technology, 1913–1963* (University of North Carolina Press, 1993). For more on rural Midwestern women, see Neth, *Preserving the Family Farm*; Jensen, *Calling This Place Home*; Mary Neth, "Gender and the Family Labor System: Defining Work in the Rural Midwest," *Journal of Social History* 27, no. 3 (1994): 563–77; Susan Sessions Rugh, *Our Common Country: Family Farming, Culture, and Community in the Nineteenth-Century Midwest* (Indiana University Press, 2001); Sonya Salamon, *Prairie Patrimony: Family, Farming, and Community in the Midwest* (University of North Carolina Press, 1992); and Murphy and Venet, *Midwestern Women* (see chapter 1, n. 15). Katherine Jellison also edited an issue of the *Middle West Review* that features a "Symposium on Midwestern Women's History." See *Middle West Review* 9, no. 2 (2023): 15–89.

44. J. L. Anderson, "'You're a Bigger Man': Technology and Agrarian Masculinity in Postwar America" *Agricultural History* 94, no. 1 (2020): 4–23.

45. Marc Dixon, *Heartland Blues: Labor Rights in the Industrial Midwest* (Oxford University Press, 2021).

46. LaGrand, *Indian Metropolis*, 11(see chapter 2, n. 46).

47. LaGrand, *Indian Metropolis*, 11–16.

48. Hoganson, *The Heartland* (see chapter 1, n. 1).

49. Gender systems among indigenous peoples varied across Midwest. See, for example, Mary Whelan, "Dakota Indian Economics and the Nineteenth-Century Fur Trade," *Ethnohistory* 40, no. 2 (1993): 246–76; Linda Clemmons, *Dakota in Exile: The Untold Stories of Captives in the Aftermath of the U.S.-Dakota War* (University of Iowa Press, 2019); and Doug Kiel, "Indigenous Agency and Resilience in the Midwest: Reclaiming the Narrative," *Middle West Review* 10, no. 2 (2024): 99–111.

50. Lisa Tatonetti, *Written by the Body: Gender Expansiveness and Indigenous Non-Cis Masculinities* (University of Minnesota Press, 2021).

51. Jim Kepner and Stephen O. Murray, "Henry Gerber (1895–1972): Grandfather of the American Gay Rights Movement," in *Before Stonewall: Activists for Gay and Lesbian Rights in Historical Context*, ed. Vern Bullough (Harrington Park Press, 2002).

52. St. Sukie de la Croix, *Chicago Whispers: A History of LGBT Chicago Before Stonewall* (University of Wisconsin Press, 2012), 73; Shirley Baugher, "Not Everyone Was Brave: Henry Gerber and the Beginning of the Gay Rights Movement in Chicago," *Living in Interesting Times* (blog), Chicago Now, April 15, 2014, http://www.chicagonow.com/my-kind-of-old-town/2014/04/not-everyone-was-brave-henrygerber-and-the-beginning-of-the-gay-rights-movement-in-chicago/.

53. Salvatore John Licata, "Gay Power: A History of the American Gay Movement, 1908–1974," (PhD diss., University of Southern California, 1978), 53; Jonathon Katz, *Gay American History: Lesbians and Gay Men in the U.S.A.*, rev. ed. (Meridian, 1992), 632. In 2001, the Henry Gerber House, located at 1710 N. Crilly Court, became a Chicago Landmark. In 2015, it became a National Historic Landmark. See "Henry Gerber House," Department of Planning and Development, Landmarks Division, City of Chicago, accessed January 16, 2023, https://webapps1.chicago.gov/landmarksweb/web/home.htm; "Old Town Site of Nation's First Gay Rights Group Designated National Landmark," *Chicago Sun Times*, June 19, 2015.

54. Timothy Stewart-Winter, *Queer Clout: Chicago and the Rise of Gay Politics* (University of Pennsylvania Press, 2016). Scholars have studied queer identities and histories in other Midwestern cities and rural areas. See Emily Kazyak, "Midwest or Lesbian? Gender, Rurality, and Sexuality," *Gender and Society* 26, no. 6 (2012): 825–48; Kevin P. Murphy, Jennifer L. Pierce, and Larry Knopp, eds., *Queer Twin Cities: Twin Cities GLBT Oral History Project* (University of Minnesota Press, 2010); Garrett W. Nichols, "Rural Drag: Fashioning Rurality and Privilege," *QED: A Journal in GLBTQ Worldmaking* 4, no. 3 (2017): 41–66. Joy Ellison examined transgender communities in the Midwest. See Joy Ellison, "Coalitions at the Crossroad: Midwest Transgender History, 1945–2000" (PhD diss., Ohio State University, 2022).

55. Karen Matthews, "Gus Hall, U.S. Communist Party Head, Dies at 90," *Seattle Times*, October 17, 2000.

56. Andy Oler, *Old-Fashioned Modernism: Rural Masculinity and Midwestern Literature* (Louisiana State University Press, 2019).

## 9

# A TALE OF TWO MURDERESSES

How Emily and Minnie Can Help Us Do
Midwestern Literary Studies

"An' the Gobble-uns 'll git you Ef you don't Watch Out!" This refrain from "Little Orphant Annie" was my earliest—and most traumatic—experience with Midwestern literature. In a futile attempt to scare some good behavior into me, my Hoosier grandmother tried to terrify me with this James Whitcomb Riley poem in the kitchen of our family home. Its ominous warning, while not effecting the intended result, is probably responsible for my lifelong aversion to James Whitcomb Riley, stoves, kitchens, baking, cooking, and food preparation in general, as well as my mantra, "A kitchen is a death trap." However, I did become concerned when I asked how "Gobble-uns" could get into our house and was told that they could come down the chimney. This revelation made for many an anxious Christmas Eve that found me peering into the fireplace, wondering, "Is it going to be Santa or 'Gobble-uns?'"[1]

I'm going to resist the temptation to make those Hoosier "Gobble-uns" a controlling metaphor for everything that is wrong with Midwestern literary studies and move on to a more benign Midwestern literary memory: Maud Hart Lovelace's Betsy-Tacy series, set in Deep Valley, Minnesota, a thinly disguised Mankato. These enchanting books were my first introduction to a democratic, inclusive, and culturally plural Midwest.[2] However, the encounter that launched my career as a Midwesternist occurred when, as I searched for a dissertation topic, someone told me that there was an obscure woman playwright from Davenport, Iowa, who had won the Pulitzer Prize. This conversation inspired my career-long engagement with the works of playwright and novelist Susan Glaspell and, especially, with *Trifles*, her most famous play and the play that features her most famous or, rather, most infamous character, a murderess named Minnie Foster Wright.

Here I call upon two infamous murderesses—the aforementioned Minnie Foster Wright of *Trifles* and also of the short story Glaspell based on that play, "A Jury of Her Peers," and Emily Grierson of William Faulkner's short story "A Rose for Emily"—to help us better understand how to do regional studies, a field that has seen much ink spilled by scholars trying to establish a region's definitive characteristics. In 1960, Thomas T. McEvoy convened a conference at the University of Notre Dame, "The Midwest: Myth or Reality?" Nearly sixty years later, the Newberry Library raised the same question with their initiative "What Is the Midwest?"[3]

Many scholars have attempted to answer this question. David D. Anderson theorizes that the myth of the Midwest—the story that defines the region—is a myth of movement and search, while David Radavich identifies five quintessential regional traits: 1) a solid and reliable, if confining, home, situated in the present; 2) a cyclical concept of time rooted in the rural growing season; 3) an emphasis on physical work and daily chores and rhythms; 4) people who are practical, capable, honest, reliable, and relatively simple; and 5) language that is quiet, forthright, and unadorned.[4] For Peter Onuf, Andrew Cayton, and James R. Shortridge, the Midwest is the most American part of America. In his seminal study *The Middle West*, Shortridge explains that the region's character was rooted in a pastoral ideal that has persisted for decades even as the Midwest has also come to be associated with parochialism, conformity, intolerance, and philistinism. Shortridge's finding corroborates Margaret Stuhr's argument for an ambiguous Midwestern identity based on the region's association with "safe," a word that evokes both an idyllic haven and a place of stultifying stasis.[5]

Southern scholars have also been at work on this project. In *The Mind of the South*, W. J. Cash conceptualizes his region as having marked tendencies toward sentimentality, "gyneolatry," romanticism, and violence. For Cleanth Brooks, Southern culture comprises a sense of place, a special conception of time that encompasses both the past and the timeless, a family- and community-focused identity, and a strong oral tradition that reflects a gift for narrative. John Shelton Reed also has defined Southern identity as a matter of culture. For Reed, the culture that Southerners share includes "some cultural conservatism, religiosity, manners, speech, humor, music, that sort of thing."[6]

These kinds of regional distinctions appear to be easily discerned in "A Rose for Emily" and "A Jury of Her Peers," two stories that have much in common. Each centers on a murderess and a murder investigation; however, they are set in different regions. Can we characterize the narrative strategies and structures of these stories, as well as the way in which each murderess perpetrates her murder and deals with its aftermath, as quintessentially Southern and Midwestern, respectively?

Are Emily's Southernness and Minnie's Midwesternness reflected in each woman's relationship to her community? Emily has been ensconced in the Grierson mansion in the center of town for decades. Her ancestors are respected Confederate officers and Southern gentlemen; after the Griersons lost their money, she finds respectable employment giving china-painting lessons to the women of the town. By contrast, Minnie, isolated on a lonely farmstead, lacks even a telephone; the two women who accompany the men to the Wright farm admit that they have lost touch with her. And does a formalist analysis reveal regional characteristics? "A Jury of Her Peers" is focalized through one character and constructed simply and directly with a straightforward chronological through line. "A Rose for Emily" features a communal "we" narrator and is built on flashbacks as it winds its circuitous way to its shocking conclusion.

Does each murderess's relationship with her victim exhibit any regional traits? Emily's victim is Homer Barron, a Yankee construction boss who fails to heed the maxim, "Never sleep with anybody crazier than you are." Homer's not just a Yankee; he's a damned Yankee—the kind that comes down South and stays there. Admittedly, though, he doesn't stay there willingly. He meets his demise after a protracted courtship, thus exemplifying the old adage that Southerners will be polite to you until they get mad enough to kill you. He isn't guilty of many of the Seven Southern Deadly Sins—atheism, sports apathy, feminism, candor, genealogy indifference, pushiness, and Yankee birth—but his failure to close the deal with Emily proves fatal. She poisons him, apparently as he lies in her bed, and there he stays until the town fathers find his moldering corpse years after his death.

Minnie's victim is her husband, John; she strangles him with a rope while he sleeps. As they examine the crime scene, the sheriff and the county attorney fail to find any clue that points to a motive. They never understand that the real clues to Minnie's state of mind and motive for murder are located in her kitchen, chief among them a strangled canary in her sewing box found by the women who have accompanied them to the Wright farmhouse and decide not to disclose this interesting discovery.

And what about the murders? Any Midwesternness or Southernness therein? Minnie kills her husband quickly and effectively and, when confronted, deals with her inquisitors just as directly. "He died of a rope round his neck," she says, a statement which, while not exactly the whole truth, is certainly accurate as far as it goes, as well as succinct and to the point. Emily kills Homer slowly and torturously, by arsenic poisoning, and plays an elaborate cat-and-mouse game with the townsmen, who succeed in gaining entrance to the crime scene only after her death.[7] And is it significant that both crimes take place in bed? If John or Homer had been a better lover, or at least used a vibrator, might they have improved their chances of survival?

I've been having a little fun with these stories to make a point: regional scholars should avoid the kind of essentialism that third-wave feminists have warned us about. While the search for a quintessential Midwesternness or Southernness has been occupying scholars for over half a century and has yielded a plethora of academic publications, none of these quests have succeeded. Such scholarship is not without merit. But while it might be amusing to think of contributions to memes such as "Things You'd Never Hear a Southerner Say" (e.g., "I didn't know that could be fried"; "Duct tape won't fix that"), this kind of essentialist investigation inevitably fails.[8]

While what we might term the first wave of regional scholarship has had heuristic value—generating conversations about the region, stimulating scholarly projects, and yielding insights about the works under study—anyone who attempts to identify the essential characteristics of the Midwest will ultimately be defeated by its complexity, diversity, and paradoxical elements as they grapple unsuccessfully with what William Barillas calls "the perpetual instability of midwestern cultural identity."[9] Despite all of the conference papers and journal articles that have attempted to discover what makes the Midwest the Midwest, we are no nearer this goal than we were in 1960 when Thomas T. McEvoy convened that conference at Notre Dame. Earlier I referred to democratic values, inclusivity, and cultural pluralism as Midwestern qualities, citing the Betsy-Tacy books. Others might just as validly name conformity, narrow-mindedness, and intolerance, citing Edgar Lee Masters's *Spoon River Anthology* (1915), Willa Cather's *O Pioneers!* (1913) and *My Antonia* (1918), Sherwood Anderson's *Winesburg, Ohio* (1919), and Sinclair Lewis's *Main Street* (1920) and *Babbitt* (1922).

During the 1970s and 1980s, feminist scholars engaged in second-wave research, recovering such marginalized writers as Sarah Orne Jewett, Nella Larsen, Ida B. Tarbell, Kate Chopin, and Frances E. Watkins Harper. In both feminist studies and regional studies, such recovery work is ongoing and more still needs to be done. Gretchen Comba's scholarship on William Maxwell, Joy Elizabeth Castro's articles about Margery Bodine Latimer, and Marilyn J. Atlas's publications on Harriet Monroe, Eunice Tietjens, and Alice Gerstenberg are examples of such Midwestern efforts. Jon K. Lauck has taken on the entire region for his recovery project, including its literature. In *From Warm Center to Ragged Edge: The Erosion of Midwestern Literary and Historical Regionalism, 1920–1965* (University of Iowa Press, 2017), he discusses little-known Midwestern authors such as Ruth Suckow, Dorothy Canfield Fisher, and August Derleth, as well as the Revolt from the Village movement.

The third wave of feminist studies got underway in the 1990s; a corresponding third wave of Midwestern literary studies developed a decade later, with intersectionality the defining feature of both disciplinary trends. In the 1970s it was perfectly appropriate for Anderson to ask about the Midwest, "what are its dimensions? Are they geographical only? Are they historical or mythical? Are there psychological and literary dimensions as well?"[10] But now it is time to ask some new questions. How does the Midwest intersect with other regions, with other nations? How is its history entangled with that of indigenous peoples, people of color, queer people, disabled people, religious minorities, immigrants, and migrants from other regions? How do transregional and transnational writers complicate our understanding of the Midwest? When the Society for the Study of Midwestern Literature was founded, Anderson pledged to encourage and support the study of Midwestern literature "in whatever directions the interests of the members may take."[11] Four directions that twenty-first-century Midwestern literary scholars have taken are 1) using poststructuralist critical approaches as lenses through which to read Midwestern texts; 2) applying methodologies from other disciplines, such as ecology and environmental science, to illuminate Midwestern works; 3) exploring how the

Midwest intersects with other regions and nations, thus creating a transregional, transnational, or global emphasis; and 4) participating in the critical turn in twenty-first-century regional scholarship. While these categories are neither exhaustive nor mutually exclusive, they do indicate some trends in contemporary Midwestern literary studies.

Near the turn of the twenty-first century, poststructuralist theory came to Midwestern literary studies. In *An American Colony* (2002), Edward Watts, using a postcolonial lens, ascribes the marginalization of the Midwest to a hegemonic Northeast that maintained "an active program of metropolitan silencing and exclusion." He positions the Old Northwest as a cultural colony of an imperialist United States, asserting that Midwestern literature is permeated with a colonial mindset that reflects the political realities of the region's status in relation to a dominant Northeastern center of culture and power and citing Hamlin Garland as a writer who could not achieve a postcolonial stance. However, he asserts that the *Spoon River Anthology, Main Street, My Antonia,* and *Winesburg, Ohio* are books in which "the East's presence is marginal and secondary and the region is central to the narratives' distinct exploration of local subjects."[12]

Another poststructuralist approach is seen in Robert Dunne's *A New Book of the Grotesques* (2005). Dunne employs Michel Foucault's theory of insanity as a departure from cultural norms to shed new light on the grotesques in *Winesburg, Ohio* and demonstrates how Gadamer and Derrida's theory of indeterminacy in language can help us understand their futile search for absolute truth and failure to communicate as functions of the limitations of language. As Dunne grounds his reading of *Winesburg, Ohio* in Foucault's view of discourse as an efficient enforcer of social norms, he emphasizes that the book can most productively be read from a multiplicity of critical approaches. "There are indeed many more Sherwood Andersons waiting to be discovered for readers of the new millennium," he predicts.[13]

Like poststructuralist theory, ecocriticism has been a trend in recent Midwestern literary studies. Four books that read Midwestern literature through an ecocritical lens are William Barillas's *The Midwestern Pastoral* (2006), David Pichaske's *Rooted* (2006), Mark Buechsel's *Sacred Land* (2014), and Christian Knoeller's *Reimagining Environmental History* (2017), all of which advocate an alternate ethos that opposes the kind of destructive social change, fueled by capitalist priorities, that commodifies and exploits Nature. Barillas focuses on how the Midwestern pastoral tradition has been re-envisioned by novelist Willa Cather, naturalist Aldo Leopold, and poets Jim Harrison, James Wright, and

Theodore Roethke. Their progressive pastoralism is positioned as an alternative to the utilitarian pastoralism of the past that elided environmental exploitation and commodification in its longing for a rural paradise of yesteryear. Barillas shows how these writers reject that kind of nostalgia while endorsing Jeffersonian agrarianism and the Romantics' veneration of Nature as a source of spiritual renewal.

Although an avowed anti-theorist, Pichaske employs a perspective similar to that of Barillas, Knoeller, and Buechsel in his examination of seven contemporary Midwestern poets. A major emphasis in his discussion of the work of Jim Harrison, Dave Etter, William Kloefkorn, Norbert Blei, Linda Hasselstrom, Bill Holm, and Jim Heynen is how their Midwestern environments have informed their identities and their poetry. Pichaske points out that their works enact a reciprocal process in which place impacts thought and art, and, in turn, art and thought shape place. He identifies a dissociation from the natural environment and the human community as "the root of postmodern anxiety" and advises that "reconstructing a sense of communal place . . . is our only real hope of regaining sanity."[14] Pichaske opines that this kind of reciprocity has the potential to heal divisions and offer, through re-established community, a remedy for the sense of loss and alienation that he sees in contemporary society.

Buechsel includes canonical Midwestern writers Sherwood Anderson, Willa Cather, and F. Scott Fitzgerald, as well as a lesser-known author, Ruth Suckow, and a contemporary novelist, Jane Smiley, in *Sacred Land*. He examines the sacramental view of Nature that these writers employ, all but one of whom were born when the promise of Jeffersonian agrarianism seemed realizable. Buechsel notes that their fiction reflects rural vulnerability to the rapid urbanization and industrialization that the Midwest endured after the Civil War and emphasizes that they not only critique these processes but also offer a remedy for their noxious impact: a sacramental approach to Nature. Like Pichaske, Buechsel sees his authors as engendering the kind of connection and community that can ameliorate the ills created by toxic capitalism and its spawn: greed, commodification, materialism, and spiritual malaise, and, like Barillas, he lauds Willa Cather for her depiction of Nature.

Knoeller looks at nine Midwestern nature writers: Gene Stratton-Porter, Paul Errington, Scott Russell Sanders, William Stafford, Louise Erdrich, Elizabeth Dodd, Diane Glancy, Paul Gruchow, and Theodore Roethke. He is concerned with how these writers deal with environmental change in their work and how their views of their respective landscapes are shaped by the tension between depredation and restoration. He asserts that each author "engages place in direct and personal ways, informed by a sense of environmental history, whether in their own bioregion or as they sojourned through less familiar terrain, as well as when contemplating the *idea* of what is ancient, indigenous, and ongoing." As does Barillas, Knoeller emphasizes the beneficial qualities of Nature in his discussion of Roethke: "Like Theodore Roethke, we believe that our spirit is inspired by what still might be thought of as wild."[15]

At the turn of the twenty-first century, Midwestern literary scholars began to look outward rather than inward, connecting the Midwest with other regions and nations and examining works that employed multiple perspectives. Two early examples of this approach are seen in Tom Lutz's *Cosmopolitan Vistas* (2004) and Timothy B. Spears's *Chicago Dreaming* (2005). Lutz advocates an ethic of cosmopolitanism: a way of holding two views simultaneously that values both the local and the global and aesthetic as well as political values. He describes this perspective as "an ethos of representational inclusiveness of the widest possible affiliation and concurrently one of aesthetic discrimination and therefore exclusivity."[16] According to Lutz, the best Midwestern writers utilize this kind of double perspective. Hamlin Garland's "Up the Coulee" (1891) presents the points of view of the two McLane brothers: Howard, who left the Midwest for a New York career, and Grant, who stayed to work the family farm. The implied author endorses neither viewpoint but encourages a sympathetic response to both. Similarly, Willa Cather's *O Pioneers!* enacts several perspectives as it portrays a cosmopolitan prairie culture comprising French, Swedish, Norwegian, Russian, and Bohemian migrants.

Spears's book also emphasizes the both/and approach, arguing that Chicago literary culture from 1871 to 1919 should be viewed within the context of many writers' migrations from the rural Midwest to the city that H. L. Mencken called "the literary capital of the United States."[17] For these provincial/sophisticates, Chicago offered a promising place to reinvent themselves; they attained personal and literary maturity while also diversifying the city. Spears asserts that the double-voiced quality in the writing of Willa Cather, Jane Addams, Floyd Dell, Sherwood Anderson, and Carl Sandburg renders their work a uniquely complex contribution to modernism: "Modern consciousness was built around the emotions associated with crossing the border from one culture to another," Spears concludes.[18]

In *Grasslands Grown* (2021), her examination of writings from the first generation of pioneer children to grow up in the northern grasslands, Molly P. Rozum combines transnational and postcolonial perspectives to show how these writers experienced place through embodied connections with animals and the environment, as well as geographic perspectives derived from travel, education, literature, and art. These commonalities link American and Canadian writers as inhabitants of a region that elides the terms "West," "Midwest," "Canadian," and "American." Rozum asserts that many of these authors felt that their early sensuous experiences of place strengthened their claims on the land: "The first generations born to settler society often made an implicit argument that they had a claim equivalent to Indigenous peoples . . . a created 'identity' rooted in the land consistent with the larger colonial project of displacing North American Indigenous populations."[19]

The critical turn in regional scholarship has been marked by a study of those works that not only evoke the ambience and character of the region but connect it with larger issues in ways that facilitate social action. In *Critical Regionalism* (2007), Douglas Reichert Powell defines region as "a social invention for describing the political, cultural, historical, and economic relationships among places" and explores the rhetorical dimensions of regionalism, asserting that "[p]laces are not things to be found out there in the world; they are ideas about spaces that are constructed by people . . . region is always at some level an attempt to persuade as much as it is to describe."[20] Though the focus of this book is Appalachia rather than the Midwest, *Critical Regionalism* offers a paradigm for understanding region that has been adopted by recent Midwestern literary scholars.

Powell explores the concept of region as constructed from rhetorical practice, analyzing the films *Deliverance* (1972), *Apocalypse Now* (1979), and *Cape Fear* (1992). All, he argues, are examples of texts that misrepresent region, portraying it as marginalized and disconnected from the cultural norm, and Powell posits *Pulp Fiction* (1994) and *Fargo* (1996) as films that challenge such misrepresentations. He offers the novels *USA* (1933), *The Grapes of Wrath* (1939), and *River of Earth* (1940) as examples of books that have linked regions to larger social entities and thus have had a transformative effect on American society. Powell asserts that critical regionalism's goal is to support projects of change. Therefore, he concludes, critical regionalism must become a pedagogy as well as a rhetorical practice, offering new perspectives and understandings that will equip students to conceptualize their own regional experiences within the context of "others near and far, both like and unlike themselves."[21]

Like Powell's book, June Howard's *The Center of the World* (2018) does not focus exclusively on Midwestern texts, although Edward Eggleston's *The Hoosier Schoolmaster* (1871) is discussed at length. She also mentions or briefly discusses fourteen other Midwestern writers, among them Hamlin Garland, Sinclair Lewis, James Whitcomb Riley, Constance Fenimore Woolson, and Zitkala-Sa. Originally a scholar of the local color movement, Howard here embraces a broader scope, exploring regionalism rather than a specific region and emphasizing that regionalism is both substantive and relational and that place and time are entangled. "[T]he local and the national and the global, the place and the planet, are never disconnected," Howard points out. "[S]uch writing shapes the ways we inhabit and imagine, not only neighborhoods and provinces, but also the world."

Howard positions the schoolteacher as a key figure in regional literature, a synecdoche for regional writing itself as this character type "negotiates between provincial and metropolitan, between local and translocal knowledges."[22] Her book is wide-ranging, considering a dizzying array of authors, books, films, articles, stories, television shows, theories, themes, and patterns. With its emphasis on making connections that will enable a beneficent social ethos, it participates in both transregional and critical regional movements.

Adam Ochonicky's *The American Midwest in Film and Literature* (2020) also takes a critical regionalist approach. Ochonicky argues that nostalgia—an "idealized imagery of the past"—has shaped our understanding of the Midwest and its significance in the larger national context, conceptualizing it as nostalgic spatiality, nostalgic atonement, and nostalgic violence. He calls the Midwest the country's "nostalgia museum," arguing that Midwesterners' desire to relive this imagined idyllic past obscures social and environmental problems as it propels a quest for an earlier, better time that is irrecoverable and may never have existed.

Ochonicky analyzes a number of nostalgic literary texts, including *Main Street, Babbitt, O Pioneers!*, Richard Wright's *Native Son* (1940), and Tim O'Brien's *In the Lake of the Woods* (1994). His discussion of nostalgia in film is more extensive; *Meet Me in St. Louis* (1944), *Badlands* (1973), *Halloween* (1978), *The Straight Story* (1999), *About Schmidt* (2002), and *Gran Torino* (2008) are among the films he considers. This nostalgic impulse, Ochonicky argues, was at the heart of the 2016 "Make American Great Again" campaign and he contends that the kind of cultural narratives about the Midwest articulated in the texts and films he discusses connect profoundly to the "restorative nostalgia" that resonate so strongly with white Midwesterners. "It becomes clear that both the propelling forces of nostalgia and deeply entrenched ideas about regional identity may be used to mobilize . . . a politics of resentment," he concludes.[23]

In *The Midwestern Novel* (2015), Nancy L. Bunge argues that the 1884 publication of *Adventures of Huckleberry Finn* marked a social turn in American literature that was especially prevalent in the Midwest, noting that the region's authors "repeatedly value the perspectives of ordinary people and fret over the damage done to both their hearts and minds by a competitive social structure."[24] Bunge discusses one hundred Midwestern novels and stories, some quite briefly, emphasizing the characters' struggles with the impact of industrialization and urbanization and pointing out that these forces foster conformity, materialism, greed, covetousness, and cutthroat competitiveness. Like other scholars discussed here, she finds redemptive potential in connection to community and Nature. She also sees such potential in the values of children, women, and African Americans and identifies *Main Street*; *Winesburg, Ohio*; *The Great Gatsby* (1925); and *Beloved* (1987), among other books, as texts that offer the correctives of compassion, empathy, kindness, and tolerance.

Britt E. Halvorson and Joshua O. Reno argue that white supremacy is embedded in the deep structures of Midwestern culture, relying in part on their analyses of canonical Midwestern books and films to make their point in *Imagining the Heartland* (2022). They argue that the Superman story, *The Wizard of Oz*, *Main Street*, W. P. Kinsella's *Shoeless Joe* (1982), Robert Bly's poetry, and the films *Halloween* (1978), *Children of the Corn* (1984), *Nightmare on Elm Street* (1984) and *Brightburn* (2019) are "coded white." Their project of critical regionalism is to show how these "white" Midwestern works facilitate white supremacy, nationalism, and imperialism. "The Midwest's perceived connection to homogeneity, whiteness, and nostalgia is a fiction that has to be actively produced and, furthermore, is productive of conceptions of nationalism and racial projects of white supremacy," they maintain.[25]

Like Halvorson and Reno's book, much of this recent scholarship explores the term "nostalgia," indicative of "a place that almost happened; a fund that almost prospered," as Phil Christman maintains in *Midwest Futures* (2020). The amorphous nature of the region's identity is also a recurrent theme in this scholarship. As Christman points out, "The Midwest is massively there, constantly eluding our grasp."[26] Also emphasized are the destructive effects of the collapse of the agrarian dream that enchanted Thomas Jefferson, inspired Frederick Jackson Turner, and motivated hundreds of thousands of homesteaders. "Violence and dissatisfaction are the production of a myth that has failed yet still reckons the nation's existence," asserts Mark Brians.[27] This mythic Midwest that occupied so many first-wave Midwestern scholars has been decentered more recently by the poststructuralist, ecocritical, transnational, and critical regionalist approaches reviewed above. Such work has often identified a communitarian ethos and a spiritual connection to Nature as remedies for the region's ills.

Another pattern in this scholarship is the centrality of Willa Cather, mentioned or discussed by Watts, Barillas, Buechsel, Lutz, Spears, Rozum, Ochonicky, and Bunge. Cather, an author who could sustain an upbeat mood and an elegiac tone in a novel that includes a cruelly duplicitous seduction, an attempted rape, a murder, three suicides, and a bride and bridegroom who are literally thrown to the wolves, is nonetheless able to emphasize beauty, virtue, and hope in its pages, despite all of the mayhem that occurs there. Near the end of *My Antonia*, narrator Jim Burden's reflections on the eponymous character, his friend from childhood, exemplify this mood and tone: "She lent herself to immemorial human attitudes which we recognize by instinct as universal and true . . . She had only to stand in the orchard, to put her hand on a little crab tree and look up at the apples, to make you feel the goodness of planting and tending and harvesting at last . . . It was no wonder that her sons stood tall and straight. She was a rich mine of life, like the founders of early races."[28] Cather's inspirational novels reassure us that, despite the region's challenges identified by the scholars discussed above, the Midwest will survive, even though its myth may be fraught, because Midwesterners are diverse, perseverant, innovative, and resilient, qualities that will ensure its continuing strength.

And as our two murderesses, Minnie and Emily, as well as Willa Cather, remind us, regional characteristics are less significant than the traits that unite us as human beings. Another author, often discussed as regional, made this point in his Nobel Prize acceptance speech. Writing five years after the atomic bomb destroyed Hiroshima and Nagasaki, William Faulkner raised the possibility of universal annihilation with this question: "When will I be blown up?" In the face of this truly existential threat, Faulkner saw a crucial role for authors: "The writer's duty is to . . . help man endure by lifting his heart, by reminding him of the courage and honor and hope and pride which have been the glory of his past." And the most famous line of this speech echoes the spirit of Cather's canonical books and reminds us of the cultural work that they perform: "I believe that man will not merely endure: he will prevail."[29]

## NOTES

1. James Whitcomb Riley, "Little Orphant Annie," in *Riley Child-Rhymes* (Bobbs-Merrill, 1920), 17–18. A very slight variation in spelling occurs in the first and fourth refrains. Riley's poem, originally published in 1885 as "The Elf Child" in the *Indianapolis Journal*, has inspired a 1924 comic strip and a 1977 musical, among other works.

2. In 1940, Maud Hart Lovelace's *Betsy-Tacy* was published in New York by the Thomas Y. Crowell Company. She completed the series in 1955 with *Betsy's Wedding*, also published by Crowell.

3. *The Midwest: Myth or Reality? A Symposium by Thomas T. McEvoy, CSC; Russel B. Nye; J. W. Wiley; Gale W. McGee; Donald R. Murphy; John T. Flanagan; and John T. Frederick* (University of Notre Dame Press, 1961); "What Is the Midwest?" Exhibition, 20 September to 31 December 2019; opening symposium, 21 September 2019, Newberry Library, Chicago, IL.

4. David D. Anderson, "The Dimensions of the Midwest," *MidAmerica* 1 (1974): 7–15, 14; David Radavich, "In the Heart of the Land: Midwestern Plays and Playwrights," in *Critical Insights: Midwestern Literature*, ed. Ronald Primeau (Salem Press, 2013), 186–97, 188–89. Due to space limitations, this review of twenty-first-century Midwestern literary scholarship excludes journal articles, articles in edited collections, book chapters, and single-author studies.

5. Cayton and Onuf, *The Midwest and the Nation*, 84–85, 123 (see chapter 6, n. 6); Shortridge, *The Middle West*, 33 (see chapter 6, n. 5); Margaret Stuhr, "The Safe Middle West: Escape to and Escape from Home," *MidAmerica* 14 (1987): 18–27.

6. W. J. Cash, *The Mind of the South* (Vintage Books, 1941), 61–89; Cleanth Brooks, "Southern Literature: The Past, History, and the Timeless," in *Southern Literature in Transition*, ed. Philip Castille and William Osborne (Memphis State University Press, 1983), 5; John Shelton Reed, "Surveying the South: A Conversation," in *Mixing It Up: A South-Watcher's Miscellany* (Louisiana State University Press, 2018), 274.

7. Susan Glaspell's "A Jury of Her Peers" was originally published in the *Washington Post*'s *Sunday Star Magazine* on March 4, 1917, and reprinted the next year in *Best Short Stories of 1917*, ed. Edward J. O'Brien (Small, Maynard, 1918). It has since been anthologized many times. William Faulkner's "A Rose for Emily" was originally published in the *Forum* magazine on April 30, 1930, and reprinted the next year in *These 13: Stories by William Faulkner* (Jonathan Cape and Harrison Smith, 1931). It, too, appears in many anthologies.

8. "10 Things You Would NEVER Hear a Southerner Say," accessed December 26, 2022, www.manbottle.com. I tried to think of ten things you would never hear a Midwesterner say, but all I could come up with was, "You say you spent your summer vacation detasseling *what*?"

9. William Barillas, *The Midwestern Pastoral: Place and Landscape in Literature of the Heartland* (Ohio University Press, 2006), 11.

10. Anderson, "Dimensions," 10.

11. Anderson, preface, *MidAmerica* 1 (1974): n.p.

12. Edward Watts, *An American Colony: Regionalism and the Roots of Midwestern Culture* (Ohio University Press, 2002), 156, 215.

13. Robert Dunne, *A New Book of the Grotesques: Contemporary Approaches to Sherwood Anderson's Early Fiction* (Kent State University Press, 2005), 115.

14. David R. Pichaske, *Rooted: Seven Midwestern Writers of Place* (University of Iowa Press, 2006), 264.

15. Christian Knoeller, *Reimagining Environmental History: Ecological Memory in the Wake of Landscape Change* (University of Nevada Press, 2017), xi, Knoeller's emphasis, 239.

16. Tom Lutz, *Cosmopolitan Vistas: American Regionalism and Literary Value* (Cornell University Press, 2004), 3.

17. H. L. Mencken, "The Literary Capital of the United States," *Nation*, 17 April 1920, 10, 92.

18. Timothy B. Spears, *Chicago Dreaming: Midwesterners and the City, 1871–1919* (University of Chicago Press, 2005), 247.

19. Molly P. Rozum, *Grasslands Grown: Creating Place on the U.S. Northern Plains and Canadian Prairies* (University of Nebraska Press, 2021), 176.

20. Douglas Reichert Powell, *Critical Regionalism: Connecting Politics and Culture in the American Landscape* (University of North Carolina Press, 2007), 67, 21.

21. Powell, *Critical Regionalism*, 8 (see chapter 9, n. 20).

22. June Howard, *The Center of the World: Regional Writing and the Puzzles of Place-Time* (Oxford University Press, 2018), vi, 51.

23. Adam R. Ochonicky, *The American Midwest in Film and Literature: Nostalgia, Violence, and Regionalism* (Indiana University Press, 2020), 3, 110, 214.

24. Nancy L. Bunge, *The Midwestern Novel: Literary Populism from Huckleberry Finn to the Present* (McFarland, 2015), 152.

25. Halvorson and Reno, *Imagining the Heartland*, 110 (see chapter 8, n. 12).

26. Phil Christman, *Midwest Futures* (Belt Publishing, 2020), 12, 15.

27. Mark Brians, "*Road to Perdition*, dir. Sam Mendes, 2022," *Middle West Review* 9, no. 1 (2022): 167–70, 169.

28. Willa Cather, *My Ántonia*, scholarly ed., ed. Charles Mignon with Kari A. Ronning (University of Nebraska Press, 1994), 342.

29. William Faulkner, "Address upon Receiving the Nobel Prize for Literature," in *William Faulkner: Essays, Speeches, and Public Letters*, ed. James B. Meriwether (The Modern Library, 2004), 119–21, 120.

CAMDEN BURD

# THE NATURE OF THE MIDWEST

Environmental History, Regionalism, and the Future
of Midwestern Studies

Held in May 2015, the inaugural conference of the Midwestern History Association corralled a group of scholars interested in grappling with the history of the
region. Its organizers argued that the Midwest lacked broader scholarly focus,
especially when compared to other regions such as the South, West, and New
England. It was not long after that first meeting when I first became involved
with the Midwestern History Association. Though I grew up in the Midwest, I
attended undergraduate and graduate schools elsewhere (Utah and New York).
I was immediately struck with diverse landscapes and environmental uses of
the places that I encountered, juxtaposing those spaces against the landscapes
of my youth. The history of the Midwestern environment, it seemed to me, was
something distinct. The complex diversity of the region's environmental history
did not always excite scholars I had met in Utah or New York, some of whom
jokingly referred to the region as "flyover country." However, I was delighted
to find individuals at regular meetings of the Midwestern History Association

who were eager to grapple with the region's nuances. Though the questions, themes, and locales differed, every scholar was interested in the same question: what historical and environmental changes made this space a distinct region and place?

These are questions well suited for environmental history. It is a field whose practitioners are interested in the historic relationship between humans and the natural world. This is not a one-sided relationship. Humans work on nature and nonhuman actors work on humans. Together, the human and nonhuman agents create space. These spaces can sometimes become places when they carry some sense of cultural meaning. One of those places is the Midwest. As with any place, scholars of the Midwest must historicize the material, and by extension environmental, conditions that informed the creation of the region. For example, the Midwest was born from two connected projects of the nineteenth century: settler colonialism and the rapid capitalist development of the North American interior centering around a singular metropole, Chicago, Illinois.[1] The experiences of these settler colonists established a shared experience among many—not all—in the region. It was at that exact moment when the *idea* of the Midwest was born. As Michael C. Steiner has argued, the "present day notion of the 'Middle West' entered the national consciousness in the thirty-year period between the 1880s and 1910s."[2] It was during this time that scholars, architects, and literary figures, embedded within those larger economic and political projects, attempted to delineate the twelve-state, middle region of the country into a cohesive whole. Their Midwest was a loosely defined region, hemmed in by the Appalachian Mountains to the east and the arid plains and rocky mountains of the American West. This vast continental "middle" was mostly flat and wet, with numerous, slow-churning rivers. That is not to say the region lacked in ecological diversity. The northern stands of mixed-coniferous forests remain a sharp contrast to the hardwood forests of the region's southeast—both of which remain distinct from the northern and southern plains that round out the region's borders.

The Midwest they described was so clearly shaped by the rise of industrial and commodity-based capitalism of the late nineteenth century. The entire region was flattened, drained, monotonized—made more economically efficient with grids, rails, roads, and market-based agriculture. It also developed into an industrial hub due, in large part, to the iron deposits in Michigan, Minnesota, and Wisconsin as well as the vast real rail network that ran through Chicago. Stippled with manufacturing sites, several large, mid-size, and small cities were born of these distinct economic forces. Those same places often also bear another hallmark of the Midwest environment: chemical waste and toxic hazards.

These political, economic, and environmental histories remind us of the temporality of regionalism, more broadly. To read a cohesive, Midwest backward from the late nineteenth century is ahistorical and ignores the varied and competing ideas of space, place, and nature that indigenous, European, and American inhabitants connected to particular landscapes. I am aware that such a position overlooks several important scholarly works dealing with environments now called the Midwest.[3] But if historians do not seriously consider the temporality of regionalism, they are peddling in myths, in search of some metaphysics of place to reinforce their version of the Midwest. The Midwest has not always been and assuredly will not always be. The conservative, reactionary, and nostalgic lament this. The regional historian knows it.

With this in mind, I intend to provide an overview of Midwestern environmental history in this chapter. First, I will survey the field of Midwest environmental history in order to get a sense of the region's place in the development of the larger discipline. I believe this historiographic overview provides an important lens to understand how regional historians might consider environmental history a foundational component of their studies. Any examination of a region—a cultural geography tied to real, physical space—is intimately tied to the organization of nature. As such, environmental history has much to offer regional historians attempting to understand the ways humans relate to a place as well as to one another. Finally, I hope to offer suggestions for further intellectual exploration of the Midwest based on the history and gaps that still persist in the scholarship. My call for research is founded on the belief that if the field of Midwestern studies is to flourish, scholars must take seriously the influence of the environment in shaping the history and broader understanding of the region.

There is a common belief among many scholars of the American Midwest that the region's history has somehow been lost, forgotten, or overlooked.[4] Such claims can be appealing. They are often a default rhetorical reflex for many who have lived in the region. But after surveying the scholarship, it is clear that there is not much truth to the claim that Midwestern topics have been overlooked or ignored by environmental historians. In fact, an examination of the past leadership of the American Society for Environmental History reveals a legacy of scholars with an interest in the history of the region. Since the Society's formation in 1977, presidents have included John Opie, Donald

Worster, William Cronon, Nancy Langston, Gregg Mitman, and Kathleen Brosnan—all of whom have published on topics related to the history of the Midwest.[5] In the decades after its founding a wide range of academics have made the Midwest or Midwestern places central to their scholarly focus. These studies have focused on a range of topics, reflecting the complex and diverse histories of the region. However, much of the work has been organized into broad categories: agriculture, extraction, conservation/environmentalism/recreation, and industry/urbanity.

## AGRICULTURE

Environmental histories of the agricultural Midwest began to flourish in the 1980s when the larger field came into being. The connections seemed obvious at first. After all, if environmental historians wanted to understand the ways in which humans have shaped, viewed, and valued the natural world, then they would have to dive deeper into the environmental implications of agricultural changes. Donald Worster led the way with his iconic *Dust Bowl: The Southern Plains in the 1930s.*[6] Worster's book, though not the first history of this environmental crisis, helped to establish what the author would later call an "agroecological perspective" of history.[7] This method tasked historians with exploring the ways in which historical agents have reorganized ecosystems for agricultural and commercial purposes. By doing so, Worster argued, historians could further explore the complex social, economic, and technological influences behind these dramatic environmental changes. Within this framework, many historians have set out to demonstrate how the influence of industrial capitalism, immigration, and technological changes have shaped the agroecological history of the region. Though several works fall under this category, David Vail's *Chemical Lands: Pesticides, Aerial Spraying, and Health in North America's Grasslands Since 1945* deserves attention. In *Chemical Lands*, Vail captures the complex systems of crop specialization, technological innovation, and human health in the American Midwest.[8] This is an agricultural history to be sure; however, Vail demonstrates the environmental implications of practices used to propagate particular crops and preserve particular economic and social relations.

More recently, scholars of the Midwest have focused on the broader economic networks that have shaped agricultural practices in the region. For example, Courtney Fullilove's *The Profit of the Earth: The Global Seeds of American Agriculture* offers insights on the transnational influences that shaped many Midwestern agricultural practices as the region came of age.[9] Fullilove's work compels historians to think more broadly about regionality as well as place-based agricultural practices. Less global in approach, Michael Lansing's work on wheat farming, carbohydrates, and cereals looks at the complex forces that shape agricultural practices in rural places. By writing a history of the popular cereal Wheaties, Lansing outlines the connected histories of wheat farming and urban industrial production within the broader story of mass consumerism.[10] Though the above works are different in scope and topic, they each answer Worster's call to consider the broader forces that have shaped the way Midwesterners viewed, restructured, and attempted to control ecological systems toward particular agricultural goals.

## EXTRACTION

Though agricultural landscapes define much of the American Midwest, the hinterlands have also been the site of other forms of resource extraction. The Upper Midwest, in particular, has a long history of mining and logging. Scholars who have focused on the mining regions of the Upper Midwest include Larry D. Lankton, Thomas W. Pearson, and Nancy Langston.[11] Jeffrey T. Manuel's *Taconite Dreams: The Struggle to Sustain Mining on Minnesota's Iron Range, 1915–2000* is representative of the potential that these histories offer scholars of Midwest. Blending environmental, economic, and legal history, Manuel tracks the history of mining communities as they experience the dwindling mining economy, the environmental movement, automation, and deindustrialization.[12] The history of logging and deforestation have also received considerable attention from environmental historians.[13] Several decades after its publication, *The Great Lakes Forest: An Environmental and Social History* still offers compelling essays that explore the interconnected histories of communities and their relation to extractive logging practices.[14] Theodore J. Karaminski's *Deep Woods Frontier: A History of Logging in Northern Michigan* tracks the long history of the logging industry in the region, demonstrating continuities in industrial pursuits alongside environmental changes in the north.[15] Moving beyond the forests and hills of the Upper Midwest, Margaret Beattie Bogue's *Fishing the Great Lakes: An Environmental History, 1783–1933* remains a field-defining resource toward understanding the development and near collapse of Great Lakes fisheries.[16] Histories of extraction are particularly important for scholars interested in the broader history of the Midwest given that the region came of age alongside the rise of industrial capitalism. Understanding the economy's influence on local environments is not just an important component of the region's history—it is a foundational component in defining the region as a distinct place.

## CONSERVATION, ENVIRONMENTALISM, AND RECREATION

The industrialized landscape of the late nineteenth and early twentieth centuries led to a wave of concern at the local, regional, and national level. As such, much of the regional environmental history has focused on topics of conservation and environmentalism. James Kates's *Planning a Wilderness: Regenerating the Great Lakes Cutover Region* documents the efforts of foresters to restore the landscapes of the Upper Midwest after farmers' failed attempts to successfully farm in the region.[17] Histories of agricultural conservation also demonstrate the unique environmental and agricultural realities of the region.[18] Though Sarah Phillips's *This Land, This Nation: Conservation, Rural America, and the New Deal* is not solely focused on the Midwest, its significance for the region should not be overlooked.[19] Her exploration of the impact of New Deal policies in conservation, water preservation, and economic development has lasting implications for the history of the region. Examinations of prominent conservationists and environmentalists offer interesting perspectives in the relationship between Midwestern places and a particular environmental ethic. Susan Flader's *Thinking Like a Mountain: Aldo Leopold and the Evolution of an Ecological Attitude Toward Deer, Wolves, and Forests* remains a thoughtful examination of Leopold and his perspective.[20] Bill Christofferson draws a connective thread between conservation and environmentalism in *The Man from Clear Lake: Earth Day Founder Senator Gaylord Nelson*.[21] Though many might recognize names like Leopold and Nelson, Gregg Mitman's research in *The State of Nature: Ecology, Community, and American Social Thought, 1900–1950* highlights the work of lesser-known ecologists from the University of Chicago whose embrace of the new science of ecology shaped their perspectives on nature and society.[22] The growing presence of indigenous voices in recent scholarship depicts a fuller and more accurate history of the region. Michael J. Chiarappa and Kristin M. Szylvian's *Fish for All: An Oral History of Multiple Claims and Divided Sentiment on Lake Michigan* as well as Nancy Langston's *Sustaining Lake Superior: An Extraordinary Lake in a Changing World* both outline the complicated histories of conservation and environmentalism of the region.[23]

As environmental attitudes shifted in the Midwest, the development of recreational landscapes began to emerge. The Upper Midwest, with its dense forests and numerous lakes, quickly garnered a reputation as a restful haven for regional

residents. Though several historians have explored this history, Aaron Shapiro's
*The Lure of the North Woods: Cultivating Tourism in the Upper Midwest* remains
exemplary.[24] By tracking the rise of the tourism industry in Michigan, Minnesota,
and Wisconsin, Shapiro historicizes the efforts of, and relationships between,
local residents, tourists, as well as state and national governmental agencies who
worked to *create* this region as a destination. Additionally, several scholars have
written histories on the various public parks of the Midwest: Brian Kalt on the
history of the Sleeping Bear Sand Dunes; Harold C. Jordahl Jr., Annie L. Booth,
and James Feldman on the history of the Apostle Islands; and Fred T. Witzig
on Voyageurs National Park.[25] There is still work to be done on the complex
history of recreational landscapes in the Midwest. Works from Lewis Walker,
Benjamin C. Wilson, and Ronald J. Stephens explore the history of Idlewild,
an African American vacation community in Michigan, and demonstrate the
racialized history of recreation and its legacy for the regional landscape.[26] The
consideration of indigenous perspectives is still underexamined in recreational
histories though Katrina Phillips's work provides a roadmap to continue to
develop these histories.[27]

## INDUSTRY AND URBANITY

In the Midwest, the connection between hinterland and urban places is especially pronounced. William Cronon's *Nature's Metropolis: Chicago and the Great
West* not only transformed the field of American environmental history but
refigured the way scholars of the Midwest understood the connection between
urban and rural histories.[28] The American city—in particular Midwestern cities—is intimately connected to the hinterland through trade, industry, and
production. Environmental histories of Midwestern cities explore the complex
matrix of business, work, transportation, and production in order to better
understand how urban spaces connect to rural ones. These ideas are further
explored in a more recent history of Chicago, *City of Lake and Prairie: Chicago's
Environmental History*, edited by Kathleen A. Brosnan, Ann Durkin Keating,
and William C. Barnett.[29] Elizabeth Grennan Browning's *Nature's Laboratory:
Environmental Thought and Labor Radicalism in Chicago, 1886–1937* explores
the divergent intellectual strands of environmental thought as industrial Chicago challenged traditional conceptions of labor, community, nature, politics,
and society.[30]

Environmental histories of the urban Midwest are also related to the field
of social history. Class, race, ethnicity, gender, and power not only shaped how

Midwesterners have lived in cities but also help us understand how different groups experienced and viewed the natural world in those places. Andrew Hurley's monumental *Environmental Inequalities: Class, Race and Industrial Pollution in Gary, Indiana, 1945–1980* outlines how residents of Gary experienced the environmental harms of the postwar industrial era. By tracking the experiences of the white middle class, the white working class, and the African American residents of Gary, Hurley argues that environmental inequality was "firmly rooted in the dynamics of postwar social arrangements and power relations."[31] The impact of Hurley's work encouraged similar studies in other American cities. Take for instance two important works on the environmental history of Detroit. Joseph S. Cialdella's *Motor City Green: A Century of Landscapes and Environmentalism in Detroit* tracks the long history of green space in the city, demonstrating that the creation of parks and gardens in Detroit reflected the unique realities of industrialization and deindustrialization, as well as racial and economic inequality.[32] Additionally, Brandon Ward's *Living Detroit: Environmental Activism in an Age of Urban Crisis* tracks the varied meanings of environmental activism in the Motor City. In doing so, he demonstrates the ways in which class, race, and work shaped views of environmentalism, activism, and, as a result, political priorities in Detroit.[33]

David and Richard Stradling's *Where the River Burned: Carl Stokes and the Struggle to Save Cleveland* further demonstrates the connection between urban politics and environmental realities in one Ohio city. By weaving together histories of the burgeoning environmental movement, the urban crisis, and the political priorities of Cleveland's first African American mayor, Carl Stokes, the Stradlings emphasize the centrality of environmental politics in that city's history. In *Landscapes of Hope: Nature of the Great Migration in Chicago*, Brian McCammack explores a defining era of Midwestern history through an environmental history lens. Settling into the Midwest, African American migrants found hope in the unfamiliar environments and industrial spaces of the Windy City. Encountering an entirely new social and often segregated landscape of the urban North, African Americans imbued many of Chicago's landscapes with a sense of optimism and hope for the future. By blending environmental, social, and cultural history, McCammack's scholarship provides an important framework to re-examine the unique experiences of African Americans throughout the urban Midwest—not only Chicago.[34]

Taken together, the environmental histories of the urban Midwest provide a fuller picture of the entire region. Binding together urban and rural, as well as extraction, production, and consumption, this subfield of environmental history offers insights into the material components that bind the Midwest together *as a cohesive region*. Furthermore, an examination of the social aspects of urban environmental history offers a more thorough understanding of the unique and complex social landscape of the region's urban spaces during periods of economic growth and decline.

## DIRECTIONS FOR THE FUTURE

Though much has been written on the environmental history of the region, there is still work to be done.[35] Though agricultural history is probably the most developed of the identified categories, there are still stories untold of particular communities, crop regimes, commodity networks, and the cultural and political histories tied directly to the soil. Additionally, the field would benefit from a deeper study of the environmental histories of the dozens of smaller and midsized urban locales of the Midwest. Not only would those histories give depth to a region often defined by a handful of metropolitan areas (Chicago, Detroit, Cleveland, St. Louis) but they might establish a connective thread between the industrial and post-industrial histories of manufacturing locales. Another space for exploration might come from an examination of the history of competing visions of environmental use between residents within the region. Urban and rural divides, in particular, are undoubtedly shaped by local environmental histories that, in turn, manifest into heated divides about the environment and land use.

Scholars of the Midwest must broaden environmental histories to include voices of residents often overlooked in histories of the region. Such work would build upon the important recovery projects already underway. Take, for instance, work of the Black Midwest Initiative to center the Black Midwestern experience as a foundational element of regional history.[36] Other scholars interested in broadening the social history of the Midwest include Edward E. Curtis IV's work on Syrian immigrants in the region.[37] The development and success of the Latinos in Chicago and the Midwest series at the University of Illinois Press also marks a positive sign for the future of the field. As of now, these initiatives do not focus on the environment, but I suspect that will change. By examining the ways in which different communities view, experience, and interact with the natural world, scholars of the region will gain a deeper understanding of what made, or makes, the Midwest Midwestern.

This brings me to my final point regarding the potential of environmental history in shaping the future of Midwestern studies. Any attempt at regional studies of the American Midwest must take into account the environmental realities that shape the region into something cohesive. The cultural geographer Yi-Fu Tuan wrote that regions are usually "too big to be directly experienced by most of its people," meaning that any region "is primarily a construct of thought."[38] The Midwest is an idea bounded together by individuals who loosely agree on what qualifies as Midwestern. What brings them together, however, requires a deeper investigation of the environments where connections are formed. "In a large unit of space people may have common experiences of nature and work, feel the same cycles of heat and cold, see the same dusk, and smell the same air."[39] In short, regionalism and regional identity is a cultural idea formed by its inhabitants based on shared experiences with real, physical space. The creation of the Midwest is, in my mind, a story of humans, the natural world, and the networks that bond certain geographies together. That is, in part, an environmental history.

I do not intend to argue for a sort of environmental determinism that places rigid rules on what "nature" defines the Midwest. However, if historians of the Midwest believe, as I do, that regionalism is formed through the social, political, cultural, and economic ties with the physical landscape, then they must consider how the environmental history of particular places helped to define those spaces as Midwestern. We have examples of this type of work, albeit on a smaller, more narrow scale. Several environmental histories narrow the scope of their studies to particular rivers, valleys, or discernible bioregions. A few notable works include Lynne Heasley's *A Thousand Pieces of Paradise: Landscape and Property in the Kickapoo Valley,* John O. Anfinson's *The River We Have Wrought: A History of the Upper Mississippi,* and a recent collection of essays, *Heartland River: A Cultural and Environmental History of the Big Sioux River Valley.*[40] In all of these works, it is the landscape, or a particular feature of it, that is used as a lens to examine communities and the cultures that develop in relation to the environment. Molly P. Rozum's *Grasslands Grown: Creating Place on the U.S. Northern Plains and Canadian Prairies* is an exemplary model for how these questions of regionalism and placemaking might be studied on a broader scale.[41] Her work combines cultural, diplomatic, and environmental history to understand how a distinct region came into being.

By asking more direct questions about the environmental history of the region and its formation, scholars of Midwestern studies might have a better understanding of its boundaries as well. Though lagging behind in number than more established regional studies, borderland histories of the Midwest are becoming more prevalent. These studies help to give shape to the region while providing more complex narratives of regional development. This is most clear when looking at environmental histories of the Great Lakes region.[42] Lynne Heasley's *The Accidental Reef and Other Ecological Odysseys in the Great Lakes* creatively explores the unique—and surprising—environmental histories of the waterways shaped by the industrial, economic, social, and political realities of a borderland region. In *Negotiating a River: Canada, the US, and the Creation of the St. Lawrence Seaway,* Daniel Macfarlane tracks a history of international relations that has profoundly shaped the environmental and economic realities of the Midwest and Canada. Extractive industries and economic trade have relied on this international waterway for over a half a century.[43] The implications are clear. Diplomatic and international relations are central forces in shaping the environmental and economic realities of much of the Midwest. Continued exploration of Midwestern borders is the focus of *The Interior Borderlands: Regional Identity in the Midwest and Great Plains.*[44] This collection of essays is not explicitly an environmental history, but many of its contributors are interested in the geographic, natural, and cultural elements that separate the Midwest from other regions. Essays by Christopher R. Laingen, Natalie Massip, Brad Tennant, Julie Courtwright, and Michael Mullin connect the environmental realities of a particular place to larger questions of regionality. As a coherent whole, the collection compels readers to consider how a sense of place, unquestionably connected to the biological world, shapes the very concept of regionalism and its blurred boundaries.

This is the promise that environmental history offers to scholars of Midwestern studies. A study of humans and their relationship with the natural world is foundational to any serious consideration of regionalism. And for a region that is often defined, first, by its natural features—its farmlands, fields, forests, rivers, and lakes—a deeper examination of humans and their environments can reveal a great deal about the historic uniqueness of this place. This requires building upon existing scholarship while continuing to ask new questions about agricultural, urban, extractive, and social histories of the Midwest. In doing so, scholars might continue the project started at the "Finding the Lost Region" meeting of the Midwestern History Association in 2015 and continue to develop Midwestern studies.

## NOTES

1. Rozum, *Grasslands Grown* (see chapter 9, n. 19). For a related but important essay on regional history, see Michael J. Lansing, "Creation as Erasure: Wallace Stegner and the Making and Unmaking of Regions," in *Wallace Stegner's Unsettled Country: Ruin, Realism, and Possibility in the American West*, ed. Mark Fiege, Michael J. Lansing, and Leisl Carr Childers (University of Nebraska Press, 2024).

2. Steiner, "Birth of the Midwest," 6 (see chapter 4, n. 23).

3. Notably, I recognize this position means ignoring incredible scholarship on colonial and early American history of the area including, but not limited to, Elizabeth Fenn, Robert Michael Morrisey, Susan Sleeper-Smith, and Richard White—all of whom have written environmental histories on topics related to spaces that would later be called the Midwest.

4. A great essay that explores this tendency in recent scholarship is Klumpp, "Not a Revival" (see chapter 7, n. 11).

5. "ASEH Presidents," *American Society for Environmental History*, December 27, 2023, https://aseh.org/Presidents. For a sampling of their works: Opie, *Ogallala* (see chapter 1, n. 16); Worster, *Dust Bowl* (see chapter 1, n. 6); Cronon, *Nature's Metropolis* (see chapter 1, n. 7); Nancy Langston, *Sustaining Lake Superior: An Extraordinary Lake in a Changing World* (Yale University Press, 2019); Gregg Mitman, *The State of Nature: Ecology, Community, and American Social Thought, 1900–1950* (University of Chicago Press, 1992); Kathleen A. Brosnan, Ann Durkin Keating, and William C. Barnett, eds., *City of Lake and Prairie: Chicago's Environmental History* (University of Pittsburgh Press, 2020); Brian Frehner and Kathleen A Brosnan, eds., *The Great Plains: Rethinking a Region's Environmental Histories* (University of Nebraska Press, 2021).

6. Worster, *Dust Bowl*.

7. This concept is further explained in Donald Worster, "Transformations of the Earth: Toward an Agroecological Perspective in History," *The Journal of American History* 76, no. 4 (1990): 1087–106.

8. Vail, *Chemical Lands* (see chapter 1, n. 6).

9. Courtney Fullilove, *The Profit of the Earth: The Global Seeds of American Agriculture* (University of Chicago Press, 2017).

10. Michael J. Lansing, "From Wheat to Wheaties: Minneapolis, the Great Plains, and the Transformation of American Food," in *The Great Plains: Rethinking a Region's Environmental Histories*, ed. Brian Frehner and Kathleen A Brosnan.

11. Larry D. Lankton, *Hollowed Ground: Copper Mining and Community Building on Lake Superior, 1840s–1990s* (Wayne State University, 2010); Thomas W. Pearson, *When the Hills Are Gone: Frac Sand Mining and the Struggle for Community* (University of Minnesota Press, 2017); Nancy Langston has published numerous articles on the environmental impacts and history of mining in the Lake Superior region. Without proper space to list her truly impressive bibliography, I will list her most recent work: Langston, *Sustaining Lake Superior: An Extraordinary Lake in a Changing World*.

12. Jeffrey T. Manuel, *Taconite Dreams: The Struggle to Sustain Mining on Minnesota's Iron Range, 1915–2000* (University of Minnesota Press, 2015).

13. Other works not mentioned here include Agnes M. Larson, *The White Pine Industry in Minnesota: A History* (University of Minnesota Press, 2007); also, Michael Williams, *Americans and Their Forest: A Historical Geography* (Cambridge University Press, 1989).

14. *The Great Lakes Forest: An Environmental and Social History*, ed. Susan Flader (University of Minnesota Press, 1983).

15. Theodore J. Karamanski, *Deep Woods Frontier: A History of Logging in Northern Michigan* (Wayne State University Press, 1989).

16. Margaret Beattie Bogue, *Fishing the Great Lakes: An Environmental History, 1783–1933* (University of Wisconsin Press, 2000).

17. James Kates, *Planning a Wilderness: Regenerating the Great Lakes Cutover Region* (University of Minnesota Press, 2001).

18. For an interesting history on cutover and attempts to transform the region into agricultural land, see Robert Gough, *Farming the Cutover: A Social History of Northern Wisconsin* (University Press of Kansas, 1997).

19. Sarah Phillips, *This Land, This Nation: Conservation, Rural America, and the New Deal* (Cambridge University Press, 2007).

20. Susan Flader, *Thinking Like a Mountain: Aldo Leopold and the Evolution of an Ecological Attitude Toward Deer, Wolves, and Forests* (University of Wisconsin Press, 1994).

21. Bill Christofferson, *The Man from Clear Lake: Earth Day Founder Senator Gaylord Nelson* (University of Wisconsin Press, 2004).

22. Mitman, *The State of Nature.*

23. Michael J. Chiarappa and Kristin M. Szylvian, *Fish for All: An Oral History of Multiple Claims and Divided Sentiment on Lake Michigan* (Michigan State University Press, 2003); Langston, *Sustaining Lake Superior.*

24. Aaron Shapiro, *The Lure of the North Woods: Cultivating Tourism in the Upper Midwest* (University of Minnesota Press, 2013).

25. Brian C. Kalt, *Sixties Sandstorm: The Fight over Establishment of Sleeping Bear Dunes National Lakeshore, 1961–1970* (Michigan State University Press, 2001); Harold C. Jordahl Jr. with Annie L. Booth, *Environmental Politics and the Creation of a Dream: Establishing the Apostle Islands National Lakeshore* (University of Wisconsin Press, 2011); James W. Feldman, *A Storied Wilderness: Rewilding the Apostle Islands* (University of Washington Press, 2011); Fred T. Witzig, *Voyageurs National Park: The Battle to Create Minnesota's National Park* (University of Minnesota Press, 2004).

26. Lewis Walker and Benjamin C. Wilson, *Black Eden: The Idlewild Community* (Michigan State University Press, 2007); Ronald J. Stephens, *Idlewild: The Rise, Decline, and Rebirth of a Unique African American Resort Town* (University of Michigan Press, 2013).

27. See an important discussion of outdoor dramas in Ohio in Phillips, *Staging Indigeneity* (see chapter 2, n. 2); Phillips, "When Grandma Went to Washington" (see chapter 2, n. 2).

28. Cronon, *Nature's Metropolis.*

29. Brosnan and Keating, *City of Lake and Prairie.*

30. Elizabeth Grennan Browning, *Nature's Laboratory: Environmental Thought and Labor Radicalism in Chicago, 1886–1937* (Johns Hopkins University Press, 2022).

31. Andrew Hurley, *Environmental Inequalities: Class, Race, and Industrial Pollution in Gary, Indiana, 1945–1980* (University of North Carolina Press, 1995), 180.

32. Joseph Cialdella, *Motor City Green: A Century of Landscapes and Environmentalism in Detroit* (University of Pittsburgh Press, 2020).

33. Brandon Ward, *Living Detroit: Environmental Activism in an Age of Urban Crisis* (Routledge, 2021).

34. Brian McCammack, *Landscapes of Hope: Nature and the Great Migration in Chicago* (Harvard University Press, 2017).

35. More recently, Jennifer Stinson and I edited a special issue of the *Middle West Review* 10, no. 1 (2023).

36. "Black Midwest Initiative," The Black Midwest Initiative, accessed December 21, 2022, http://www.theblackmidwest.com.

37. Edward C. Curtis IV, *Muslims of the Heartland: How Syrian Immigrants Made a Home in the American Midwest* (New York University Press, 2022).

38. Yi-Fu Tuan, "Place: An Experiential Perspective," *Geographical Review* 65, no. 2 (1975): 158.

39. Tuan, "Place," 159.

40. Lynne Heasley, *A Thousand Pieces of Paradise: Landscape and Property in the Kickapoo Valley* (University of Wisconsin Press, 2005); John O. Anfinson, *The River We Have Wrought: A History of the Upper Mississippi* (University of Minnesota Press, 2005); Lauck, *Heartland River* (see introduction, n. 27); see also Lauck and Whitney, *North Country* (see introduction, n. 7).

41. Rozum, *Grasslands Grown.*

42. For an early essay calling for more investigation of the Great Lakes region, see James Feldman and Lynne Heasley, "Re-Centering North American Environmental History: Pedagogy and Scholarship in the Great Lakes Region," *Environmental History* 12, no. 3 (2007): 951–58.

43. Daniel Macfarlane, *Negotiating a River: Canada, the US, and the Creation of the St. Lawrence Seaway* (University of British Columbia Press, 2014). Another notable collection of essays is Lynne Heasley and Daniel Macfarlane, eds., *Border Flows: A Century of the Canadian-American Water Relationship* (University of Calgary Press, 2016); see also Ramya Swayamprakash, "Flotsam: Garbage Dumping, Pollution, and Legal Tensions in the Detroit River," *Water History* 12 (2020): 361–71.

44. Lauck, *Interior Borderlands* (see introduction, n. 24).

TIMOTHY G. ANDERSON

11

# THE AMERICAN MIDWEST AND THE GEOGRAPHIC IMAGINATION

The more one thinks about the Middle West, the more muddled the regional identity seems to become.[1]

James R. Shortridge, *The Middle West* (1989)

American geographers characterize the Midwest as a prime example of what are known as "perceptual" regions, places whose boundaries and geographic extent are informal or ambiguous, sometimes not codified legally or politically, and often open to debate and critique. But while it may not exist as a formalized region, few would argue with the assertion that many of the powerful images, tropes, and discourses associated with the Midwest—Main Street; the Corn Belt; bucolic rural landscapes; conservatism—are deeply embedded in the American consciousness and its idealized identities. That is, for many Americans the Midwest is at once "real" and "perceived," something both concrete and imagined. This chapter examines such concepts through a synopsis of how academics and other authors—but cultural and historical geographers in particular—have approached the Midwest as both a place and as representation.

## DEFINING AND DELIMITING THE REGION

Where is the Midwest? What are its defining characteristics? These are two of the most vexing questions that arise in both historical and contemporary academic research and writing about the region. Unlike some other federally recognized regions, the geographic extent of the Midwest is rather loosely defined by the federal government.[2] Even so, it is clear that the "idea" of the Midwest occupies a central place in the country's national consciousness and in the collective memories connected with the nation's rural, agricultural past. In his seminal study of how the region came to loom large in our national archetype, cultural geographer James Shortridge contends that American perceptions of the Midwest developed out of a deep nostalgia for a highly romanticized, pastoral ideal that came to be (and continues to be) linked with life in the Corn Belt.[3] In a similar vein, the noted historian Andrew Cayton suggests that by the early twentieth century the region for many Americans "seemed to be more a state of mind or attitude than a specific place." Cayton speculates that, together, the landscapes and people of the Midwest "refle[c]t the combined impact of the democratic revolutions of the nineteenth century. No other place on earth brought so many different human beings together in such a short period of time to negotiate and fashion new ways of life."[4] With time, the Midwest as both a real place on the map and as a perceived, constructed ideal grew to be associated with a set of compelling populist themes and images, rooted in an idyllic rural and small-town way of life evocative of Jefferson's conceptualization of a new "American" worldview grounded in the labor and virtues of the "yeoman" farmer.[5]

Approaches to the geographic analysis of the Midwest have changed markedly over the past several decades, reflecting broader paradigmatic shifts with respect to dominant themes and research methodologies in the social sciences and the humanities. Between the 1920s and roughly 1990, American cultural and historical geographers focused much of their attention on documenting and assessing the significance of geographic patterns and processes associated with the settlement of North America by various population groups, especially Euro-American and Anglo-American settlers. Much of this research produced prior to the "quantitative revolution" of the early 1970s reflected the influence of "traditional" empirical concepts and methods, was preoccupied with folk culture and rural settlement, and tended to focus on the documentation of changes in cultural landscapes associated with successive episodes of human settlement. A central goal (some may say *the* central goal) of such research over roughly the seven decades between 1920 and 1990 involved the identification and analysis of American "culture" regions. It has been said that the region is to geography as the period or era is to history. Historically, maps were the central "tool" of the discipline, what geographers use to organize and analyze spatial patterns associated with various phenomena. At the same time, and perhaps ironically, cultural geographers during this era were not particularly interested in defining culture or writing extensively about the cultural characteristics of the regions they were drawing on maps, opting instead to focus on the documentation of material culture artifacts (houses, barns, fences, and the like) as proxies for identifying the location of a given cultural group. In this sense, a culture region was contextualized as a space within which there is cultural homogeneity of some sort, a place where a certain "way of life" (how cultural anthropologists historically defined "culture") predominates.

In this line of reasoning, then, the "Midwest" was one of many distinct sub-culture regions of the United States, each characterized by a certain set of cultural landscape features—specific house types and barn forms, for example—that reflected the settlement of that area by specific groups of people. Only a handful of cultural geographers have focused their attention on defining the normative social qualities and attributes that might define the Midwest as a region. Without question, the most prolific geographer to approach the Midwest from this vantage point is James Shortridge, whose research and writing on the region spans nearly three decades, culminating in a monograph that remains the only book-length analysis of the Midwest by a geographer.[6] Relying on both empirical analysis and more humanistic assessments, Shortridge's scholarship identified a number of social and cultural characteristics that he contends sets the Midwest apart. Foremost among these are the association of the Midwest with a pastoral, rural ideal that flows deep through the American psyche, and the notion of the Midwest as a "metaphor" for nationalistic tropes (such as wholesomeness, self-sufficiency, and rugged individualism) that define and encompass the American experience.[7] At the same time, his research makes clear that the ideals associated with the region have always been debated, contested, up in the air, so much so that Midwesterners themselves are often ambiguous about their own character traits. This ambiguity, according the Shortridge, propagates a complex, uncertain—even insecure—regional identity. So too, the region and its people have been "plagued" by a series of contradictory images:

wholesomeness vs. "narrow conservatism"; self-sufficiency vs. dependence on outside governmental interests; hard work and resiliency vs. "embitterment" and parochialism; rural cornfields vs. gleaming postmodern cities. Shortridge traces such contradictions in part to the complex settlement history of the region. Compared with the East Coast culture regions, the Midwest's earliest settlers hailed from a variety of places, including New England, the mid-Atlantic, the Upland South, and a range of European countries, bringing with them a plurality of social, economic, and cultural attitudes. Indeed, Shortridge infers that such complexity, ambiguity, and insecurity is in fact one of the central, defining characteristics of the Midwest.[8]

In one of the first studies to attempt an empirical delimitation of the geographic extent of the Midwest, Shortridge (with the aid of faculty colleagues around the country) administered just under two thousand questionnaires to undergraduate students from across the country in which respondents were asked to draw a line around where they believed the "Midwest" to be on a map of the United States. The students were also asked to name the primary attributes with which they associated the "Midwest." Unsurprisingly, the resulting cognitive maps confirmed the ambiguous nature of the region's perceived boundaries. Roughly 70 percent of the students perceived the heart of the Midwest to be centered on Nebraska, Kansas, and Iowa. Only half placed Chicago, often hailed as the "capital" of the Midwest, in the region. As many students perceived Wyoming and Arkansas to be a part of the Midwest as they did Ohio. Students from the five states of the Old Northwest (Ohio, Indiana, Michigan, Illinois, and Wisconsin) generally agreed that those states were in the Midwest but placed the actual "core" of the region several hundred miles west, beyond the Mississippi, centered on Nebraska. With respect to perceived social and cultural traits associated with the region, the results were not surprising: roughly seven in ten respondents linked the Midwest with pastoral themes: farming, corn, wheat, ranching, cattle, and small towns.[9] Perhaps not unexpectedly, the most recent and largest survey of Midwestern identity, conducted in 2023 by *Middle West Review* and Emerson College Polling, largely mirrors Shortridge's poll results from 1985, (re)affirming a basic geographic pattern of regional affiliation that has remained essentially the same over nearly forty years: a "core" bounded by Ohio to the east, Michigan, Wisconsin, and Michigan to the north, the Dakotas and Nebraska to the west, and Kansas and Missouri to the south, with a strong but "frayed" Midwestern identity around the edges, especially in areas to the west (Wyoming) and south (Oklahoma) of the core.[10]

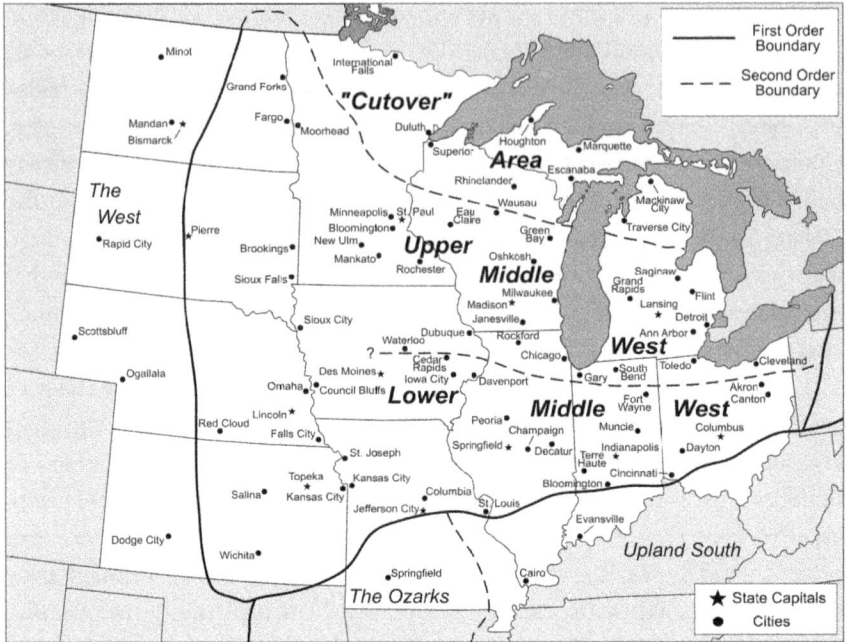

Map 11.1. Midwestern subculture regions as defined by Wilbur Zelinsky.
Source: Zelinsky, *Cultural Geography of the United States*, 118–19.
Cartography by author.

A decade before Shortridge's attempt to empirically demarcate the boundaries of the Midwest, Wilbur Zelinsky, another prolific and oft-cited cultural geographer, produced one of the most well-known maps of American culture and subculture regions (map 11.1).[11] Zelinsky centered the "Middle West" in Illinois and Indiana, and stretching from northwestern Pennsylvania in the east to roughly the 100th meridian (bisecting each of the Great Plains states) in the west. Notably, the southern portions of Ohio, Indiana, Illinois, and Missouri are not included; he places these areas in the "Upland South" subculture region. Most significantly, Zelinsky proposed a national culture area map characterized by a nested hierarchy of regions (delimited by "first-order" borderlines) and subregions (delimited by "second—and third-order" borderlines). The Middle West is itself divided into three subregions: an "Upper Middle West," a "Lower Middle West," and the "Cutover Area" of northeastern Minnesota, northern Wisconsin, and the Upper Peninsula of Michigan. Zelinsky's regional and subregional boundaries are based upon who the "first effective settlers" in an area were, and from where they hailed in the American East or Europe. This concept is exemplified in his so-called "Doctrine of First Effective Settlement:" "Whenever an empty territory undergoes settlement, or an earlier population is dislodged by invaders, the specific characteristics of the first group able to effect a viable, self-perpetuating society are of crucial importance for the later social and cultural geography of the area, no matter how tiny the initial band of settlers may have been . . . thus, in terms of lasting impact, the activities of a few hundred, or even a few score, initial colonizers can mean much more for the cultural geography of a place than the contributions of tens of thousands of new immigrants a few generations later."[12] As such, Zelinsky subdivides the Midwest into three separate subregions according to the "major sources of culture" in each: New England and nineteenth-century Europe for the Upper Middle West; the Middle Colonies, upstate and western New York, and nineteenth-century Europe for the Lower Middle West; and the Upper Middle West and nineteenth-century Europe (primarily Scandinavia) for the "Cutover Area."

Notwithstanding contemporary critiques of the Doctrine of First Effective Settlement (were the indigenous populations of North America not "viable, self-perpetuating" societies?), it is clear that Zelinsky's formulations influenced a number of subsequent writers. Two of the most well known are journalists who wrote immensely popular books that attempted to explain contemporary regional differences in everything from voting patterns to food preferences. In *The Nine Nations of North America*, Joel Garreau argues that conventional state boundaries are artificial abstractions that cannot explain regional cultural and economic differences. He proposes nine separate North American "nations," large groups with common "tribal" identities and cultural affinities, as well as distinctive geographic distributions whose boundaries supersede state (and even international) political boundaries.[13] Garreau's map accompanying the book situates the heart of the region conventionally known as the Midwest at the intersection of three of his nine nations: The Breadbasket; The Foundry; and Dixie (map 11.2).

In *American Nations*, Colin Woodard draws heavily from the scholarship of American cultural geographers (especially Wilbur Zelinsky) and historian David Hackett Fisher to construct a narrative synthesis that explores how contemporary regional identities can be traced to regional differences in the colonial era (e.g., New England, the Middle Colonies, and the Tidewater South, among others).[14] Each "nation" shared a common "culture" and geographic origin, and as populations moved west out of the original colonial locales they

Map 11.2. Midwestern subculture regions as imagined by Joel Garreau.
Source: Garreau, *Nine Nations of North America*. Cartography by author.

brought these common cultural proclivities with them. Like Garreau, Woodard shows how the borders of his eleven nations cut across state and international boundaries, and he contends that the national borders are a more accurate explanatory tool for understanding current national political, economic, and social divides. Woodard's map of the eleven "rival" national culture regions is highly precise, with the county as the unit of analysis, resulting in more highly detailed and sharper national boundaries. Like Zelinsky and Garreau, Woodard maintains that the Midwest is better understood as consisting of three different "nations:" "Yankeedom," with its population (and cultural) origins in colonial New England; the "Midlands," with an origin in southeast Pennsylvania and the lower Delaware valley; and "Greater Appalachia," originating in the Chesapeake Tidewater region of colonial Virginia and Maryland (map 11.3).[15]

## MATERIAL CULTURE

As noted above, an earlier generation of American cultural geographers prior to the early 1980s devoted much of their scholarly attention to the identification

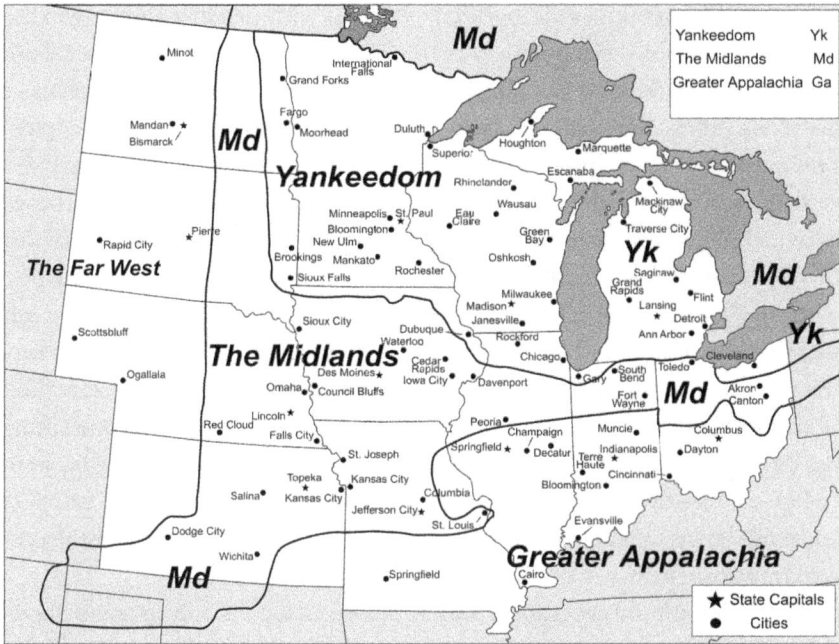

Map 11.3. Midwestern subculture regions as delimited by Colin Woodard.
Source: Woodard, *American Nations*. Cartography by author.

and analysis of material culture features in order to uncover processes at work
in the formation of culture regions.[16] The Midwest was the setting for much
of this kind of scholarship, focusing on the geographic distribution of various
iconic regional landscape elements—field patterns, land survey systems, grain
elevators, windmills, fencing, houses, barns, and the like.[17] Although much of
this kind of research focused on highly detailed empirical analyses of forms
and functions, a broader takeaway from this long line of scholarship is how
such material objects are imbued with a powerful and lasting nostalgia for an
earlier, pastoral past.

Of the various elements that make up the Midwestern rural landscape, barns
are perhaps the most iconic and evocative symbols of the region. Although
many Americans associate barns with the rural Midwest and with a past that
is distant yet somehow still viable, most of us encounter them only in a fleeting
way as we observe them from interstate highways. Few Americans have ever
set foot in one or thought deeply about why a particular barn looks the way it
does or how it is constructed, or what these may reveal about its builders or

users. Employing the idea of "invented tradition," historian Eric Hobsbawm has observed that "objects or practices are liberated for full symbolic and ritual use when no longer fettered by practical use."[18] Most of us no longer use barns or live in log cabins, but such objects are often associated with a former, "simpler" time and imbued with highly symbolic meaning and value in American popular culture. Accordingly, they convey meaning far beyond the utilitarian purposes for which they were built.[19] The popularity of television programs such as *This Old House*, *Antiques Roadshow*, and *Barnwood Builders* reflects our fascination with "old" objects and our nostalgia for the past that they represent. Through such objects we can be linked to or even transformed into the past. Perhaps this is an important clue in understanding why the Midwest is seen as an idealized past place for so many Americans. But as geographer David Lowenthal has observed, the past, like the present, is not static and unchanging because "when we identify, preserve, enhance, or commemorate surviving artifacts and landscapes, we affect the very nature of the past . . . To appreciate the past is to transform it."[20]

The noted cultural geographer John Fraser Hart, second only to James Shortridge as the geographer most often associated with scholarship on the Midwest as a region, asks us to think about material objects like barns—construction techniques, styles, regional typologies—within the context of their function and the needs of those who built them. But part of the difficulty in "reading" such objects is that the original functions they served in an earlier time are often difficult to understand or reconstruct and thus become lost to antiquity.[21] Hart reminds us of a simple fact: "On a modern farm the barn is a relict feature; the hayloft is obsolescent, the threshing floor is obsolete, and who needs stalls for horses?"[22] Historically, regional variations in barn types reflected regional variations in agricultural systems. In the Midwest, however (as in most other regions of the country for that matter), the rise to prominence of industrial agriculture ("agro-industry"), shifting market structures, and the adoption of newer technologies have significantly altered the nature of agricultural production. The nineteenth-century Corn Belt agricultural system that focused on mixed crop and livestock farming has been replaced with cash-crop farming concentrated on corn and soybean production. Accordingly, large livestock "feeder barns" with spaces for hay and grain storage, livestock, and machinery are no longer worth the labor and capital necessary to build them. Barns are now needed primarily to house large, expensive machinery, and wooden barns based on floor plans and styles diffused from the East Coast and Europe centuries before are being

replaced with cheaper multipurpose metal structures. So too, regional variations in material culture such as barns and houses that were once more readily
discernible have been replaced by standardized forms that are reproduced
everywhere, eroding regional distinctions.

## HISTORICAL SETTLEMENT GEOGRAPHY

A third major tradition in scholarship on the Midwest by cultural and historical geographers involves detailed analyses of the settlement of the region by
various populations from the East Coast and Europe during the nineteenth
century. Such studies appeared between roughly 1970 and 1990 as American
historical geographers shifted their attention to a more thorough and nuanced
understanding of the spatial processes underlying the regional and national
patterns in material culture identified by an earlier generation of geographers.
One of the dominant themes of these studies was the documentation of cultural
transfer resulting from the European and African settlement of North America
and the analysis of cultural "divergence" in the interior of the continent. Often
informed by detailed analysis of archival and statistical data (such as census data),
a central goal was to better understand how "American" cultural landscapes
and settlement systems evolved from Old World antecedents.[23]

Another primary goal of this line of scholarship was the documentation
and cartographic depiction of migration streams into the incipient Midwest
from East Coast locales in the early nineteenth century. A number of studies
employed places of birth recorded in the 1850 census to map the geographic
origins of populations at the multi-county or state level.[24] The analysis of census data alone, however, provides only a partial picture of the nativity and
geographic origins of the population of a given place because this information
was only recorded at the state (or national) scale. Accordingly, researchers
interested in a fuller understanding of the regional origins of the Midwest's
frontier populations or looking to better understand larger-scale social and
historical processes at work in inter-regional migrations turned to other data
sources to fill the gaps in the census record. Foremost among such researchers
is John Hudson of Northwestern University. Hudson turned to the biographical
sketches of residents found in county histories that were immensely popular
in Midwestern locales in the late nineteenth century. These histories often
included up to several hundred biographical sketches of the county's residents,
including sometimes very specific information at the local level related to place
of birth. These records are not without biases: women and those of modest

income, for example, are highly underrepresented. Nevertheless, they are rich sources for determining the place and date of birth of significant numbers of frontier settlers. In his study of nearly 32,000 biographical sketches contained in 175 county histories from twelve Midwestern states, Hudson produced highly detailed birthplace maps for the two hundred earliest residents of each county; these maps revealed distinctive migration fields. Drawing on both statistical and cartographic techniques, isolines connecting places of birth with places of death were fashioned that, when analyzed, demonstrated that migrations from East Coast colonial regions (New England, the Mid-Atlantic, and Virginia) to Midwestern locales were largely latitudinal (i.e., east–west) in nature.[25] These latitudinal migrations are apparent in the culture region maps produced by Zelinsky, Garreau, and Woodard that accompany this chapter.

More recently, technological advances have afforded the compilation of very large electronic databases of genealogical and genetic data that can be accessed by almost anyone. Working within a new genre that has been coined "genealogical geography," geographers and demographers have been especially proficient in exploiting such databases that can contain up to hundreds of millions of names. These new studies are revolutionizing our understanding of the migration geographies of multiple generations of people linked by kinship and ancestry.[26] Some of the most detailed scholarship of this kind has been carried out by Samuel Otterstrom, a geographer at Brigham Young University. Working from the premise that "individuals are tied together in time and space by their biological connections," Otterstrom and his colleagues have developed a spatial-temporal model of intergenerational migration across North America utilizing detailed statistical algorithms and GIS mapping techniques that query the New FamilySearch genealogical database of over 800 million names.[27] As these groundbreaking technologies are applied to the problem of documenting the geographic origins of Midwestern frontier populations, and as newer, larger databases are tapped (including databases of genetic information), we will likely be able to uncover previously unrecognized settlement patterns and processes, helping us to more fully understand the origins of the iconic and evocative characteristics that define this most important of American culture regions.

## AN EVOCATIVE REGION AND LANDSCAPE

A common denominator—a leitmotif—running through the long line of scholarship on the Midwest by American cultural geographers involves attempts to define the region as a place unified by a distinctive settlement history and an attendant characteristic cultural landscape. This landscape, it is argued, includes physical manifestations in the form of iconic material culture elements (barns, windmills, silos, vast fields of corn and soybeans, etc.). For many Americans, this landscape came to evoke a variety of iconic images and tropes that over time became synonymous with the Midwest in American popular culture: fertility, frugality, authenticity, self-reliance, social and political conservatism. Numerous prominent writers and artists employed these sorts of perceived "positive" themes in works that celebrated the landscapes and images of the region. Contrasting with such affirmative images, however, is an array of competing, darker metaphors lying just below a seemingly sublime surface: xenophobia, hypocrisy, pessimism, backwardness, and, more recently, "flyover" country. In Grant Wood's well-known painting *American Gothic*, for example, the strength and determination that so many Americans associate with rural and small-town America is juxtaposed with the stoic, stiff appearances of the elderly Midwestern farmer and his daughter.[28] So too, the characters in Sherwood Anderson's *Winesburg, Ohio* inhabit a seemingly ideal Midwestern farming community, but their obstinance in holding to Midwestern principles in the face of drastic social and economic changes produced by industrialization and modernity leads to alienation and dysfunction. An aching nostalgia for a former, preindustrial way of life, anchored by the bonds of community and a common sense of purpose and meaning, compounds the characters' sense of loss and isolation.[29] And in *Lake Wobegon Days* and his radio program *A Prairie Home Companion*, Garrison Keillor evokes (and celebrates) a Midwestern "complex duality" in which traits such as frugality, tidiness, and skepticism of modern urban life are contrasted with the "piety and parochialism, . . . self-doubt and pessimism" of the region's inhabitants.[30] It should be noted, however, that this "revolt from the village" trope—the cynical and at times satirical appraisal of Midwestern values by artists born and raised in the region such as Anderson, Keillor, Sinclair Lewis, and Carl Van Doren—has been challenged and critiqued as of late by a number of prominent Midwest specialists, most notably (and most recently) Jon K. Lauck, one of our most prolific contemporary scholars on Midwestern history and identity. In his latest book, *The Good Country*, Lauck recenters the "place" of the Midwest in the nation's history, arguing that many of the nostalgic collective memories with which it is associated are in fact grounded in reality, at least historically. In doing so, he demonstrates how the Midwest became perhaps the most democratically advanced place in the world during this period and was the setting for the development of a rich, stable society grounded in rather progressive social norms that placed a high value on education, the arts, and civic virtue.[31]

It can be argued that the Midwest plays a prominent role in the ongoing "culture wars" that dominate our contemporary national discourses, a process in which competing tropes fight for primacy in defining American identity in the early twenty-first century. Even though less than 2 percent of the American labor force is made up of farmers, the current political divisions and the narratives surrounding these divisions make it clear that many in the "flyover" country of the "West" beyond the Mississippi still identify with social and political norms perceived to be associated with a rural, small-town way of life. For such people, these kinds of norms and values are represented by the idea of the Midwest, a place where it is perceived that community bonds and "traditional" values are still important. But such powerful, nostalgic discourses are increasingly challenged by a newer set of attitudes stemming from—and anchored in—bicoastal narratives in which values such as progressiveness, inclusivity, diversity, and plurality are forwarded as a set of superior "American" standards.[32] Drawing on the recent work of Steven Conn, historian Amy Fluker asserts that the cultural and political identity of many rural Midwesterners is rooted in and fueled by "grief over [a] wounded sense of regional identity" and a profound sense of loss—institutions, businesses, people, farms—that surrounds them on a daily basis.[33]

Perhaps it is because of the real and perceived loss of "important" things associated with an earlier time that we continue to instill value and meaning in objects such as barns, old houses, and in small-town "Main Street" ideals. Written at the height of the rural banking crisis of the 1980s, sociologist Robert Bellah and his team of co-researchers identified this deep nostalgia for a supposed ideal past embodied in—and inexorably linked to—small-town social values in their groundbreaking study of American public and private life: "The erosion of meaning and coherence in our lives is not something Americans desire. Indeed, the profound yearning for the idealized small town is a yearning for just such meaning and coherence . . . but . . . the yearning for the small town is nostalgia for the irretrievably lost."[34] In objects instilled with such meaning, geographer Richard Francaviglia asserts that "we see *time* (change or stasis and preservation) and *space* (patterns of local, regional, national, even international traits) interacting. These help individuals create and sustain social networks as they in turn create *place* in America."[35] Places such as the Midwest and the "old" objects associated with them are material manifestations of our values and ideals, our perceptions about our past, and as such reflect our cerebral constructions of time, space, and place.[36]

## NOTES

1. Shortridge, *The Middle West*, 3 (see chapter 6, n. 5).

2. For example, the federal government defines the Appalachian Regional Commission (ARC) as comprising 432 officially designated counties across thirteen states. The Midwest is in fact one of the Census Bureau's four statistical administrative regions but is itself subdivided into two divisions: East North Central and West North Central. There is a general consensus (at least among academics) that the Midwest is comprised of the twelve states in the region as delimited by the Bureau, even if there is less agreement as to where the region "ends" around the edges. Interestingly, while Chicago is the regional office location for eleven of these states, Ohio is part of the Philadelphia regional office administrative region. For details, see https://www.census.gov/about/regions.html.

3. Shortridge, *The Middle West*, 70–82.

4. Andrew Cayton, "General Overview," in *The American Midwest: An Interpretive Encyclopedia*, ed. Richard Sisson, Christian Zacher, and Andrew Cayton (Indiana University Press, 2007), xvix, xxii.

5. Timothy G. Anderson, "Introduction," in *Barns of the Midwest*, ed. Allen G. Noble and Hubert G. H. Wilhelm (Ohio University Press, [1995] 2018), xiii.

6. Shortridge, *The Middle West*.

7. The development of these themes over time is detailed in, James R. Shortridge, "The Emergence of 'Middle West' as an American Regional Label," *Annals of the Association of American Geographers* 74, no. 2 (1984): 209–20. The idea of the Midwest as metaphor is most fully developed in Shortridge, *The Middle West*, 134–44.

8. Shortridge, *The Middle West*, 2–3. For an extended discussion of these themes, see Kent C. Ryden, "Writing the Midwest: History, Literature, and Regional Identity," *Geographical Review* 89, no. 4 (1999): 511–32.

9. James R. Shortridge, "The Vernacular Middle West," *Annals of the Association of American Geographers* 75, no. 1 (1985): 48–57.

10. For a thorough discussion of the results of this poll, see Jon K. Lauck, "Introduction: Finding the Boundaries of the American Midwest," *Middle West Review* 10, no. 2 (2024): xi–xx.

11. Wilbur Zelinsky, *The Cultural Geography of the United States: A Revised Edition* (Prentice Hall, [1973] 1992), 118–19.

12. Zelinsky, *Cultural Geography of the United States*, 13–14.

13. Joel Garreau, *The Nine Nations of North America* (Houghton Mifflin, 1981).

14. David Hackett Fischer, *Albion's Seed: Four British Folkways in America* (Oxford University Press, 1989).

15. Colin Woodard, *American Nations: A History of the Eleven Rival Regional Cultures of North America* (Penguin Books, 2011). For an example of how Woodard employs this

American nations model to analyze contemporary social and political debates, see Colin Woodard, "Abortion's Regional Divide," Nationhood Lab, May 24, 2024, https://www .nationhoodlab.org/abortions-regional-divide/.

16. For archetypal examples of such research, see Carl O. Sauer, "The Morphology of Landscape," *University of California Publications in Geography* 2 (1925): 19–54; and Fred Kniffen, "Folk Housing: Key to Diffusion," *Annals of the Association of American Geographers* 55 (1965): 549–77.

17. Examples include Glenn Trewartha, "Some Regional Characteristics of American Farmsteads," *Annals of the Association of American Geographers* 38, no. 3 (1948): 169–225; John Fraser Hart, "Field Patterns in Indiana," *Geographical Review* 58, no. 3 (1968): 450–71; Susan Ridlen, "Bank Barns in Cass County, Indiana," *Pioneer America* 4, no. 2 (1972): 25–43; Allen G. Noble, "Barns and Square Silos in Northeast Ohio," *Pioneer America* 6, no. 2 (1974): 12–21; Laurence Kruckman and Darrell L. Whiteman, "Barns, Buildings, and Windmills: A Key to Change on the Illinois Prairies," *Journal of the Illinois State Historical Society* 68 (1975): 257–66; Robert W. Bastian, "Indiana Folk Architecture: A Lower Midwestern Index," *Pioneer America* 9, no. 2 (1977): 115–42; Hildegard Binder Johnson, *Order Upon the Land: The U.S. Rectangular Land Survey and the Upper Mississippi Country* (Oxford University Press, 1978); Leslie Hewes, "Early Fencing on the Western Margin of the Prairie," *Annals of the Association of American Geographers* 71, no. 4 (1981): 499–527; Warren E. Roberts, *Log Buildings of Southern Indiana* (Trickster Press, 1984); and Allen G. Noble and Hubert G. H. Wilhelm, eds., *Barns of the Midwest* (Ohio University Press, 1995).

18. Eric Hobsbawm, "Introduction: Inventing Traditions," in *The Invention of Tradition*, ed. Eric Hobsbawm and Terence Ranger (Cambridge University Press, 1983), 4.

19. James Deetz, *In Small Things Forgotten: An Archaeology of Early American Life* (Anchor Books, 1977), 4.

20. David Lowenthal, "Age and Artifact: Dilemmas of Appreciation," in *The Interpretation of Ordinary Landscapes: Geographical Essays*, ed. D. W. Meinig (Oxford University Press, 1979), 124–25.

21. John Fraser Hart, *The Rural Landscape* (Johns Hopkins University Press, 1998), 193.

22. John Fraser Hart, *The Look of the Land* (Prentice Hall, 1975), 136.

23. Exemplary examples of such studies include: R. Cole Harris, "The Simplification of Europe Overseas," *Annals of the Association of American Geographers* 67 (1977): 469–83; Robert D. Mitchell, "The Formation of Early American Cultural Regions: An Interpretation," in *European Settlement and Development in North America*, ed. James R. Gibson (University of Toronto Press, 1978); and Terry G. Jordan and Matti Kaups, *The American Backwoods Frontier: An Ethnic and Ecological Interpretation* (Johns Hopkins University Press, 1989).

24. Hubert G. H. Wilhelm, *The Origin and Distribution of Settlement Groups: Ohio, 1850* (Cutler Printing, 1982); Gregory S. Rose, "Major Sources of Indiana's Settlers in 1850," *Pioneer America Society Transactions* 6 (1983): 67–76; Gregory S. Rose, "Information Sources for Nineteenth-Century Midwestern Migration," *Professional Geographer* 37

(1985): 66–72; Russel L. Gerlach, *Settlement Patterns in Missouri: A Study of Population Origins with a Wall Map* (University of Missouri Press, 1986); Gregory S. Rose, "Upland Southerners: The County Origins of Southern Migrants to Indiana by 1850," *Indiana Magazine of History* 82 (1986): 242–63; Douglas K. Meyer, *Making the Heartland Quilt: A Geographical History of Settlement and Migration in Early-Nineteenth-Century Illinois* (Southern Illinois University Press, 2000); Timothy G. Anderson, "The Creation of an Ethnic Culture Complex Region: Pennsylvania-Germans in Central Ohio, 1790–1850," *Historical Geography* 29 (2001): 133–57.

25. John C. Hudson, "North American Origins of Middlewestern Frontier Popula-tions," *Annals of the Association of American Geographers* 78, no. 3 (1988): 395–413.

26. For a rich collection of essays on this topic, see Dallen J. Timothy and Jeanne Kay Guelke, eds., *Geography and Genealogy: Locating Personal Pasts* (Ashgate, 2008).

27. Samuel M. Otterstrom and Brian E. Bunker, "Genealogy, Migration, and the Intertwined Geographies of Personal Pasts," *Annals of the American Association of Geographers* 103, no. 3 (2013): 544–69.

28. James Kelly, "Grant Wood's *American Gothic*," in Sisson, Zacher, and Cayton, *The American Midwest*, 117–18.

29. Timothy G. Anderson, "Sherwood Anderson's *Winesburg, Ohio*," in Sisson, Zacher, and Cayton, *The American Midwest*, 112–13.

30. Cynthia Miller, "Garrison Keillor's Lake Wobegon," in Sisson, Zacher, and Cayton, *The American Midwest*, 108–9.

31. Lauck, *The Good Country* (see chapter 4, n. 25); see Lauck, pages 197–98 for a detailed discussion of the "revolt from the village" trope. Although now dated, perhaps the best overall treatment of this subject remains Anthony Channell Hilfer, *The Revolt from the Village, 1915–1930* (University of North Carolina Press, 1969).

32. Anderson, "Introduction," xiv.

33. Fluker, "'A Ghost Among Regions,'" 73; Steven Conn, "It's the Geography, Stupid; Or Why the Democratic Party Should Stop with its Appeals to the White Working Class," *Belt Magazine*, January 30, 2018, https://beltmag.com/its-the-geography-stupid. Conn develops such ideas more extensively in *The Lies of the Land: Seeing Rural America for What It Is—and Isn't* (University of Chicago Press, 2023).

34. Robert N. Bellah, Richard Madsen, William M. Sullivan, Ann Swidler, and Steven M. Tipton, *Habits of the Heart: Individualism and Commitment in American Life* (University of California Press, 1985), 282–83.

35. Richard F. Francaviglia, *Main Street Revisited: Time, Space, and Image Building in Small-Town America* (University of Iowa Press, 1996), 192 (emphasis in the original).

36. Much of this section is taken from Anderson, "Introduction," xiv–xvi.

## 12

# MIDWEST METONYMY

## A Linguistic and Historical Inquiry

In the late 1980s cultural geographer James R. Shortridge of the University of Kansas pondered a research dilemma tough enough to tax even his virtuoso intellect. Years earlier he had received a Guggenheim Fellowship to study perceptions of the Midwest, but by 1987 he was determined to dive more deeply into American regional labels. Did average Oklahomans consider themselves Midwesterners or Westerners? Did Ohioans embrace the label "Easterner" or prefer "Midwesterner" as an emblem of regional fealty?

Short of a US census question posing the regional identity question directly to Americans, Shortridge feared his study would be doomed by insufficient data until a chance discovery by KU colleague Robert Nunley opened the floodgates.[1] Nunley had recently purchased a Cobra brand radio, and had been asked to complete the warranty card with his home address, age, sex, size of home community, and "community location." Consumers completed their product registration by selecting one of four options—East, West, South, and Midwest.

Sensing synergy, Nunley contacted Cobra on behalf of his colleague in the geography department, and shortly thereafter the company sent Shortridge thousands of warranty cards for products sold between 1979 and 1980. Here was the dataset Shortridge had longed for—some twenty thousand Americans sharing their self-reported regional identity practically and unsentimentally, unaffected by experimental bias.

Gifted with an unexpected windfall of data points from across the nation, Shortridge set himself to the difficult task of determining the boundaries of America's vernacular regions and "transition zones."[2] Transition zones were the borderline places where two or more regional identities bumped up against one another. In Kentucky, for example, if a preponderance of Cobra radios buyers checked "Midwest" instead of "South" on their warranty cards, it might suggest that the citizens of the commonwealth affiliated more strongly with the Midwest. When a particular zip code yielded a mixed response—for example, if warranty card holders effectively split their responses between "Midwest" and "South"—the geodemographic data would suggest a liminal zone betwixt and between regional identities. As expected, some boundaries, particularly those in more remote areas of the Great Plains and the Ozarks, yielded insufficient data. Others—like the Texas Panhandle and the Kentuckiana region encompassing Cincinnati, Ohio—were characteristically conflicted, reporting affiliations split among three identities. Still, the outlines of Shortridge's Cobra radio-derived regional maps corroborated boundaries well documented in the existing literature, tracing the front range of the Rocky Mountains as the line between "Midwest" and "West," for example, and the Ohio River on Pennsylvania's southeastern border as a key delineator between "Midwest" and "East."

For all the study's insight, however, the consumer data proved nonrepresentative in several key ways. First, buyers of Cobras products skewed male. Second, the warranty card data lacked controls for socioeconomic variables.[3] While Shortridge's ingenious inquiry into regional allegiances had surely transcended the anecdotal, it needed a larger sample size and considerably less "noise" from outlier participants who had, for example, failed to check off a box for home region, or who had checked off two separate boxes, for example, "West" and "South," to signify a hybrid affiliation such as "Southwest." A more nuanced metric set was required, one capable of tracking subtle shifts over time.

Such place-based affiliations proved protean rather than enduring, shifting along with migrations in and out, and with inevitable ebbs and flows of a region's stature and esteem in the court of public opinion and relative to other rival regions. Whether individuals living in a single state identified with the Midwest or with the South, for example, might seem a matter of merely academic concern, but as Frederick Jackson Turner points out, the distinct "sections" of America inevitably vie with one another for prominence much as words vie for expression;[4] the region that attracts the most citizens to live within its borders and advocate for its concerns in effect wins by subscription.

## MIDWEST N-GRAMS

In December 2010 Google released its eagerly awaited Google Books Ngram Viewer, an online search engine that charts the frequencies of search strings using a yearly count of n-grams found in digitized print sources published between 1800 and 2019. Developed by Jon Orwant and Will Brockman, the computer program was hailed as a potential difference-maker in the study of cultural change over time. Early studies by Jean-Baptiste Michel at Harvard claimed it would be a game-changing technology in what Michel and his colleagues called "culturomics," the statistical study of linguistic and cultural phenomena. Lexicography, the evolution of grammar, collective memory, the adoption of technology—culturomics, the study's authors claimed, would "extend the boundaries of rigorous quantitative inquiry to a wide array of new phenomena spanning the social sciences and the humanities,"[5] including cultural geography.

In theory, Michel's culturomics could, if thoughtfully applied, help confirm or deny the general feeling among regional scholars in the early twenty-first century that the Midwest had quietly become what regional historians Timothy R. Mahoney and Wendy Katz called "a ghost of region."[6] By 2013 Jon K. Lauck invoked the so-called "lost region" in his book of the same name, one in which he argues that the Heartland had, in effect, been shelved if not mothballed, destined to function "as an antique" rather than a "critical region of the republic."[7] If the region had indeed become ghosted, forgotten, or lost, such epitaphs as these tacitly implied that it had once been found, like an elder who in their glorious youth had once been "famous among the barns" as the poet Dylan Thomas once put it.[8] If so, when did that halcyon fame end; when does the barn begin to weather and warp, bowing under its own weight? And by what metric might we hope to measure when a flame that once burned brightly begins to flicker?

In Google n-gram vernacular a two-word search string is a "bigram," while a one-word strand is a "unigram." When users search for a bigram or unigram, the search engine scours the entire Google Books corpus, returning a graph of the gram's use over time from 1800 to 2019. The y-axis shows what percentage of all the words in the selected Google Books corpus consist of the chosen search string. When, for example, a cultural geographer enters the word "Midwest" into the Google Ngram Viewer, they see a visual representation of the use of the word since 1800 as a plotted line viewed in profile with tell-tale peaks and valleys similar to a NASDAQ Composite Index or an EKG. Peaks in the graph mark moments in time when the use of the term, as a percentage of all terms scanned in the English corpus (alternately, the searcher can specify American English or British English), increases.

The Ngram Viewer promised to shed new light on many of the questions Shortridge and other cultural geographers attempted to answer with the limited datasets of the 1980s. While Cobra's twenty thousand warranty cards (about nine thousand of which ultimately proved unusable) might have seemed a data windfall in the Reagan era, they could scarcely compare with the half a trillion words across more than fifteen million scanned publications searched by Google Ngram.[9] While the Ngram Viewer could not address the many emotional and subjective resonances of regional identity, it could, for example, determine when regional calling cards like "Midwest," "Midlands," "Midsection," and "Heartland" began appearing in books and periodicals in statistically significant ways. In this fashion it could corroborate analog methods of literature review and lexicographical analysis that attempted to show when, for example, the term "Midwest" entered common usage. Ngram Viewer's graph of the case-sensitive word "Midwest" from 1800 to 2019 tracks closely with more analog and anecdotal methods employed by earlier generations of regional historians and cultural geographers, confirming use of the term as rare in print until about 1908, when a steady upward trend commenced, rising to a decided peak in 1991, before dropping off precipitously to the year of last available data, 2019, by which time its percentage usage dropped to a rate more typical of 1939.[10] In sum, the Ngram graph reveals that the term "Midwest" has been in a marked, steady decline for more than three decades.

Reasonable scholars might disagree about what such a precipitous drop in the usage of a key regional moniker might mean. Some would argue that the Ngram offers definitive lexicographical proof of a truth many Midwestern historians and literary critics have claimed for decades: that the region has suffered a steady slide in cultural prominence and visibility that began in the Reagan years. With 2019 registering the smallest percentage use of the unigram in print since 1938, the relative decline in the usage of "Midwest" testifies to a probable cultural devaluing of the region in the early twenty-first century. Scholars who discount the precipitousness of the decline might point to the proliferation of more useful synonyms over time as a plausible explanation for the diminished percentage share of "Midwest" as appellation in the English corpus. As useful neologisms (new coinages) emerge, or as existing synonyms become more germane to public discourse, they, in theory, outcompete the alternatives, effectively reducing the share of all words represented by the single word "Midwest." Thus, each time a writer opts for the less common "Flyover Country" (coined in 1980 according to the *Oxford English Dictionary*), the use of "Midwest" might register a corresponding decrease as a competing synonym.

Those skeptical of the abundant linguistic evidence for the cultural devaluing of the Midwest further argue that a drop-off in the usage of a term as shown in the Ngram Viewer may not necessarily equate with a decline in mindfulness of the term or its referent, for the writer referring to the region as "Flyover County," for instance, in their book or article nevertheless writes to, and about, the target region. Fair enough. However, precipitous declines in the use of a particular term not otherwise suffering from what John Ellison Kahn calls "semantic taint" (for example, in the event "Midwest" came to be viewed as impolitic or otherwise inappropriate) and minus a concomitant, statistically significant rise in the use of a synonym such as "Flyover Country" point to a real and meaningful decline in the cultural currency of the region as reflected in the corpus.[11]

## THE SMALL GODS THEORY

In his popular science fiction *Small Gods*, British novelist Terry Pratchett creates a universe populated by as many small deities as there are words in English. The numberless gods are "thick as herring roe" though the vast majority of them are too small to see and fail to attract much notice.[12] These myriad minor deities linger, for instance, in "the spirits of places where two ant trails cross" and in the "microclimates down between grass roots." For their very existence the small gods depend on use—on human belief. If a small god is believed in—in other words conjured by name—they grow in strength, "the belief of its worshippers raising it upwards like a thousand tons of rocket fuel."[13]

Pratchett's analogy is apropos, as each of the half trillion words searched via Google Ngram is, in a sense, analogous to a small god competing for usage and space in a swarm of words akin to billions of stars in the multiverse. When a word like *Midwest* is used frequently, its Ngram plotline rockets upward; its use as *mot juste* affirms its utility, as it has been picked from all words because the writer deemed it best. In the same way geo-demographers claim citizens "vote with their feet" by moving to places in which they will prosper,[14] the writer-thinker casts their vote by choosing the words that give expression to their consciousness, or that best capture the contents of their minds and render them intelligible for others. Seeking clarity, they opt for the word or words—the unigrams or bigrams—that most exactly, precisely, and transparently convey their thinking.

This, at any rate, is the long-accepted premise of literary scholars, linguists, and lexicographers who, for example, insist a valuable window into Shakespeare's heart and mind can be had by compiling a literary concordance of the words used in the complete plays. What does it say about the Bard that he uses the word "love" approximately ten times as much as its antithesis, "hate"?[15] Shakespeare uses the words "death" and "life" with nearly equal frequency, but each occurs less than half as often as "love." If the scholar of Midwestern studies applies a similar logic to the corpus of English indexed by Google Ngram, it stands to reason that the dramatically declining use of "Midwest" from approximately 1991 to 2019 could mean that scribes and scholars of the twenty-first century have quietly turned away from the Midwest and its many resonant meanings.

## "HEARTLAND" IN DECLINE

While dated synonyms such as "Midlands" and "Midsection" strike most twenty-first-century ears as antiquated monikers for the American Midwest, the term "Heartland" persists in common usage, providing an alternate linguistic lens through which to consider both the relative predominance of the term "Midwest" as a signifier for the twelve-state region as well as the utility and accuracy of the n-gram method as a barometer of cultural change over time.

Similar to the uppercase "Midwest," "Heartland" is of overwhelmingly American conception and coinage. While other countries outside the United States—most notably Britain—also refer to their "midlands" or "heartland," the capital "H" in "Heartland" typically connotes a distinct geographic and cultural place in America. So while the *Oxford English Dictionary* grants the lowercase versions of the word two independent listings, respectively defined as "a place where love resides" and a more generic geographic concept connoting "an inner part of a country, region or area," the capitalized version of "Heartland" almost exclusively connotes the American Midwest to writers publishing works indexed within the Google Ngram American English corpus. Thus, a search for the case-sensitive unigram "Heartland" within the corpus of American English should largely avoid conflation with the rarer, alternate, or antiquated meanings of the same term. Indeed, an n-gram search reveals three periods of increased usage of the word prior to the sharp increase that commenced in the mid-1980s and lasted until 2000—the first from approximately 1854 to 1861; the second more significant bump from 1878 to 1885; and a third smaller increase from 1916 to 1922. For those versed in Midwestern history, these date ranges correspond with anomalous periods of national attention directed at the region, as the period 1854 to 1861 takes in such Midwest-centric national events as the Kansas-Nebraska Act, Bleeding Kansas, and the statehood of Minnesota in 1858 and Kansas in 1861. A more pronounced though fleeting increase in the use of "Heartland" next occurred from 1878 to 1885, dates that include the immediate lead-up to statehood for Dakota Territory, the farm protest crusade against railroad monopolies and Eastern plutocrats, and the contentious rise of early populist reform organizations and political parties such as the Farmers' Alliance.

From 1917 to 1922, the use of the unigram "Heartland" increased briefly a third and final time prior to a period of dramatic increase beginning in the mid-1980s. The years 1917 to 1922 saw the first stirrings of the Midwestern Regionalist movement and, in the eyes of many scholars, constituted a high-water mark in the production of regional literature with the publication in close succession of Willa Cather's *My Antonia* (1918), Sherwood Anderson's *Winesburg Ohio* (1919), and Sinclair Lewis's *Main Street* (1920). During these same years Will Rogers became a Hollywood darling and a syndicated newspaper wit, while Iowa's popular evangelist Billy Sunday preached to millions.[16] Middle America had found its national voices. However, these more modest bumps pale in comparison to the spike in the use of "Heartland" the Google Ngram Viewer depicts from 1984 to a peak in late 2000. These years encompass Illinois native Ronald Reagan's re-election and second term, the countless soul-searching books and articles generated by the 1980s Ag Crisis—including *Broken Heartland* by Osha Gray Davidson—and the auto industry recession in Michigan famously chronicled by documentarian Michael Moore in his popular film *Roger and Me*. Use of "Heartland" continued to rise apace until its absolute apogee in the contested George Bush vs. Al Gore election in 2000, a statistical dead heat that drew national attention to Midwestern swing states such as Iowa and Wisconsin in which the margin of victory proved less than 1 percent.[17]

Following the contested election of 2000, however, the Ngram plotline registers a sharp decline in relative percentage of print mentions of both "Midwest" and "Heartland," suggesting a diminishing awareness of the region in published texts and, subsequently, in the public mind. By 2019, use of the term "Heartland" in the American English corpus had declined to percentages not seen since the early 1980s, giving back the gains in usage the word registered from 1984 to 2000. Meanwhile, use of the corollary term "Midwest" in American English dropped to levels not seen since the American entry into World War II in 1941. In general, the use of both terms had been at all-time highs at various points between 1984 and 2000, suggesting the volume of attention paid to the region, by name, during those boon years.

If one subscribes to the "Small Gods" theory, the use of a word in print to reference a place amounts, metaphorically speaking at least, to a small invocation or prayer—a token of cultivated consciousness and an artifact of concerted attention. By extension, a dramatic decline in the percentage use of a word in a single generation might reflect a potential loss of faith in the place or idea the term represents, or at the very least a cultural forgetting or devaluing. Skeptics might argue that the dramatic decline in use of both the "Midwest" and "Heartland" unigrams in the roughly twenty-year period from 2000 to 2019 merely reflects the inevitable calm after the storm; that after such seismic Midwest-centric national events as the Ag and Auto Crises, the Reagan years, and the contested election of 2000, perhaps a characteristically reticent region willingly retreated into the background, preferring not to invite so much outside attention.

By comparison, if one replicates the parameters of the n-gram search for "Heartland" and "Midwest," and searches instead for the term "South" in the corpus of American English, one finds use of the unigram to have experienced a similar, though less dramatic, year-by-year decline since about 1988. However, use of the term in 2019 was many times more common than "Midwest," for example, registering a percentage of approximately .01 percent of all words scanned and plotted by the Google Ngram Viewer. Since Google does not publish the exact number of unique words indexed in the American English corpus, we will use the 155 billion-word estimate cited by English-Corpora.org. 155,000,000,000 multiplied by a percentage of approximately .01 suggests that the word "South" in its capitalized form might be expected to appear in print in the books and periodicals scanned by Google Ngram approximately 1.5 billion times in 2019. For the sake of comparison, "East," used in print at a percentage of about .0063 percent, adds up to more than 976 million estimated uses in 2019. By contrast, the term "Midwest," at approximately .00022 percent, would register an estimated 34 million uses, and "Heartland," at about .000026 percent of all n-grams overall in the 2019 American English corpus, could be expected to yield just over four million occurrences in print. The magnitude of the math can be somewhat abstract until one realizes that the total usage of the terms "Midwest" and "Heartland" in 2019, at about 38 million instances combined, is roughly 2.5 percent of the approximately 1.5 billion uses of the uppercase version of "South."

Small gods indeed.

Google's Ngram Viewer, like any search engine, is far from perfect; for example, because its calculations depend on OCR software, scan errors do occur. And because the engine's search results cannot always account for the precise context in which the search word appears, conflation does happen. Still, even conceding its imperfections, Google Ngram Viewer unambiguously shows the percentage use of the terms "Midwest" and "Heartland" in books and periodicals scanned by Google in a period of precipitous decline over the last two decades.

## MIDWEST METONYMY

"Metonymy" is defined as a figure of speech in which an object, idea, or place is referred to by the name of something closely associated with it, and involves a word or phrase substituting for, or standing in for, another word or phrase. Examples of metonymy used in toponomy (the study of place names) are among the most common examples of the figure of speech, ranging from "Silicon Valley" as a sobriquet signifying the greater San Jose metropolitan area, to "Madison Avenue" to refer to the American ad industry, to "Wall Street" as a substitution by association for the New York Stock Exchange. Such metonymic swaps render known geographies more memorable and familiar, both to those who experience them directly and to those who observe them from a distance. As a metonymic substitution for the Midwest, "Heartland" merits special attention, as it derives its figurative resonance not just from metonymy but from the anthropomorphic sense of the nation as a body. The *OED* acknowledges the figurative roots of the toponymic expression in its definition, referencing "The central states of the United States, esp. regarded as representing traditional social attitudes and moderately conservative politics."[18] In its plural sense, the word is frequently attributive, as in "heartland America, heartland values, etc." The word in lowercase can refer to "a region which is especially important to or associated with a particular activity, organization, or ideology." For example, scholars have long labeled rural America as a "heartland of evangelism."[19]

Metonymy and anthropomorphism both qualify as figures of speech, and poetic ones at that; thus, the writer opting to refer to the nation's midlands as the "American Heartland" purposefully connotes a feeling or emotion connected to a place believed to be essential and without which the rest of the body politic would surely die. Used in this sense the term seeks to associate the region by metonymy with what Nick Carraway calls the nation's "warm center" in F. Scott Fitzgerald's *The Great Gatsby*.[20] Such metaphoric conceits aim to bathe the place in an amber glow, attributing to it the positive feeling and life-giving centrality of the human heart.

In an unsentimental age one would expect the use of metonymy in regional place-naming to decrease, and indeed lexicographical analysis suggests our growing discomfort in assigning the word "Heartland," and all its connotations, to the twelve states the US census defines as comprising the American Midwest. In 2019 for example, the Google Ngram Viewer registered approximately four million uses of "Heartland" in Google Books; by comparison, as recently as the year 2000, the figure was closer to ten million. If each use of the term "Heartland" amounts to a vote for the word, and, thereby, the concept or feeling the word evokes, it is reasonable to conclude that in the metaphoric election where writers vote with their words, "Heartland" loses in a landslide. Its decline stands in sharp contrast to the use of other common metonymic place names such as "Silicon Valley" and "Wall Street," which charted near-record highs in usage in 2019.

If the dramatic decline in the use of "Heartland" reveals some attendant loss of affection or esteem for the heartbeat region of the nation, from whence does this loss of affection stem? Logically, any decrease in the percentage use of the term must originate with the writers and thinkers who produce the works digitized in Google Books, which in turn comprise the English corpora searched by the Google Ngram Viewer. As positive associations with farmers and conventional commodity crop agriculture decrease, and as the region's famed political and cultural pluralism is systematically replaced by popular representations of the place as noninclusive and nonrepresentative, the emotive connotations of "Heartland" feel to many like an increasingly poor fit, perhaps explaining why a search for the adjacent bigram "heartland values" produces a similarly shaped plotline, one showing a dramatic rise in the 1980s, a peak in the early 2000s, and a precipitous decline from about 2007 to 2019.

While the use-value of "Heartland" undergoes a period of conspicuous decline, another analogous metonymic place name for the region, "America's breadbasket," remained at or near its peak in the early to mid-2010s, its usage significantly greater as a percentage circa the year 2013 than in the period from 1941 to 1948, during which America's breadbasket fed the world via the Marshall Plan. The sustained contemporary usage of the bigram "America's breadbasket"—ostensibly associated more with 1950s Middle American prosperity than with the present Digital Age—surely also speaks to America's concomitant aversion to "Heartland" and "heartland values" in particular, since "America's breadbasket" has experienced no commensurate declines in usage during the past two decades.

## FOLLOWING THE WORD-STREAM FORWARD

Language lay at the heart of James R. Shortridge's pathmaking research into regional identity. While he was not the first cultural geographer to glean insights from linguistic and lexicographical analysis, his innovative interdisciplinary methods remind us of the importance of words as artifacts of cultural identity. Simply by attending to the terms people used to describe their allegiances, he could begin to construct a kind of cognitive map that described how his subjects thought about themselves relative to region. For example, if a mid-Missourian affiliated with the South, there was a de facto sense in which they had become Southern irrespective of any formal geographic classification or categorization. Vernacular geography, rather than formal or functional geography, conveyed a sense of place as revealed in ordinary people's language.

Google's American English corpus and other similar digital corpora offer a next-level projection of that paradigm, one that promises the most comprehensive quantitative method yet for determining what words and phrases writers turn to, and away from, en masse and over time. While it cannot necessarily explain why the scribes whose words are scanned and indexed in the corpus would help make unigrams such as "heartfelt," "heartwarming," and even the seemingly antiquated "heartstrings" more common than ever while simultaneously putting the heart-words connoting region—words like "Heartland" and "heartland values"—in a nosedive, it can offer valuable statistical data concerning the words individuals contribute to the collective word-stream while indexing and aggregating that word-stream for analysis.

Ngram Views offer today's historians an invaluable glimpse into word-clouds past and present, transporting them back in time to the chatter of a year or a decade, making them privy to the Babble of billions. In a current cultural moment era characterized by crowdsourcing, regional histories vested in language become, more than ever, popular histories, as the words professional and citizen writers generate and publish by the trillions beget a buzzing, pulsing universe, a whirling cloud nebulae of sentiment, notion, and opinion. If in our crowded, crowdsourced multiverse, regional appellations like "Midwest" and "Heartland" decline in print, while mentions of "Iowa" and "Iowan" likewise decrease in terms of percentage usage, could such reductions signify corollary declines in regional consciousness, state fealty, or even a steady erosion of federalism? Do words like these—words the Ngram Viewer shows we increasingly reject in lieu of others that seem more apt, accurate, or apropos—help free us, finally, from the chains of outmoded geodemographic identity (i.e., why refer to oneself merely or generically as an "Iowan" when a twenty-first-century Iowan might instead describe themselves more specifically using words the Ngram Viewer shows are more popular than they have ever been, words like "vegetarian," "libertarian," or even "Hawkeye"?). Do the aggregate word choices of our post-postmodern era, when graphed, chart our growing sense of placelessness? Or is the apparent twilight of the small gods of our regional words, thoughts, and feelings just that—a picture of a Heartland in repose, an EKG of a region, and a regional consciousness, captured by snapshot in temporary diastolic retreat—on the offbeat—awaiting inevitable resuscitation?

What then is the region-loving scholar to do in a world where the once-venerated gods of place have experienced a kind of *Ragnarök*? Lauck would have us push against subordination and toward revival, reclaiming a "a healthy component of American pluralism" while "recognizing regionalist currents and finding regional voices to express them."[21] He worries, with good cause, that the forces of globalization and mass culture have caused regionalism to retreat "into the recesses of the historical imagination." Too much of this kind of "national uniformity," Frederick Jackson Turner predicted at the dawn of the twentieth century, would ultimately provoke a compensatory regionalist resurgence as a counterweight to mass consolidation and homogeneity. Regions of the country, he posited, would aggressively reclaim their cultural sovereignty, in effect reasserting their voice, and via that voice, their distinctive identity.

Agrarian Wendell Berry suggests a similar antidote to the loss of shared regional feeling and fealty, quoting Ralph Waldo Emerson's notion that we must reinvigorate it in such a way that the "dumb abyss becomes vocal in speech."[22] While critics charge that such voice and language-based prescriptions for sectional revitalization are naive at best, I argue that they are in fact the essence of communal, place-based thinking—one that reminds us that language is the locus for the most pernicious forms of cultural hegemony and assimilationist forms of forgetting. If scholars can rightly be said to love their subjects, and if love and loss are inextricably, linguistically bound, when we summon by name something we fear is losing, liminal, or nearly lost, we offer it, at that moment in time, new life.

## NOTES

1. James R. Shortridge, "Changing Usage of Four American Regional Labels," *Annals of the Association of American Geographers* 77, no. 3 (September 1987): 326.

2. Shortridge, "Changing Usage," 327.

3. Shortridge, "Changing Usage," 226.

4. Frederick Jackson Turner, "Is Sectionalism in America Dying Away?" *American Journal of Sociology* 13, no. 5 (March 1908): 670–73.

5. Jean Baptiste Michel et al., "Quantitative Analysis of Culture Using Millions of Digitized Books," *Science* 331, no. 6014 (2010): 176, https://dash.harvard.edu/bitstream /handle/1/8899722/MichelScience2011.pdf.

6. Timothy R. Mahoney and Wendy Jean Katz, *Regionalism and the Humanities* (University of Nebraska Press, 2008), 99.

7. Lauck, *The Lost Region*, 2 (see chapter 4, n. 22).

8. Dylan Thomas, *The Poems of Dylan Thomas* (New Directions, 2003), 225.

9. Michel, "Quantitative Analysis," 176.

10. All n-gram searches were conducted using the Google Ngram Viewer available at https://books.google.com/ngrams/.

11. John Ellison Kahn, "Polysemania, Semantic Taint, and Related Conditions," *Verbatim* 12, no. 3 (1986): 1–3.

12. Terry Pratchett, *Small Gods* (Harper, 2009), 6.

13. Pratchett, *Small Gods*, 7.

14. Bill Bishop, *The Big Sort: Why the Clustering of Like-Minded America Is Tearing Us Apart* (Mariner Books, 2009), 199.

15. "Open Source Shakespeare," accessed January 6, 2023, https://www .opensourceshakespeare.org/concordance/.

16. Richard Martin, *Hero of the Heartland: Billy Sunday and the Transformation of American Society* (Indiana University Press, 2002), 49.

17. University of California Santa Barbara, "The American Presidency Project," accessed January 6, 2023, https://www.presidency.ucsb.edu/statistics/elections/2000.

18. *Oxford English Dictionary Online*, s.v. "Heartland," accessed December 10, 2022, https://www.oed.com/view/Entry/85107.

19. R. Stephen Warner, *A Church of Our Own: Disestablishment and Diversity in American Religion* (Rutgers University Press, 2005), 273.

20. F. Scott Fitzgerald, *The Great Gatsby* (Charles Scribner's Sons, 1925), 3.

21. Lauck, *From Warm Center*, 101 (see introduction, n. 21).

22. Wendell Berry, "Writer and Region," *The Hudson Review* 40, no. 1 (1987): 28.

JASON WEEMS

# RE-MEMBERING THE LAND

## Toward an Artistic Anatomy of the Midwest

"We are the land; the land is us."

An Iowan farm daughter, eighth grade, 1996

In summer 1996, I returned to the Midwest from my first year of West Coast graduate study to work on a farm near Iowa City. It was an important return for me as I had just spent the lengthiest period of my life outside the region. It was also complicated. The farm family I worked for, who had also employed me during my undergraduate studies at the University of Iowa, was undergoing a period of friction of a sort common to multigenerational operations. Although the drama was among people, I was struck by another presence in the family's dynamics: the farm itself, the land. As had been the case with my own family during the farm crisis of the 1980s, the land loomed large at every moment, sometimes out in the open and other times implicitly. For people whose identities derived from lifelong inhabitation and multigenerational husbandry, whose deeper selves were rooted in Jeffersonian landholding as well as modern agribusiness, the land was not merely the setting but rather a central player in the family drama. That same summer, I visited the exhibition *Plain Pictures: Images of the American Prairie*, which was on display in Iowa City and curated by the art historian Joni Kinsey.[1] This large-scale and groundbreaking exhibition chronicled roughly two centuries of Euro-American efforts to identify, envision, and compose the prairie region. As a self-identified Midwesterner, I also perceived in these images (perhaps only inchoately at the time) a meaning that was more intimate and familiar, and perhaps only accessible to those whose lives were shaped by their ties to the region. From this vantage, the land seemed almost human: not just a site but an all-too-humanized actor in the story of being and becoming portrayed in the works.

From early prairie illustrators to contemporary earthwork artists, the Midwestern landscape has been frequently analogized to the human figure—so much so that the transposition of the two forms is arguably the key foundation for Midwestern identity. Pioneers likened the open horizon to the human spirit and the plow-resistant sod to their own hardened bodies and determination—a feeling captured by the Nebraska pioneer photographer Solomon Butcher. A generation later, the anthropomorphized landscape became a cipher for the experiences of economic, technological, and social modernization, especially in the sensual and sentimentally laden hillsides of the regionalist painter Grant Wood. For postwar contemporary artists such as the Cuban émigré Ana Mendieta, the human form served as a model for remolding the prairie soil to evoke the possibilities and foreclosures of the Midwestern social body in relation to issues of gender, race, and belonging. Less mythologized but equally important, the correlation of landscape to human body played forward in the ongoing processes of dismemberment and atrophy that have guided the region's modern social and economic life: from the rending of human and nonhuman bodies enacted by industrial scale meatpacking to the homogenization of the environment produced by monocrop agriculture.

How and to what degree has this Midwestern analogy of human figure to landform (and vice versa) constituted the region, and more importantly to what ends? Perhaps more than ever the figure of the region is shrouded and its form eroding. Working across the region's post Euro-American settlement history, this chapter will explore the landscape to human figure analogy to offer a new critical understanding of Midwestern identity and, moreover, a call for a more subtle and multifaceted anatomization of the ways that we perceive the region and shape our understanding of its past, present, and future. What might be gained if we moved beyond analogy and metaphor and take seriously the possibilities of analyzing the region—in addition to and alongside its inhabitants—as a materially defined and moreover embodied subject? In doing so, how must we redraw the relationship between the region's human, living nonhuman, and nonliving elements? What new understandings of land and body must the region's inhabitants embrace for the future? And finally, in what instances have the region's artist-inhabitants already anticipated these figures and forms? In the argument that follows, I propose that the propensity of Midwestern image makers to envision the region as a living and often anthropomorphized form is born of (and in that way embodies) an array of unusually visceral and psychologically laden affinities that arise when a landscape and its inhabitants act upon each other in equally constitutive and often ineffable ways. In other words, to really capture the history and meaning of the Midwest requires more than simply recognizing that a tight connection exists between people and the land. Rather, we must unlock this relationship through recognition of its two-way character. This means moving beyond frameworks that focus only on human authority over the land, to instead perceive how the land also exerts power over and sometimes against its human inhabitants, and how those inhabitants respond to its capacity to do so.

## EMBRACING THE PRAIRIE

It is well documented that from the outset the prairie astounded early explorers and travelers with its unprecedented terrain, while in turn confounding their efforts to perceive themselves in relationship to it. As US literature scholar Wayne Fields observes in the foreword to Kinsey's exhibition catalog, the seemingly infinite, indefinite, and, from the Euro-American perspective, featureless surface of the prairie form left early explorers struggling to compose descriptions of the land.[2] Over and again, people found themselves lacking the words and experiential frameworks to describe what they saw and felt as they encountered (and in many early instances endured) the grasslands. The inability of newcomers to describe and relate to the land was of course not a new thing, especially in the context of New World exploration and colonization.[3] But on the prairie the need for familiarizing analogies seemed inescapable. Bereft of the language to convey their experiences directly, they formulated comparisons to recast the prairie terrain in terms of more familiar things. Among the most common correlation was to the sea and the desert, each of which captured the sense of

Figure 13.1. George Catlin, *Nishnabottana Bluffs, Upper Missouri*, 1832, oil on canvas, 11 ¼ × 14 ⅜ in (28.6 × 36.6 cm). Smithsonian American Art Museum, Gift of Mrs. Joseph Harrison Jr., 1985.66.402.

unfixity people perceived in undulating grass and featureless topography, as well as the precarity Euro-Americans felt when upon them.[4] Inhabitation, at least at first, seemed almost impossible. In visual terms, the early explorer and artist of the prairie George Catlin was among the first to convey this sense of the unfixed character of the natural prairie terrain in his 1832 oil painting *Nishnabottana Bluffs, Upper Missouri* (fig. 13.1). Here, Catlin depicted the land as a continuous green surface that spans the entire lower half of the picture plane, while the downward motion of his brushstrokes conveys the rolling motion of a sea swell or drifting sand. The rounded peaks of the background bluffs seem to take the form of additional waves or dunes, while the curling gusts of ochre paint in the upper portion trace out the blustering winds that blew unimpeded across the land. Yet even with these allusions to other known landscapes, Catlin's painting is also remarkable for the way that it does not congeal as a landscape, at least in the early nineteenth-century sense. Indeed, to our modern eyes the painting is perhaps most striking for its formal and conceptual abstraction.

To early Euro-American explorers, most of whom understood their relation to the land as transitory, the comparison of the terrain to inhospitable places like the sea and desert likely proved sufficient, and Catlin's sense of abstraction apt. For the region's first settlers, however, the view was different. These people staked their lives on their ability to transform the raw, seemingly ungoverned land into an inhabitable and productive countryside. Reflecting upon these settler experiences, Midwestern novelist Willa Cather understood the unique challenge that the prairie form represented to expectations and ambitions. In her saga *My Antonia*, Cather introduced her emigrant protagonists' encounter with prairie terrain by first listing the things they expected to see but did not. Even though it was in the process of settlement, to Cather's eye the land appeared featureless, offering up no perceptible hills, trees, roads, or fences upon which to stake a view. Instead, Cather focused on the land's seemingly overwhelming features: its abstraction and formlessness: "There was nothing but land: not a country at all but the material out of which countries are made."[5] As Kinsey observes, Cather's words captured the fundamental dualism of lack and possibility that would become the basis of Euro-American settlement. According to Kinsey, the land in its natural form was "so formless as to be unintelligible," which means paradoxically that "it can be defined only by what it may become."[6]

We commonly say that people come to embody the character of the land they inhabit. But what does that mean if at the inception of its settlement that land was defined largely by its featurelessness? One answer would be to imagine that those who inhabited that land became featureless themselves. For some first-generation Midwesterners, this perception did indeed prove to be a source of angst and indictment. Himself a child of Midwestern settler-farmers, the writer Hamlin Garland lamented the mean barrenness of his Wisconsin childhood, noting especially how the unrelenting labor and isolation of settler farming rendered his rural Wisconsin family and neighbors bitter, trapped, and unimaginative (Garland, like Cather, had left the Midwest upon reaching adulthood).[7] An image of a Nebraska pioneer family produced by the late nineteenth-century photographer Solomon Butcher appears to visualize Garland's claim (fig. 13.2). A homestead portrait, the image situates the family in front of a low-slung sod house they had erected from bricks of sod cut literally from the surface of the land around them.[8] The structure, along with the homesteaders' spare possessions—a team of horses, a few hand tools, and the youngest child's proudly displayed toy rocking horse—convey a sense of isolation. A single glass-paned window is the only visible opening in the thick earthen

Figure 13.2. Solomon Butcher, *The Huckleberry House, near Broken Bow, Custer County, Nebraska*, 1886; circa 1982–84 (from glass plate negative in the Nebraska State Historical Society Collection). Gift of John Carter, Museum of Nebraska Art, Kearney, Nebraska.

walls of the home. Unwittingly perhaps, Butcher's image discloses some of the stark realities of the first-generation settler life as it was shaped by the isolating emptiness of the countryside and, alternately, the dark claustrophobia of the home. The emotionless faces of the family, especially the stiffly seated woman, seem to instill the perception of the environment's emptiness into the sitters' figures, and by extension their lives.

There is a stark, inscrutable poetry in how Butcher's photograph intertwines the austerity of both land and inhabitant. While both the photographer and his sitters were doubtlessly drawn to this effect, evidence suggests that they also simultaneously perceived it in a more positive light. Between 1886 and 1892, Butcher captured hundreds of photographs such as this one and compiled an equal number of pioneer family narratives with the intent of creating an illustrated history of Custer County. He self-published the book in 1901 under the title *Pioneer History of Custer County and Short Sketches of Custer County*.[9]

He advertised the volume specifically to the inhabitants of the county and the first edition of a thousand copies sold out prior to publication, with a second edition issued that same year. The local popularity of the volume, which was never marketed on a broader scale, demonstrated that settlers appreciated the photograph and must certainly have perceived their characterization of pioneer life in positive terms. The featurelessness and inscrutability of the land that so challenged earlier explorers had become, via the hands-on process of settlement, a meaningful and even intrinsic element of Midwestern settler identity.

The ready acceptance by Butcher and his Custer County audience of the prairie's openness, and moreover their embrace of this condition as both ingredient and metaphor of their own character, speaks to the second component of Kinsey's prairie dualism, that of potential. As Kinsey elaborates, the prairie might have seemed empty, but that also meant that it was open to be transformed into something of value.[10] This optimism grew as settlers cut through the thick sod and discovered the rich fertility of the land and its capacity, once remade, for agricultural production. It was this promise that first drew settlers to the region from the East, even though they knew the land only abstractly through the boosterism of promotional literature that was usually accompanied by picturesque agrarian illustrations and, equally importantly, via the conceptual geometry of survey lines protracted over the landscape by the US government surveyors.[11] This system of "nested squares" platted the countryside—site unseen—into small, undeveloped parcels that could be acquired inexpensively by those willing to work them. The method was cadastral, but the purpose political, founded on the democratic Jeffersonian philosophy that, according to geographer Yi-Fu Tuan, "possessing such land, [a small farmer] could become truly independent, unbeholden to arbitrary authority."[12] In this sense, the desolate and hard-edged quality of Butcher's photograph must also be measured against the graphically inscribed aura of availability and potential for self-definition that infused survey maps that circulated widely among settlers before, during, and after settlement (fig. 13.3). For Butcher's subjects, the undefined and abstract quality of the prairie was the embodiment of their hopes for a self-invented sense of being.

In the context of early Euro-American settlement of the North American continent, the scholar Kenneth Olwig has demonstrated that landscape operated as both a means for describing and an instrument for shaping the conceptual "body politic."[13] Thinking primarily at the scale of national identity, this meant to Olwig that the settled form that eventually materialized upon nature was in substantial ways an already imagined projection of cultural values and desires.

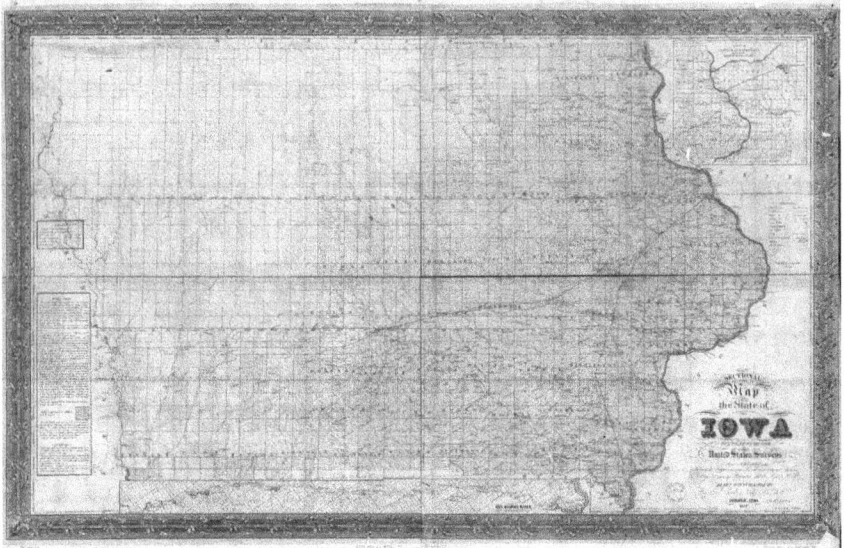

Figure 13.3. Carleton Guy, *Sectional map of the state of Iowa, compiled from the United States surveys also exhibiting the internal improvements, distances between towns & villages, lines of projected rail roads &c. &c.; drawn and published by Guy H. Carleton, Dep. Sur. U.S.* Dubuque, Iowa, 1850. Map in 4 parts, each 13 ⅚ × 21 ⅓ in. Library of Congress, Geography and Map Division.

The analogization of the resulting form to an implicitly human body was not merely expedient but rather purposeful. As Olwig demonstrates, such language had long been used in the European context to cement the understanding that a successful countryside was inherently a human rather than a natural form. Evidence suggests that prairie settlers especially took this embodiment to heart. In 1817, traveler John Bradbury articulated the common uncertainly as to whether the "vast" prairie could not be "peopled by civilized man." His response was that it would "not only be peopled, but cultivated," and thereby "become one of the most beautiful countries in the world."[14] The key term in Bradbury's pronouncement is the verb cultivation, by which he situated human action—rather than conceptualization—as the key to making the prairie. My point here is that while some aspects of shaping the prairie were mental and ideational—on the order of imagining the land as a body politic—for many Midwesterners the work was at least in equal measure based upon direct manual engagement with it. From this perspective, it is possible to shift the perspective of Olwig's body politic analogy by making it smaller in scale and more personal. What matters is not only the human figure as abstract social form but also the reality of actual human bodies working on, and to push the point further *with*, the land.

As nationally known Midwestern writers like Garland and Cather made clear and countless local writers and diarists vouchsafed, for most settlers the strain of manual labor on the land was perhaps the most ubiquitous and insistent facet of prairie life.[15] People toiled with often limited success to establish their homesteads, clear the land, and make it produce.[16] Women worked in at least equal measure to provide for their families, while children often sacrificed their schooling to labor alongside their parents.[17] Most tasks were physically taxing and could be dispiriting, with the landscape perceived as an almost animate presence that either aided or stymied the settlers' efforts. Yet they were also deeply engaging and remarkably tactile. The slow and monotonous back and forth of guiding a plow across the prairie sod gave the plow driver maximum time to take measure of every aspect of the land, from the form of the terrain and consistency of the soil to the depth of the plant roots. It was undoubtedly the case that farmers personalized these qualities as a means for characterizing their own experiences. Land that resisted the plow became the antagonist in the farmer's self-perceived drama of life on the land. The all-surrounding earth of the sod home became both protection and prison to those, especially women, whose lives were defined within it.[18] Both Garland and Cather alluded to this sense of relationality between the land and inhabitant. Repeatedly they used language that described both the people and land responding to events and circumstances in similar ways—describing how both soil and skin parched in a drought, for example, or how crops and settlers blossomed similarly in the summer sun.[19]

The tactile relationship of settler life to the land is vital to understanding the early experience of the prairie precisely because of the intimate connections that it brought forth. As the writers' parallelisms profess, those who worked the land physically could not help but understand it through the terms of direct contact, and moreover in ways that moved beyond the rotely physical to imbue the contact with a sense of emotional and psychological closeness. Given the extent to which settlers' every experience emanated from intimate contact with the land, from a day spent plowing to a night in sod-walled home, it is not surprising that settlers found it difficult to draw hard distinctions between it and themselves. Nor is it surprising that their descriptions of the land became in many respects projections of their own thoughts and actions. Part of this was simply a commonplace deployment of metaphor as a communication device. In this sense, we can imagine that as prairie inhabitants struggled for the means to describe the unprecedented form of the natural prairie and their equally unprecedented encounters upon it, drawing analogies to their lives as means to characterize the land simply made sense. At the same time, one can sense in such expressions the insinuation of a deeper correspondence between the two, whereby the personification of the land is not merely rhetorical but indicative of an increasingly palpable and personal affinity that inhabitants perceived between themselves and the land. The effect was so powerful that many inhabitants began to think of the land not only as part of themselves but also like themselves (and they like it). In other words, they perceived the land as an embodiment of their own sought-after identities, yet also possessing a stubborn character uniquely its own.

Returning to Butcher's photograph, I believe that quality previously described as its poetic inscrutability is in fact the visual manifestation of the deep and mutual entanglement between settler and prairie that I have been describing—which I believe Midwestern historians must both recognize and analyze. I am not alone in sensing something extra at play in these images, as other scholars have noted the unusual quality of Butcher's homestead photographs, which Kinsey describes as "not so much portraits in the traditional sense as they are portraits of states of existence."[20] But whereas Kinsey notes that the combination of people, possessions, and prairie might best be interpreted as an effort to convey the "pride and ambition" of the settler subjects, I propose a less transparent and more psychologically entangled interpretation. Intentional or not, Butcher's settler subjects communicate a sense that they viewed the land and their situation on it as something that they were in the process of making, yet also understood to be making them. The evidence lies in the raw and unfinished quality of all elements perceived within the photograph. Certainly, intended as a symbol of permanence, the rough earthiness of the sod house and the haphazard way that the family's rudimentary possessions surround it also convey strong sense of a place still inchoate. This effect is mirrored in the picture's open foreground, where the sparse, twiggy natural vegetation vies with rough pathways demarcating routes of human activity. The family members' countenances are equally varied and in-process, with the female figure sternly seated with her chin sharply tucked in, the man trapped somewhere between propriety and the uncouth with his smoothed hair and bushy beard, and the two boys registering looks and gestures that seem to vacillate between pride and uneasiness. Indeed, even Butcher's photographic technique seems itself

Figure 13.4. Sally Cover, *The Homestead of Ellsworth Ball*, 1880s, oil on canvas, 19 ½ × 23 in. Nebraska State Historical Society.

unsettled. The scene is meticulously staged with the homestead at dead center, the horse team hitched and on display, and a chair and rocking horse brought purposefully outdoors to invoke a sense of domestic refinement. Yet the image also displays Butcher's limitations as cameraman, especially in the blurriness that creeps around the edges of the foreground and the hazy grey blankness of the distant horizon and sky.

In sum, Butcher's photograph captures the reality of a landscape and its inhabitants in a process of mutual becoming in which neither element is determinant, and each is dependent upon the other. The frankness of this equity—and uncertainty—makes Butcher's photograph unique among settlement pictures, which overall exhibit an uneasiness at such precarity and tended toward idealization of both landscape and human subjects. An 1880s painting by the artist Sally Cover of a Nebraska homestead demonstrates this claim (fig. 13.4). Seeking to envision the process of prairie transformation in a more secure light, Cover transformed it as an idealized fait accompli, with the open prairie already fully transformed into an impossibly picturesque garden.[21] Equally significant, she de-emphasized the human labor and hardship required to achieve that end, with the daunting process of breaking the land for cultivation reduced into the figure of a minute plowman whose presence is almost undetectable in the image's center-right portion, and whose implement seems not even to engage the soil.

For all its charm, Cover's painting rehearses an idealized (and ideological) narrative that naturalizes human domination over the land, whose formlessness is coaxed into fecundity by and the innate goodness of the settlers and their vision. There is a quaint and childlike idealism to the image, a charm that that seems intended to imply that prairie society came into being without toil or disturbance. This may have been the narrative that prairie settlers wanted to believe, and perhaps even did in retrospect. In comparison, Butcher's imagery expresses a less masterful but more meaningful reality that upends the subject–object relationship of settler to prairie to recognize the degree to which these two forms acted upon one another, with each transformed in turn by the other. This sense of reciprocity required a level of personification of the land, and a co-identification with it, that became an unconscious and, in many ways, ineffable quality of the region's emerging identity.

## EXERCISING REGIONAL EMBODIMENT

By the start of the twentieth century, very little open prairie land capable of supporting settlement remained. Memories of the settler experience endured for a time, along with inhabitants' sense of their coming into being alongside the land. Yet prairie inhabitants, whose identity since the close of the frontier had begun to coalesce under the sectional term Midwest, had little direct experience of the open prairie. Born into an already established countryside, their engagement with the land took a different shape than that of their forebears. In particular, the widespread industrialization of agriculture that had been present since the post–Civil War era, but became concentrated in the 1920s, significantly altered the personality of the land along with that of the culture upon it. The challenge for Midwesterners was to adapt their conceptual and psychological frameworks to encompass the new conditions as they refigured the forms through which they represented the region. As Kinsey observes, these efforts invested heavily in the meaning of the land as culturally determinant. "Not since the heyday of landscape painting in the 1850s and 1860s had there been so much attention to and appreciation of the American scene's symbolic value."[22] Yet in the Midwest it was not simply symbolism at stake, since we have seen that for prairie inhabitants, the connection between the land's identity and their own was more deeply and even viscerally co-determinant. They sensed modernization in the changing circumstances of their own being and equally— almost sentiently—in the land.

Perhaps more than any other artist, the Iowa Regionalist painter Grant Wood understood and moreover cherished the existential relationship between the two. An Iowan, Wood grew up on a small farm in rural Iowa and identi- fied those earthy experiences, for example walking barefoot in the furrows while his father plowed his fields, as formative to his own sense of being.[23] He also recalled his fascination with the body of late nineteenth-century pioneer imagery, from land plats to family photographs that had made the meaning of the land tangible to him. The trauma of his family being forced to leave the farm for town upon the death of his father certainly sharpened his awareness of the land's significance to Midwestern identity. Upon adulthood, he trained in the arts in both Chicago and Europe; when he returned to Iowa to make his career, he also returned to the agrarian landscape and people as his grounding subjects. His subsequent efforts as artist, teacher, and even homespun cultural philosopher centered on these two forms that he, like his settler forbears, saw to be innately interconnected.

This perceived affinity was in Wood's mind essential and shaped his endeav- ors. When the artist founded a rural art colony in Stone City, Iowa, during the summers of 1932 and 1933, he suggested that participants live nomadically in horse-drawn ice wagons, which was undoubtedly intended as both a recogni- tion of first-generation pioneer experience and to ensure the most direct con- nection between students and the countryside. Several years later, he put his name to a written statement of his philosophy, entitled *Revolt Against the City*, in which he proclaims the need for a national artistic culture that eschews the call of international and metropolitan centers in favor of investment in regional culture. In Wood's case, this requires recognition of the co-eval, intertwined relationship of land and inhabitant. Describing his home Midwestern region, he states: "Each section [of the country] has a personality of its own, in physi- ography, industry, psychology." His characterization of the Midwest's core inhabitant, the farmer, states the relationship even more clearly. He writes that "The farmer is not articulate . . . He is almost wholly preoccupied with his struggle against the elements, with the fundamental things of life."[24] Perhaps searching for words of greater sensitivity to the human–land relationship, the

Figure 13.5. Grant Wood, *Portrait of John B. Turner, Pioneer*, 1928–30, oil on canvas, 37 × 31 ¾ in. Cedar Rapids Museum of Art, Gift of John B. Turner II and Happy Young, 76.2.2.

artist turned to his friend and Iowa poet Jay Sigmund, quoting his description of the farmer as "brother to the soil."[25]

If Wood's writing insinuates his perception of the subjectivity shared between land and inhabitant, his painting binds it. In a painting that is among the most significant of his pre-1930s works, a 1928 portrait of the Cedar Rapids, Iowa, businessman and Wood benefactor John Turner, the artist positions his sitter

Figure 13.6. Grant Wood, *Young Corn*, 1931, oil on Masonite panel, 24 × 29 ⅞ in. Collection of the Cedar Rapids Community School District, on loan to the Cedar Rapids Museum of Art.

alongside a nineteenth-century local map illustrated with idealized scenes of local homes, farms, and buildings (fig. 13.5). Upon seeing the portrait, Turner would describe it as a scene of "two old maps," thereby demonstrating his sense that he and the landscape were equals, and moreover that each embodied the influence of the other.[26] Wood's more celebrated Iowa landscapes push this sense of shared subjecthood further through a now literal rather than merely associative anthropomorphization of the Midwestern countryside. For example, in the 1931 painting *Young Corn* the artist conjures an agrarian countryside into a molded surface whose bulging hillsides, planted crops, and clustered trees are so deeply anthropomorphized that they appear not simply to resemble a human form but instead to constitute one (fig. 13.6). There can be little doubt that Wood is consciously inviting such identification of the land at least as humanlike. The bulging hill in the upper center shows an undeniable resemblance to a human torso, with the fence lines running both horizontally and diagonally across it evoking the waistline and zipper of work trousers. The valley makes a veiled

Figure 13.7. Alexander Hogue, *Erosion Number 2: Mother Earth Laid Bare*, 1938, oil on canvas, 44 × 56 in. Philbrook Museum of Art, Tulsa, Oklahoma.

allusion to the human groin, with the prominent tree in the center positioned playfully as if to cover the erogenous zone where, incidentally, an adult farmer and his two children work in the field. Though less directly figural, other elements of the land share similar affinities to the human form, such as the stand of just sprouted corn in the foreground that take on the quality of hairs on a forearm.

From the outset, those who saw Wood's landscapes recognized their allusion to the land as a human body. Many chose to interpret the effects in metaphorical terms, imputing that Wood's goal was to reference conventional, long-standing allegories of the landscape as a female figure.[27] Such was the case for fellow 1930s Regionalist painter Alexander Hogue, who in 1938 appropriated Wood's anthropomorphic style to emblematize the catastrophe of soil erosion via the symbolically naked female figure "laid bare" by aggressive and shortsighted agricultural practices (fig. 13.7).[28] While Wood was not averse to such overt, and in Hogue's case politically engaged, symbolism, the subtle sensuousness of his representation evinces a deeper and more affective set of motivations. *Young Corn*, for example, does not emblematize the landscape as passively suffering under human action. Rather, it conveys Wood's quest to represent the possibility of a deeper communion between land and inhabitant. It is no accident that in

Wood's most celebrated Midwestern landscapes—additional examples include his iconic *Stone City* (1930) and *Spring Turning* (1936)—the visual perspective is distant and all encompassing, while human figures are small. The effect of this compositional decision is to put the landscape firmly into an equal, if not leading, role in the composition. Yet because the land's shape is no longer wholly natural but instead cultivated, the end result of Wood's painting is to convey a sense of co-subjectivity between the land and those that reside upon it. In this sense, Wood's hillsides are not inert bodies to be rendered by human actors but living forms that both give shape to and take it from their human cultivators as part of a mutually engaged, generative process of placemaking.

## RE-MEMBERING THE LAND

Given the psychological resonance of Wood's landscapes, there is little doubt that that the artist was touched by the land in almost equal measure to how it was touched (and thereby transformed) by him. A painter's touch upon the landscape may readily be characterized as purposeful and authoritative; we regularly describe the subjective will behind the brushstroke and the thoughts that motivated it. A farmer's touch may be treated analogously, with the blade of the plow in place of the paintbrush. Yet inversely, it remains unclear how far we should go in characterizing the land as possessing a self-assertive, animate agency like that ascribed to human subjects. In most instances, we as historians are uncomfortable in asserting that land's touch upon the human subject might also be interpreted as an active force. Throughout most of Western thinking, agency has been taken for granted as the unique and autonomous property not just of living beings but particularly of human beings. Only recently have scholars begun challenging such anthropocentrism. In particular, theorist Jane Bennett has advocated for a new model of "distributive agency" that affirms the relational character of human and nonhuman matter by positioning human embodiment as "one site of agency within and across a multiplicity of other material bodies and formations."[29] While not seeking to go so far as to flatten the real distinctions between human beings and material forms, Bennett's approach holds forth a new potential for grasping the heretofore ineffable entanglement of Midwestern land and culture. After all, the expressions of those who reside on the land, from Butcher's pioneer photographs to the words of late twentieth-century farm daughter, reveal not dominion but rather a relationship—one where the land is repeatedly interpreted as having something at least akin to animate and assertive characteristics. To ignore this evidence is to artificially delimit our understanding of both human and nonhuman agency, and particularly the assertive capacity of the land in human–land relationship. It is also to risk underestimating the meaning of Midwesternness, both historically and in the current moment.

In 1961, a twelve-year-old Cuban emigre Ana Mendieta was sent by her parents to Dubuque, Iowa, as part of Operation Peter Pan, a program for Cuban children to flee the Castro government. Eight years later as an art student at the University of Iowa, she began to create life-sized performative pieces that she described as "earth-body" sculptures. The sculptures involved a combination of actions in which Mendieta both placed her body on the land and sculpted it into the soil as a life-sized silhouette. Mirroring her experiences, she enacted these works in landscapes that were formative to her, including sites in Iowa, Florida, Cuba, and Mexico. A photograph of one such piece enacted at Old Man's Creek in Iowa City documents the potent mixture of bodily presence and absence that shaped Mendieta's thinking. Initially, the artist's living body was present on the land as she laid herself onto the riverbank and sculpted her silhouette into it. Thereafter, the mode of Mendieta's presence shifted, however, with her body remaining perceptible only via the figure she had outlined in the soil (fig. 13.8). While it is possible to understand this figural outline simply as a record of the artist's now removed body, the more potent consideration is how even with her physical absence her presence remains. It does so not in the flesh but rather as embodied in the animate soil, which we can imagine both conformed to and pushed back against Mendieta's body as she lay upon it. The end effect of Mendieta's work at Old Man Creek is a powerful and complicated evocation of a shared sense of being—one in which the land carries the history of its interaction with its human inhabitants and vice versa, even when earthen matter is the only body present.

Mendieta's story is both old and new. In some respects, her effort to enact a relationship in and with the land echoes those of the Euro-American emigrant settlers who had undertaken similar work in the century before. No less than those forebears, Mendieta's descriptions of her work convey how she felt the prairie earth press back against her own body with its own animated sense of being. Yet for that artist and in the last decades of the twentieth century, the circumstances were different from before. Mendieta, of course, came to the region as a Cold War Cuban refugee and in that way encountered a region whose developed patterns and politics held her in abeyance. For this reason, the connection to the land she sought was more transcendent. She imagined her art as

Figure 13.8. Ana Mendieta, *Untitled: Silueta Series, Iowa*, 1978, Color photograph. © The Estate of Ana Mendieta Collection, LLC. Licensed by Artists Rights Society, New York. Courtesy Galerie Lelong & Co., New York.

communing with a mythic and primordial earth—a body that she could draw strength from as an analeptic to the strictures of mainstream Middle American life. It was no accident, perhaps, that she crafted her artwork in the transient soil of creekbanks and riverbeds. This was the land accessible to her: unclaimed, fugitive, and fluxing places that could not be reconciled with the region's increasingly displacing conditions of technology, property, and productivity.

■ ■ ■

In spending the formative years of her adolescence and collegiate artistic training in Iowa, Mendieta identified with the Midwest's rural and Main Street cultural mythos only guardedly, if at all. In the land, by contrast, she found a more meaningful partner. The land, of course, did not exert agency in the human sense in her work, or that of the others we have discussed. It did in all cases, however, manifest a vital animacy that made it something more than an object that Mendieta and others acted upon. If we take seriously the belief that the land is a vital and ongoing basis of regional identity, it behooves us to reformulate how we understand the relationship between it and its inhabitants. This means reframing the Midwest a place where agency emerges through configurations of human and nonhuman forces—all of them so deeply entangled as to be vitally interdependent. Standing as we do at a possible crisis point, where the status the region's ecology, demography, and politics leave us uncomfortable in our surroundings, to reshape our relationship to the land is to reshape ourselves. "We are the land; the land is us."

## NOTES

1. Joni Kinsey, *Plain Pictures: Images of the American Prairie* (Smithsonian Press, 1996). The exhibition took place at the University of Iowa Museum of Art, August 17 to November 3, 1996.

2. Wayne Fields, "Foreword: The American Prairies and the Literary Aesthetic," in Kinsey, *Plain Pictures*, ix.

3. On the development of descriptive frameworks for European colonial encounters in the New World, see Patricia Seed, *Ceremonies of Possession: Europe's Conquest of the New World* (Cambridge University Press, 1995). On the coincidence of European colonialism and the emergence of landscape as an artistic category, see W. J. T. Mitchell, "Imperial Landscape," in *Landscape and Power* (University of Chicago Press, 1994), 5–34.

4. Fields's analysis of the use of metaphor in the literary description of prairie landscape is instructive. Inversely, Fields also provides evidence that the prairie itself came to serve as a metaphor to explain other great unknowns in US culture, such as Melville's

description in *Moby Dick* of the white whale's vast forehead as a "prairie." Kinsey, *Plain Pictures*, x. For other influential discussions of metaphor as a determinant factor for American landscape study, see Annette Kolodny, *The Lay of the Land: Metaphor as Experience and History in American Life and Letters* (University of North Carolina Press, 1975) and Leo Marx, *The Machine in the Garden: Technology and the Pastoral Ideal in America* (Oxford University Press, 1964). For the classic study of the pervasiveness of metaphor in everyday life, see George Lakoff and Mark Johnson, *Metaphors We Live By* (University of Chicago Press, 1980).

5. Willa Cather, *My Antonia* (Houghton Mifflin, 1988 [1917]), 7–8.

6. Kinsey, *Plain Pictures*, 5.

7. In one short story Garland describes the effect of a life-long prairie inhabitation on a female character: "A grey haired woman was sitting in rocking chair on the porch, her hands in her lap, her eyes fixed on the faintly yellow sky, against which the hills stood, dim purple silhouettes, and on which the locust trees were etched as fine as lace. There was sorrow, resignation, and a sort of dumb despair in her attitude." Note how Garland's prose entangles the description of landscape and inhabitant. Hamlin Garland, "Up the Coolly," in *Main Traveled Roads* (University of Nebraska Press, 1995 [orig. pub. 1891]), 52–53. Recently, Jon K. Lauck has argued that early in his career Garland played up the hardship of Midwestern life to meet the expectations of national audiences. Lauck shows that later in life the author softened these views. See Lauck, *From Warm Center*, 11–36 (see introduction, n. 21).

8. For a comprehensive history of sod houses in Nebraska, see Robert Welsch, *Sod Walls: The Story of the Nebraska Sod House* (Purcells, 1968). For a sociologically based study of material conditions of settler house construction and inhabitation on the North American plains, see Sandra Rollings-Magnusson, "Sod, Straw, Logs, and Mud: Building a Home on the Canadian Prairies, 1867–1914," *Journal of Family History* 40, no. 3 (2015): 399–423. The theme of the "homestead portrait" is undoubtedly a democratization of the long-standing European tradition of the aristocratic estate portrait. The format took hold early in visual culture on the plains and prairie and became codified Midwestern art by the twentieth century in the work of numerous painters such as Iowan Grant Wood or the South Dakotan Harvey Dunn.

9. Solomon Butcher, *Pioneer History of Custer County, Nebraska, and Short Sketches of Early Days in Nebraska* (S. D. Butcher and Ephraim Finch, 1901).

10. Kinsey, *Plain Pictures*, 17–18.

11. For an analysis of the survey process, especially in relations to its visual culture component, see Jason Weems, *Barnstorming the Prairies: How Aerial Vision Made the Midwest* (University of Minnesota Press, 2015), 11–18. See also Johnson, *Order Upon the Land* (see chapter 11, n. 17).

12. Yi-Fu Tuan, "Foreword," in Kenneth Olwig, *Landscape and the Body Politic: From Britain's Renaissance to America's New World* (University of Wisconsin Press, 2002), xvii. For a political and legal history of the Land Ordinance survey, see John Opie, *The Law of the Land: Two Hundred Years of Farmland Policy* (University of Nebraska Press, 1994). For a provocative reappraisal of plains homesteading in the wake of the

Homestead Act of 1862, see Richard Edwards, Jacob Friefeld, and Rebeccá Wingo, *Homesteading the Plains: Toward a New History* (University of Nebraska Press, 2017).

13. Olwig, *Landscape and the Body Politic*, xxiii and passim.

14. John Bradbury, *Travels in the Interior of America* [1817], quoted in Kinsey, *Plain Pictures*, 79.

15. Garland, *Main Traveled Roads* and *Son of the Middle Border* (Penguin, 1995 [1917]); Cather, *My Antonia* and *Oh Pioneers* (Quality Paperback Club, 1995 [1913]). Local newspapers offer a rich source of reports and reflections on the conditions of settler life, though none are cited here. Unpublished settler diaries may be found in numerous state historical archives. For an historical characterization of farm work from the perspective of paid laborers, see David Schob, *Hired Hands and Plowboys: Farm Labor in the Midwest, 1815–1860* (University of Illinois Press, 1975).

16. For a provocative reappraisal of plains settlement in the wake of the Homestead Act of 1862, including a striking reassessment of its level of success, see Edwards et al., *Homesteading the Plains.*

17. On women's labor, see Barbara Handy-Marchello, *Women of the Northern Great Plains: Gender and Settlement on the Homestead Frontier* (Minnesota Historical Society Press, 2007). See also the groundbreaking study of women's responses to successive US frontiers: Annette Kolodny, *The Land Before Her: Fantasy and Experience of the American Frontiers, 1630–1860* (University of North Carolina Press, 1984).

18. While the atypical materials of the sod house render it in some ways a special case, we may surmise that many non-sods pioneer first dwellings were equally austere.

19. Garland, "Among the Corn Rows," in *Main Traveled Roads*, 97–98.

20. Kinsey, *Plain Pictures*, 84. Kinsey's description is paraphrasing historian John Carter's analysis. See Carter, *Solomon D. Butcher: Photographing the American Dream* (University of Nebraska Press, 1985), 12–14

21. For a critical look at the artistic idealization of early US agrarian life, see: Sarah Burns, *Pastoral Inventions: Rural Life in Nineteeth-Century American Art and Culture* (Temple University Press, 1989).

22. Kinsey, *Plain Pictures*, 121.

23. Grant Wood/Park Rhinard, "Return from Bohemia," unpublished manuscript with handwritten notations, 204 (the text appears on microfilm as D24, frames/pages 165–295), Grant Wood Papers, Archives of American Art, Smithsonian Institution, Washington, DC. Although often attributed to Wood alone, the text was ghostwritten by Wood's longtime confidante Rhinard. More recently it has been published in full as an appendix to Sue Taylor, *Grant Wood's Secrets* (University of Delaware Press, 2020), 193–280.

24. Wood, *Revolt from the City*, 232–34, reprinted in James Dennis, *Grant Wood: A Study in American Culture* (University of Missouri Press, 1975).

25. For a poignant reflection on Sigmund's largely forgotten body of work, see Zachary Michael Jack, "Exhuming the Regionalist Body," in *The Haunt of Home: Journey Through the America's Heartland* (Northern Illinois Press, 2020). Zachary's great grandfather is the Iowan Walter Thomas Jack, who as an Iowa farmer also divined the emotional,

subjective ties between Midwesterners and the land. See Walter Thomas Jack, *The Furrow and Us: Essays on Soil and Sentiment* (Dorrance and Company Press, 1946).

26. See Weems, *Barnstorming the Prairies*, 156.

27. For a critique of use of the female form as a metaphor for the violation of nature in the 1930s, see Kolodny, *Lay of the Land*, 146–47.

28. Soil erosion was a major concern in both regional and national Thirties culture, as highlighted by the dustbowl. See Weems, *Barnstorming the Prairies*, 61–84.

29. Gulshan Ara Khan, "Vital Materiality and Non-Human Agency: An Interview with Jane Bennett," in *Dialogues with Contemporary Political Theorists*, ed. Gary Browning, Raia Prokhovnik, and Maria Dimova-Cookson (Palgrave Macmillan, 2012), 42. For a full accounting of Bennett's ideas, see Jason Bennett, *Vital Matter: A Material Ecology of Things* (Duke University Press, 2010).

## 14

# THE MIDWESTERN SMALL TOWN

An Interpretive Problem of Mythical Proportions

*I HATE THIS SMALL TOWN FULL OF SMALL MINDED PEOPLE
WHO SUFFOCATE ME WITH EMPTY PROMISES AND SPITEFUL
COMMENTS ABOUT THE WAY I LOOK AND ACT*

Internet meme

I grew up in a Midwestern town of around a thousand people.[1] It was received opinion among my friends that we needed to get out if we could. The place was supposedly stultifying and boring, though the facts on the ground did not prove this so much as the way in which we interpreted them. From television to film, from popular music to the poetry my English teacher assigned, outside factors pushed me out the door. Even John "Cougar" Mellencamp's famous song sounded defensive. There wasn't supposed to be much for me there.

Now I live in a small Midwestern city of around 25,000 people. We have a revitalized downtown that aspires to a memory of small-town charm. Main

Street is lined with a couple of cafés, quite a few restaurants, boutiques, and resale shops. Even the old barbershop, two generations in business, has made the jump from necessity to icon. Main Street cultivates wholesomeness. And the city council keeps the big-box stores at bay.

Behind these two versions of the Midwestern town lies a century of history, much of which has been revived by a generation of historians who have sought to counter clichés of insularity and homogeneity. John E. Miller captures the era when Midwestern small towns slid into stereotype after World War II through figures like Alvin Hansen, Bob Feller, James Dean, Meredith Wilson, and Walt Disney, each of whom, in their own way, shepherded the small town into an era when the "myth seemed more potent than the reality."[2] Contrary to myths of homogeneity, Colin Johnson reveals that "small-town Americans" embraced "normalization of the discourses of gender and sexuality" over the course of the last century.[3] Against traditions of a white rural Midwest devoid of racist violence, Brent Campney finds a homegrown history of lynching and resistance.[4] Kristin Hoganson bucks claims of Midwestern parochialism by discovering "that coastal areas had no edge on continental centers when it came to connectivity."[5] Jon K. Lauck recently reminded us that the Midwest cannot fit into the easy, monochromatic stereotypes of the past century: while "so much diversity . . . coalesced" into an "'American Civil Religion,'" the Midwest also witnessed "of all [the] developments in modern democracy, the most advanced and most enduring and perhaps the most forgotten."[6] This chapter fits within current historiographical trends in Midwestern studies that take the integrity, diversity, complexity, and historical significance of the region seriously.[7] But instead of exploring the history of the Midwest *as it was*, I invite a critical approach to the Midwest as it was *perceived to be* by excavating the myth of a well-known place: the Midwestern small town.

By the middle of the last century, the Midwestern small town had popularly become representative of the nation itself, a synecdoche of the whole. This chapter traces three seemingly disparate trends that laid a foundation for this synecdoche: the formation of "Main Streets" out of Midwestern settlement patterns, the maturation of the Midwestern industrial-agricultural economy in the late nineteenth century, and two literary trends during the generation that bridged the nineteenth and twentieth centuries. Then, I analyze the way this synecdoche proved adaptable after 1945 and offered both a bulwark of American identity against economic and social flux, as well as a seat for self-actualization in the face of a supposedly repressive dominant culture. Finally, I consider the "othering" of the small town in twenty-first-century popular media. Throughout, I draw upon my book *Spoon River America: Edgar Lee Masters and the Myth of the American Small Town* (2021), to trace the ways in which popular culture confected economic and social changes into a trope where the Midwestern small town proved normative as a place both wholesomely American and wholly repressive. Like all myths, this one served certain purposes, most of which did not accurately portray the Midwest itself. Nevertheless, unpacking its origins, life-cycle, decline, and modern variants advances an accurate and robust Midwestern history by situating the mythologized Midwestern town within a discrete historical context, and thereby undermining the seeming timelessness of its claims. By doing so, I also hope to inspire further avenues of research.

Several factors prepared the Midwest for settlement patterns which gestated the small towns that came to characterize the region. Starting with the Land Ordinance of 1785, the grid pattern of six-by-six square-mile townships aided in the relatively cohesive system of land sales that prefaced the distinctive system of property lines apparent across the Midwest today. The Ordinance also required surveying *before* public sale, which, according to James E. Davis, "led to orderly land sales . . . and helped [the region] . . . escape the . . . squabbling . . . over sales that marred . . . other states."[8] By the end of the second decade of the nineteenth century, the Midwest's structured settlement and relatively thorough removal of native peoples laid the foundation for synergy between town and farm. By 1818, the year Illinois became a state, fourteen of its fifteen counties contained a county seat with a land office, as well as "a courthouse, jail, and tavern, and possibly a general store."[9]

With an eye to transparent land sales, Midwestern towns tended to be laid out according to a grid pattern mapped to the Land Ordinance. Accordingly, residential housing often expanded along lines west of the town's center to take advantage of the generally easterly wind patterns.[10] This contributed to residential districts with straight streets that ran perpendicular and parallel to a main street, reserved for businesses and municipal institutions.[11] According to Andrew Cayton and Peter Onuf, after the 1830s, proponents of "full-blown . . . bourgeois capitalism" created towns of "shopkeepers, professionals, merchants, and other people of middling rank."[12]

After the Civil War, the railroad, local banks, grain elevators, and the city of Chicago came to seem for some rural Midwesterners an aberration on the relatively recent vision of the region as a haven for independent farmers and towns.[13] When the value of staple crops fell after production outstripped demand in the 1870s, many Midwestern farmers accused economic elites of benefiting from their economic plight. New financial and transportation networks proved easily reducible to a trope that pitted hardworking farmers against local town elites and, later, faraway cities like Chicago and New York.[14] To seek redress, Midwestern farmers in the 1870s organized Granger parties, and, by the 1880s, state-level "Alliance" parties that won control of state legislatures, stood poised to shape national legislation, and paved the way for the unified People's (or "Populist") party of the 1890s.[15]

Midwestern literary "realism" sought to portray the region as distinct after the Civil War. Joseph Kirkland drew from European precedents like Émile Zola and Thomas Hardy to "reproduce, on American soil . . . , unflinching realism."[16] E. W. Howe portrayed the Midwestern town of Twin Mounds as a place where "[N]o one in the great outside world talked about it, and no one wrote about it."[17] As agrarian reform politics grew from its Midwestern base to national influence in the 1890s, a parallel transformation reframed Midwestern literary realism into critiques of social and economic dislocation. Wisconsinite Hamlin Garland's *Main-Travelled Roads* (1891) offered the best example of this kind of reform realism, which he later described as a portrayal of Midwestern farmers' struggle against "the selfish monopolistic liars of the towns."[18] Edgar Lee Masters's bestselling *Spoon River Anthology* (1915) likewise drew upon these populist sentiments and, influenced by the imagist poetry in Harriet Monroe's *Poetry: A Magazine of Verse*, bridged Midwestern realism, popular audiences, and the nation's literati, helping to transform Midwestern regional literature into a national myth where a Midwestern town's normal-seeming exterior veiled underlying pathologies.

Six years after Edgar Lee Masters published *Spoon River Anthology*, the book editor of the *Nation* and fellow Illinoisan Carl Van Doren declared in an article called "Revolt from the Village: 1920" that "[t]he newest style in American fiction dates from the appearance . . . of 'Spoon River Anthology.'"[19] In his characterization of Masters as the vanguard of a new "style," Van Doren helped reconceive the Midwestern town at the dawn of the 1920s, and laid the foundation for the mythology that characterized it for the next generation. According to Van Doren, the literature of Masters, Sherwood Anderson, Sinclair Lewis, and Floyd Dell, among others, exposed Midwestern communities' quiet tragedy and churning avarice underneath a placid exterior, portraying them as battlefields in a culture war between the modern and the traditional. And while even the authors themselves denied Van Doren's terms,[20] the persistent tradition of a literary revolt against rural communities in the 1920s marked its impact on the evolving popular myth of the Midwestern town.

Scholars since have rejected Van Doren's characterization of a literary village revolt.[21] Jon K. Lauck reminds us that Van Doren himself undermined his thesis in recollections of his Illinois boyhood.[22] And while elements of Van Doren's characterization echoed changing conceptions of a late-Victorian ethos of progress, character, and community, his attack on contemporary bromides required a mythologized place of preternatural, but ultimately hollow, American values. In this regard, the mythologization of the Midwestern town tracked changing norms in middle-class culture beyond the bounds of the Midwest itself. Barry Gross reminds us that the "revolt" was not against any specific place but against "the *myth* of the . . . great good place."[23] The Midwestern small town, therefore, stood in for the nation as a place whose claims to be "simple and innocent, pure and virtuous, democratic and egalitarian" proved fraudulent once one looked under the surface.[24]

Intellectual trends provided support for this characterization, largely by reconfiguring assumptions about human psychology. The popularization of Freud's theories of sexual repression since the 1910s provided the means by which to overturn perceived notions of the small town as a "great good place." Freud's visit to the United States in 1909 led to the dissemination of his ideas, especially after the translations of *Selected Papers on Hysteria and Other Psychoneuroses* (1909) and *Three Essays on the Theory of Sexuality* (1910). These translations, according to Richard Skues, transformed Freud's reputation from "a psychotherapist who had adopted a new method" to a psychologist with a cohesive "body of thought."[25] By 1927, the literary critic Vernon Louis Parrington characterized middle-aged readers as "in the unhappy predicament of [having] . . . [t]heir counsel . . . smiled at as the chatter of a . . . generation that knew not Freud."[26] And while Freud's theories of human psychology and psychoanalysis have been discredited by the medical community today, his ideas of innate psychological struggles and the neuroses they produced proved compelling during the middle two-quarters of the last century, and applicable to subjects beyond Freud's intention.

By the middle of the 1920s, a largely urban middle-class cross-section of the reading public opened a discursive space that imagined the rural Midwestern town as the symbolic home of contemporary anxieties, where moral hypocrisy proved to be a manifestation of social neuroses. H. L. Mencken's rhetorical war against the rural "booboisie," "village editors, clubwomen, [and]

Fundamentalists," mocked them to scorn.[27] Thorstein Veblen found greed at the heart of small-town life that fed its ethical contradictions.[28] Robert and Helen Lynd's *Middletown* (1929) turned the methods of social science on small-town Indiana.[29]

In this historical context, the Midwestern town proved vulnerable to a vulgarized Freudian analysis like Van Doren's: it exhibited anxieties that arose from the repression of its municipal id. According to Van Doren, after the authors of the "village revolt" published their works, "[t]he roofs and walls . . . were gone; the closets were open and all the skeletons rattled undenied; . . . and set the most private treasures out for the most public gaze."[30] Even though Edgar Lee Masters, Sherwood Anderson, and Sinclair Lewis rejected the idea that their work represented a "revolt" against Midwestern communities, Van Doren's appellation waxed and waned in popular culture for the rest of the century.[31] In this regard, Van Doren and his ilk created a cultural mold, where diverse stories and situations could be made to fit the myth of a repressive municipality that threatened individual self-actualization. This mold also became increasingly region-less, maintaining attributes of its Midwestern origins but applied generally as a narrative trope for understanding complex economic and cultural conflicts in the second half of the century.

After 1945, for example, the town was reconceived as the battlefield between retrograde economic elites and regular Americans who sought decent housing. Since the 1930s, family formation had been a risky proposition, while the Great Depression and World War II incubated contemporary ideals of family life that had remained largely static since the nineteenth century. With memories of intractable unemployment during the Depression, American policymakers marshaled federal policies to prevent the economy from spiraling back into depression.[32] The Servicemen's Readjustment Act of 1944 smoothed the transition back to civilian life by broadening the role of the Federal Housing Authority to insure mortgages for returning soldiers.[33] This benefit induced banks to invest in new housing primarily for white male veterans, many of whom could not have acquired mortgages before the war.[34] This shift in federal policy toward single-family homes led to an explosion in housing starts in the half-decade after the war, from 114,000 in 1944 to over 1.6 million by 1950.[35]

In this context, films like *The Best Years of Our Lives* (1946) and *It's a Wonderful Life* (1946) reinterpreted the American town as the field upon which elites and regular people battled, thereby soothing anxieties about the war's aftermath in a familiar setting. Needless to say, the prodigal sons in *The Best Years of Our*

*Lives* represented only a narrow slice of the American people: male, white, and war-experienced (tellingly, the only African American character is a porter). The veterans of the film return to the fictional Midwestern town of Boone City to build a postwar consensus against the avaricious bankers of the Corn Belt Loan and Trust. This consensus was justified by the wartime service of these men, exiled for a time from their communities, and rewarded upon their return with homes and stable families.[36]

Likewise, Frank Capra's *It's a Wonderful Life* (1946) further nationalized a stereotype forged in the Midwest, that of a small-town Main Street with a friendly surface and underlying threats. George Bailey, the proprietor of the Bailey Building and Loan in rural New York, assured the townspeople's rights to a "roof and walls and fireplace," but Mr. Potter, the banker, threatened to repress the natural urge for homeownership. In a fantasy of a Bedford Falls called "Pottersville," George careens in shock through a town of flophouses, juke joints, and drunks, all the fruit of Potter's greed. When George's Building and Loan is saved, the promise of homeownership for the citizens of the Bedford Falls is assured.

And yet, as suburbs expanded in the 1950s (founded overwhelmingly on the ideals of homeownership exhibited in films like *The Best Years of Our Lives* and *It's a Wonderful Life*) descendants of Van Doren's critique revived the myth of revolt and nationalized it. As C. Wright Mills put it in *White Collar: The American Middle Classes* (1951): "[n]ow there are no centers of firm and uniform identification. Political alienation and spiritual homelessness are widespread."[37] Significantly, much of the suburban concept of "togetherness," first formulated by the magazine *McCall's* in 1954,[38] grew out of an urge for ready-made attributes of Midwestern towns. Outdoor malls, for example, with a central thoroughfare of shops, emulated the retail district of Midwestern main streets. And Disneyland, USA, which opened in 1955, solidified the image of the Midwestern town as primarily a retail space that exuded comfortable and timeless charm.[39] Both of these descendants of the Midwestern model, according to Grace Elizabeth Hale, generated a counter-discourse to municipal "togetherness," a "romance of the outsider," where white, middle-class Americans pitted visions of inviolable identity against a supposedly repressive community.[40] In this romance of the outsider, suburban and rural communities threatened an indelible personality that struggled to actualization and "authenticity."[41] Applied in this way, the romance of the outsider by the 1950s fed popular forms of psychology, literature, media, and fashion, since flourishing meant finding one's inner self in the community, or conversely, *against* the community when it demanded sublimation of the authentic self.[42]

Popular media from the era exploited anxieties over alienation into dramas of repressive municipalities and the individuals who escaped them, reprising a familiar narrative of the "village rebels," though in locales far removed from the Midwest. Two examples from mid-century exemplify this trend: *All that Heaven Allows* (1955) told the story of an affluent widow, Cary Scott, whose staid suburban life was turned upside down when she fell in love with Ron Kirby, her gardener; and *Rebel Without a Cause* (1955), which followed the disaffected Jim Stark through Los Angeles as he struggled to define himself against his parents, community, and peers.[43] These films recruited the audience to liberation through the power of self-actualization: Cary, a symbol of suburban ennui, moved in with Ron against her community's wishes; Jim, Judy, and Plato, symbolizing every teenager mistreated by teachers, parents, and peers, exposed the immorality of the normal by being true to themselves and each other.

By mid-century, the Midwestern community itself had become increasingly difficult to conceive of as a universal home against which to rebel. The fraught years between 1955 and 1970 of activism, legislative progress, urban riots, police violence, and "long, hot summers" accentuated the sheer regionality of the village revolt in Midwestern terms.[44] But small towns in the Midwestern mold did not disappear from popular portrayals in the late twentieth century. Films like *Breaking Away* (1979)—where Dave, a high school student and amateur cyclist in Bloomington, Indiana, fantasizes about Italian cycling and, along with his working-class friends, beats the local university team in a bicycle race—echoed populist portrayals of the Midwest by authors like Garland and Masters. *Footloose* (1984), where Chicagoan Ren McCormack moves to rural Utah and teaches the town to appreciate rock music and dancing, challenged the efficacy of moral elites in ways that reflected the sensibility of Van Doren's "revolt." Likewise, *Back to the Future* (1985) revisited some of the themes of *Rebel Without a Cause*, with a fair dose of nostalgia and less angst. And *Heathers* (1988), a black comedy about an oppressive clique of high school students, their rebellious friend, Veronica, and her psychopathic boyfriend, J.D., takes place in suburban "Sherwood," Ohio, a likely nod to Sherwood Anderson and *Winesburg, Ohio*. But none of these films consciously established their small communities as synecdoche. Instead, they augured two broad changes in the popular portrayal of small towns in the Midwestern mold: small towns were either exotic or surreal.

Garrison Keillor's radio show *A Prairie Home Companion* (1974–2016) represented one of the longest-running examples of the "exotic" Midwestern town. Keillor's portrayal of Lake Wobegon, Minnesota, as a kind of timeless community of ironic and humorous residents spanned forty years of syndication on National Public Radio. Tellingly, Keillor's show was initially rejected by NPR for national syndication since the network president, Frank Mankiewicz, feared that the way *A Prairie Home Companion* portrayed small towns as locales of timeless charm might alienate rural residents and "cement our status as elitist."[45]

Likewise, films like *Fargo* (1996) and *Three Billboards Outside Ebbing Missouri* (2017) portrayed their respective communities as insular and unusual. Each film revolved around a murder whose mystery is wrapped in the mores of the community: in the case of Ethan and Joel Coen's *Fargo*, the overweening niceness of the Upper Midwest, and in Martin McDonagh's *Three Billboards*, the turgid conformity and latent violence of small towns in the lower Midwest. In both, McDormand marshals egalitarian righteousness to undercover a community's hidden crimes while, at the same time, personifying the eccentric quirks of each community. Conversely, the narrative conceit of Bill Dubuque and Mark Williams's Netflix series *Ozark* (2017–22)—about the Byrde family, Chicago suburbanites, who are forced to move to the Ozarks to launder money for a drug cartel—is dependent upon the juxtaposition between the suburban Byrdes and the colorful locals around them. In *Ozark*, portrayals of rural communities as exotic invite spectatorship from the audience who are entertained and dismayed by the antics of rural residents.

In the decades before and after the millennium, popular media also portrayed small towns as places where the surreal and freakish happened. John Carpenter's *Halloween* (1978) depends upon the juxtaposition between sedate Haddonfield, Illinois, and the serial killer who terrorizes it. Phil Alden Robinson's *Field of Dreams* (1989) takes place in rural Iowa, where the ghosts of the Chicago Black Sox inspire a middle-aged son to build a baseball field in his father's honor.[46] *The Messengers* (2007) follows a Chicago family to rural North Dakota and the horror of living in an isolated farmhouse haunted by ghosts of the murdered previous residents. More recently, the Netflix series *Stranger Things* (2016–25), by Matt and Ross Duffer, portrays Hawkins, Indiana, as afflicted by a sinister alternate dimension and exploitation by a hidden government lab, further situating the small Midwestern town as a community with secrets, in this case, supernatural ones.

The various myths of the Midwestern small town and its inheritors have served many purposes, none of which has proved particularly useful to the region itself. In the twentieth century, in the aftermath of the growth of the economic and social influence of the Midwest, the small town was imagined as a representative but contested place, where conceptions of the traditional and the modern, the individual and the community, struggled to lay claim even beyond the region itself. By the early twenty-first century, the Midwestern small town was reimagined as a place where localism abided in an increasingly interconnected society, an insular place of charming peculiarities or backward notions, and sometimes a place where the supernatural emerged from the woods or fields. In this regard, the Midwestern town is still often portrayed as a location of native ways in the interior, for better or worse. Consider HBO's series *Somebody Somewhere* (2022), where Sam returns to Manhattan, Kansas, to engage in an ambivalent love affair with her home town, a place where, according to the show's website, she "discover[s] herself and a community of outsiders who don't fit in but don't give up, showing that finding your people, and finding your voice, is possible. Anywhere. Somewhere."[47] But recent works like Julianne Couch's *The Small-Town Midwest: Resilience and Hope in the Twenty-First Century* (2016) and Jon K. Lauck's *The Good Country* (2022) reject these easy applications of well-worn tropes.[48] It is perhaps finally time to move on from the myth of the Midwestern small town as representative, and consequently reject the idea that it is a place for revolt or self-discovery, a cage or refuge. Our towns are, instead, actual places, no more or less representative of contemporary cultural anxieties or nostalgia than anywhere else. In this brief genealogy, I have tried to undermine the abiding nature of myths about the Midwestern small town by tracing their historical origins and trajectory. Other popular misconceptions of the region will benefit from similar treatment.

## NOTES

1. Portions of this chapter are drawn from *Spoon River America: Edgar Lee Masters and the Myth of the American Small Town*. Copyright 2021 by the Board of Trustees of the University of Illinois. Used with permission of the University of Illinois Press.

2. John E. Miller, *Small-Town Dreams: Stories of Midwestern Boys Who Shaped America* (University Press of Kansas, 2014), 234.

3. Colin R. Johnson, *Just Queer Folks: Gender and Sexuality in Rural America* (Temple University Press, 2013), 2.

4. Campney, *Hostile Heartland* (see chapter 2, n. 14).

5. Hoganson, *The Heartland*, 199 (see chapter 1, n. 1).

6. Lauck, *The Good Country*, 21 (see chapter 4, n. 25), also see pp. 51–85; C. Robert Haywood, *Victorian West: Class and Culture in Kansas Cattle Towns* (University Press of Kansas, 1991), 91, quoted in Lauck, *The Good Country*, 25.

7. For the latest in historiography of the Midwest, see *Middle West Review* 10, no. 2 (2024) for an issue dedicated to the state of the field. Also see Jon K. Lauck, "Introduction: The Endangered Ecosystem of Midwestern Studies," *Middle West Review* 10, no. 1 (2023): 1–10.

8. Davis, *Frontier Illinois*, 93 (see chapter 6, n. 22); also see Gregory H. Nobles (cited in Davis, *Frontier Illinois*, 441), "Straight Lines and Stability: Mapping the Political Order of the Anglo-American Frontier," *Journal of American History* 80, no. 1 (1993): 34, who argues that structured settlement was perceived as a bulwark against anarchy in the West. Also see Johnson, *Order Upon the Land* (see chapter 11, n. 17), especially 143–48 on the "checkerboard" pattern of allotments. John E. Miller notes that De Smet, in modern South Dakota, was laid out in a similar pattern in the 1880s, with Main Street forming the base of a "T" and the railroad forming the "crossbar." John E. Miller, *Laura Ingalls Wilder's Little Town: Where History and Literature Meet* (University Press of Kansas, 1994), 23–25.

9. Solon Justus Buck, *Illinois in 1818* (The Illinois Centennial Commission, 1917), 60.

10. Davis, *Frontier Illinois*, 459.

11. Davis, *Frontier Illinois*, 459.

12. Cayton and Onuf, *Midwest and the Nation*, 44, 50–51 (see chapter 6, n. 6).

13. Cronon, *Nature's Metropolis*, 74 (see chapter 1, n. 7).

14. See Charles Postel, *The Populist Vision* (Oxford University Press, 2007) for the most recent synthesis of populism.

15. See Lauck, *The Good Country*, 154–62. For differences between Midwestern Alliance politics and those of the "more-radical Southern Alliance," see Lauck, *The Good Country*, 162–63.

16. Joseph Kirkland, *Zury: The Meanest Man in Spring County, a Novel of Western Life* (Houghton Mifflin, 1889), 4.

17. E. W. Howe, *The Story of a Country Town* (Howe, 1883), 1.

18. Though he chose after *Main Travelled Roads* to "avoid the fault of mixing my fiction with my polemics." Hamlin Garland, *A Son of the Middle Border* (P. F. Collier and Son, 1917), 416–17. Jon K. Lauck notes that Garland, in his 1917 book, *A Son of the Middle Border*, portrayed a less tragic vision of the Midwest, one that was more "supportive of regionalist voices than conventional wisdom would suggest," and reminds us that Garland warned Midwestern writers against "going Hollywood" in their pursuit of adulation from the popular media centers in the East and West. Lauck, *From Warm Center*, 46–47 (see introduction, n. 21).

19. Carl Van Doren, "Contemporary American Novels: X. The Revolt from the Village: 1920," *The Nation* 113, no. 2936 (October 21, 1921): 407–412, 407. Van Doren revisited this theme in "On Hating the Provinces," in *The Roving Critic* (Kennikat Press, 1923). See also Van Wyck Brooks, *Letters and Leadership* (B. W. Heubsch, 1923).

20. See August Derleth, *Three Literary Men: A Memoir of Sinclair Lewis, Sherwood Anderson, Edgar Lee Masters* (Candlelight Press, 1963), especially the chapter on Masters.

21. It is impossible here to thoroughly discuss the half-century of scholarship that interrogates the idea of a village revolt. See, for example, Henry Steele Commager, *The American Mind: An Interpretation of America* (Yale University Press, 1950), 248; Barry Gross, "The Revolt That Wasn't: The Legacies of Critical Myopia," *CEA Critic* 30, no. 2 (1977): 4–8; and Jon K. Lauck, "The Myth of the Midwestern 'Revolt from the Village,'" *MidAmerica* 40 (2013): 43. The "Revolt from the Village" entry by Marcia Noe, in *Dictionary of Midwestern Literature: Vol. II: Dimensions of Midwestern Literary Imagination,* ed. Philip A Greasley (Indiana University Press, 2016), provides an excellent review of this scholarship.

22. See Lauck, *The Good Country,* 195–98.

23. Gross, "The Revolt That Wasn't," 5 (emphasis in the original).

24. Gross, "The Revolt That Wasn't," 5.

25. Richard Skues, "Clark Revisited: Reappraising Freud in America," in *After Freud Left: A Century of Psychoanalysis in America,* ed. John Burnham (The University of Chicago Press, 2012), 75–76.

26. Vernon Louis Parrington, *Main Currents in American Thought, Vol. III: The Beginnings of Critical Realism in America* (Harcourt, Brace, 1930), 401.

27. Lauck, "The Myth," 44. Also see Lauck's *From Warm Center to Ragged Edge: The Erosion of Midwestern Literary and Historical Regionalism, 1920–1965* (University of Iowa Press, 2017), 11–37.

28. Thorstein Veblen, "The Country Town," *The Freeman,* July 11, 1923, 417–20, and July 18, 1923, 440–43, quoted in Veblen, *Absentee Ownership and Business Enterprise in Recent Times: The Case of America* (George Allen and Unwin, 1924), 142–65. For a historical analysis of Veblen's arguments, see Lewis E. Atherton, "The Midwestern Country Town: Myth and Reality," *Agricultural History* 26, no. 3 (1953): 73–80.

29. Henry May, "Shifting Perspectives on the 1920s," *The Mississippi Valley Historical Review* 43, no. 3 (1956): 405–427, 408.

30. Van Doren, "The Revolt from the Village, 1920," 407.

31. See Lauck, *From Warm Center,* 11–37 and Stacy, *Spoon River America,* 129–31.

32. David Kennedy, *Freedom from Fear: The American People in Depression and War, 1929–1945* (Oxford University Press, 1999), 637.

33. May, *Homeward Bound,* 151 (see chapter 5, n. 57).

34. Lizabeth Cohen, *A Consumers' Republic: The Politics of Mass Consumption in Postwar America* (Alfred A. Knopf, 2003), 122.

35. May, *Homeward Bound,* 151.

36. To help solidify this consensus, middle-class working daughters and wives returned to their roles as homemakers in the film. See May, *Homeward Bound,* 56–62.

37. C. Wright Mills, *White Collar: The American Middle Classes* (Oxford University Press, 1951), 332.

38. Laura J. Miller, "Family Togetherness and the Suburban Ideal," *Sociological Forum* 10, no. 3 (1995): 393–418, 394.

39. See James E. Miller's chapter on Walt Disney in *Small-Town Dreams*, 310–27.

40. Grace Elizabeth Hale, *Nation of Outsiders: How the White Middle Class Fell in Love with Rebellion in Postwar America* (Oxford University Press, 2014), 5.

41. See, for example, Mills, *White Collar*, 332.

42. See Medovoi on "identitarianism" in the 1950s. Leerom Medovoi, *Rebels: Youth and the Cold War Origins of Identity* (Duke University Press, 2005), 49–51, specifically, 50.

43. James Dean was, himself, a native of Indiana. See Miller, *Small-Town Dreams*, 277–87.

44. For less mythological histories of race in the Midwest see Campney, *Hostile Heartland*, Thomas Sugrue's *The Origins of the Urban Crisis: Race and Inequality in Postwar Detroit* (Princeton University Press, 1996), and more recently, Lauck, *The Good Country*, 120–54.

45. See Cokie Roberts, Susan Stamberg, Noah Adams, John Ydstie, Renee Montagne, Ari Shapiro, and David Folkenflik, *This is NPR: The First Forty Years* (Chronicle Books, 2010), 102.

46. Originally a novel called *Shoeless Joe* (1982) by W. P. Kinsella.

47. HBO, *Somebody Somewhere*, accessed February 16, 2023, https://www.hbo.com /somebody-somewhere.

48. Julianne Couch, *The Small-Town Midwest: Resilience and Hope in the Twenty-First Century* (University of Iowa Press, 2016).

ANDREW SEAL

15

# LOVE IT OR LEAVE IT

The Past Ten Years of Midwestern Intellectual History

In writing this chapter, my remit is to survey the last ten years of Midwestern intellectual history. These have been years of growth and change for Midwestern intellectuals, but also years of crossed signals and some false starts. It has been a decade of infrastructure building—particularly in the academic field of history and the business of publishing—and it has been a decade of emerging voices whose conjectures about the Midwestern past and ambitions for the Midwestern future intertwine with forthright admissions of confusion about the Midwestern present.[1]

Politically, it has been a decade of earthquakes and wildfire for the region. The eyes of the world have turned to the Midwest for answers to two of the most dramatically unexpected events of the past thirty years: the election of Donald Trump as President in 2016 with the pivotal support of Ohio, Michigan, Iowa, and Wisconsin; and the emergence of the Black Lives Matter movement in Ferguson, Missouri, in 2014, and its re-emergence in Minneapolis, Minnesota, in 2020. Coupled with two deeply important water-related crises—the lead poisoning of Flint, Michigan, throughout this decade, and the Standing Rock protests led by members of Oceti Sakowin (the Sioux nation) in the Dakotas beginning in 2016—these events have spurred an overdue reckoning with a history of white supremacist violence and control that white Midwesterners have seldom been eager to learn about or even acknowledge.[2]

On the intellectual balance sheet of the past decade or so, we can happily mark down as an asset the increasing availability to all Midwesterners of a more honest and inclusive history of the region and a more open discussion of many of its continuing problems. But that balance sheet also contains several liabilities that many Midwesterners seem determined not to discharge, which they compulsively keep paying in the coin of effort and attention. Or, to be more charitable and more accurate, most Midwestern writers encompass both of these tendencies. They have begun to experiment with forms of self-examination and self-critique that are genuine breakthroughs in the history of Midwestern intellectual life, and they also return to the fixations of prior generations of Midwesterners, to alluring dead-ends that promise insight but deliver only repetition.

As an example, it has always mystified me why so many Midwestern writers have felt (and continue to feel) the need to begin their books or essays by constructing a roster of those states or parts of states that are properly in the Midwest. Such prominence signifies that this is a matter of great importance, yet the subject almost never comes up later in any of these books or essays. In practical terms, very few Midwestern writers *need* a precise cartographic definition of the Midwest to do their intellectual or imaginative work. Moreover, when I have heard a Midwesterner object to the right of, say, a Missourian to call themselves Midwestern, the protest has always been jocular, not genuine.

"Where does the Midwest end?" is an argument that no one is determined to win, but it is one Midwesterners feel they must have, over and over again. Midwesterners are so sure that their region has been lost or overlooked (but by who?) that they can never stop refinding it.[3]

It so happens that I have not lived in the Midwest for any of the past ten years. For all but the first two, I have been a New Englander, and I have, I am afraid, absorbed this region's propensity for abrupt frankness. Rather than proceed with tactless candor, however, I will first take a Midwestern route and make use of an anecdote to reveal my little theory.

I have a t-shirt that I bought in Bloomington, Indiana, at TIS, one of the stores that specializes in IU apparel. The shirt is supposed to be cream and crimson but is a few shades off by now. It bears the outline of the state of Indiana and letters spelling out a minatory command: LOVE IT OR LEAVE IT. (Notably, the shirt does not identify the outline as Indiana—you are expected to recognize its shape.)

I purchased the shirt because I was amused by the thought of wearing it outside the Midwest. What is the meaning of such a shirt floating around New England? When I wear it outside Indiana, does it automatically mean that I don't love the state? But why would a person who left the state because they do not love it be wearing a shirt with its image?

Realistically, none of the people I encounter are likely to have any of these thoughts. After all, they are New Englanders and are appalled by the slightest twinge of nosiness. Noticing my shirt and trying to decode its message is something Midwesterners might do, but it will never be done by a New Englander.

But then, perhaps that is the point. Perhaps, in my heart of hearts, I wear the shirt as a beacon for other Midwesterners washed ashore in this craggy region; it is an invitation for a fellow Hoosier—or, *faute de mieux*, an Iowan or Michigander—to break with Yankee brusqueness and say hello.

That Midwesterners have an intense curiosity about other people is a gross generalization and a cliché, but the best supporting evidence for its validity is how surprised Midwesterners are when someone from elsewhere fails to reciprocate their earnest and benevolent inquisitiveness. Midwesterners' assumption that everyone is as gregarious as they are plays a sort of trick on them. They believe that if they have been snubbed by a non-Midwesterner, it is a sign that the other person is only being aloof to *them*: probably to everyone else that non-Midwesterner must be ordinarily congenial. Culturally and intellectually, these awkward interactions scale up into persistent patterns of thought about far more important things like power and authority, elitism and populism.

Enough beating around the bush. Here comes the New England candor.

Midwestern intellectuals have entangled themselves in a long, repetitive, frequently self-referential debate about how snubbed, derided, and abandoned they are. They have created a series of rhetorical morasses that new writers about the region feel obligated to trudge through before they can write anything original. And they feel compelled to do this because almost no one seems to recognize that the whole question of whether the Midwest ought to be given more attention or better representation in national media, in popular culture, and in academia is not a dialogue in which anyone is answering "no," but instead a monologue in which Midwesterners fill in the lines that they assume a snobby elitist *would* say. I am not saying that Midwesterners do not sincerely feel demeaned; I am saying that this feeling has emerged from a Midwestern echo chamber.

Yes, the Midwest is occasionally on the receiving end of a snide dismissal or a mean-spirited joke, but more often than not, the origin of these barbs is a Midwestern malcontent, not a person born outside the region. Midwesterners are mostly unaware of how seldom non-Midwesterners think about the Midwest. Of course, one of the things that irritates Midwesterners about "coastal elites" is precisely that indifference, but what they fail to understand is that indifference is not always a symptom of condescension; oftentimes the worst you can say about indifference is that it comes from incuriousness, which is not quite the same thing as disdain. There are infinite things about which every person is incurious simply because they either do not have the opportunity to know about them in the first place or to learn about them in a more than superficial manner. This is a fact of life, not a unique condition of Midwesternness.

Midwesterners prefer to believe that they play an essential role in the mental lives of all Americans, but they are especially anxious to be noticed by people from New England and the Mid-Atlantic. They often imagine that the Midwest and the East Coast are reciprocally locked in a tango of self-definition: simplicity contrasting with urbanity. What they do not realize is that Boston does not need Indiana to feel cosmopolitan; it has New Hampshire. New York City does not have to mock Topeka when it wants to feel superior; it has Albany.

What I will do in the rest of this chapter is examine a series of intellectual and cultural products and point out two kinds of things. First, I think it is necessary to substantiate my claim that Midwesterners often get so caught up in an internal monologue about cultural elites' condescension that they confuse it for a genuinely two-sided debate—a debate that, ironically, those cultural elites have little interest in joining.

Second and more positively, I want to draw attention to some examples of what I believe is the most promising intellectual development of the past ten or fifteen years: Midwestern writers looking more deeply into one of the more difficult subjects for a Midwesterner to write about—their own ambivalence about or even alienation from the region.

Midwestern intellectuals are like intellectuals anywhere: they often mistake symbolism for significance. Because the Midwest is used so often as a symbol (and for so many different things—innocence, parochialism, tedium, conviviality, authenticity), they assume that any decision to use the region as a setting must be a deeply meaningful decision, a communication from the creator to the audience to really think about what the Midwest stands for. But often symbols are just narrative shortcuts.

Consider the Netflix series *Stranger Things* (2016–present), which is set in Hawkins, Indiana. Indiana is not particularly essential to the plot of the series; even the geographic Midwest adds nothing irreplaceable. *Stranger Things* would almost certainly not have looked very different had it been set in upstate New York or the Ozarks or any non-metropolitan part of about a dozen different states. To suggest a translation of it into Florida, however, or Texas or New Jersey (states that Americans truly love to hate) is to set off a chain of negative associations that are highly specialized, that would force the show to incorporate quite specific horror elements connected to popular perceptions of what is bad or defective about those states. Indiana, on the other hand, comes with only a generic stock of archetypal problems or dangers—the showrunners are free to invent monsters that could come from almost anywhere.

Midwesterners often resent this anonymity. But they also tend to misread it, tend to see it as more intentional and less incidental than it really is. It might be helpful to ask, if *Stranger Things* were set in upstate New York, would a Utican be quite so perturbed that their home region was considered featureless enough to be a common denominator? There may be worse things to be than bland— would it be better to be Florida?

Regional animus does (as I just demonstrated) exist, but not only are Midwesterners a bit trigger-happy when it comes to identifying examples of it, they also often fail to distinguish the genuine article from a peculiar ritual that is in fact an expression of Middle American camaraderie. I am going to steal an example of this ritual from the recent book *Imagining the Heartland: White Supremacy and the American Midwest*, by Britt E. Halvorson and Joshua O. Reno, where they incorrectly interpret it precisely by missing its hidden character.

Orson Welles was a frequent guest on late night talk shows in the late 1960s and early 1970s—he was between projects, more or less—and it happened that one night in May 1970 he appeared on *The Dick Cavett Show* on ABC. Trying to create a little human interest, Cavett ribbed Welles by treating his Midwestern roots as a shocking discovery: "If you were to ask, I think, the average person 'Where is Orson Welles' hometown?' I have a feeling that you would get a guess that would go all over the globe, probably starting with Budapest or something, and the fact that it's Kenosha, Wisconsin . . ." After some laughter from Welles and the audience, Cavett finished his question: "[it's] the most startling . . . That's the truth, isn't it?"[4]

In *Imagining the Heartland*, the authors read this momentary exchange as an exemplary staging of cosmopolitan arrogance. Cavett, they suggest, could not picture the "painfully ordinary . . . average, plain, and homogeneous" Midwest producing a sophisticated genius like Orson Welles.[5]

But if you know something about Dick Cavett, you have probably surmised my punchline. Like Jack Paar, Johnny Carson, Arsenio Hall, Craig Kilborn, and David Letterman, Cavett was himself a Midwesterner, born and raised in Nebraska.

With such firsthand experience of a life's journey from tractors to TV studios, was he really then so shocked by Welles's roots in the Badger State? Or was he feigning surprise to flatter the prejudices of an audience that really did have trouble fitting Welles's imperious persona into the modest banality of Kenosha, Wisconsin? Or was there yet another possibility: that Cavett, Welles, and his audience were all equally "in on the joke?" Perhaps "Orson Welles is from Kenosha" was not really a difficult fact for anyone to assimilate, but everyone knew that it was customary to act as if it were, that it was part of the comic routine in which they were participants.

It is easy to misidentify moments like this as examples of condescension toward the Midwest—it is, after all, quite difficult to know who in the public eye is or is not a Midwesterner. But that difficulty is what makes an interaction like the one between Cavett and Welles meaningful: it is an intensely Midwestern experience to feel pleased at finding a fellow Midwesterner outside the Midwest, and that joy is not diluted by the fact that it happens pretty darn often. On the other hand, Midwesterners are unlikely to always express their joy straightforwardly. It might come out in peculiar ways, including the self-effacing drollery we can observe in Cavett.

Phil Christman's *Midwest Futures* is persistently excellent at capturing nuances of Midwestern life, and in it he describes a variation on what Cavett and Welles were doing as "a kind of exquisitely light condescension that is well-known among Midwesterners, not the obvious kind practiced against them, but the subtle kind they practice back. 'Oh, you'd be surprised how nice it is here! The newspaper is just top-notch!' they say."[6]

Yet Christman still needs to imagine this moment as one of regional conflict: he places the Midwesterner next to an "unbelieving New Yorker at the dinner party." The "exquisitely light condescension" practiced by the Midwesterner is a kind of bait—if the New Yorker takes it, the Midwesterner gets some private satisfaction. Maybe New Yorkers are not so sharp after all!

Christman's little scene is, in its own way, as archetypally empty as *Stranger Things*'s Hawkins, Indiana. Changing the New Yorker to someone from Silicon Valley would alter the angle of its critique by a degree or two—no more. The dinner party might take place anywhere. The only details that are specified and essential are the existence of a regional contrast between the two characters and the culturally inferior position of the Midwesterner.

But notice what does not happen. The Midwesterner does not confront Mr. Cosmopolitan about his snobbery. He does not make a good-faith effort to convince the New Yorker of the value or importance of the Midwest. Not only has Christman invented this dialogue but he does not even turn it into an open debate.

On the other hand, is a debate about the merits of the Midwest what anyone is looking for? There has undeniably been over the last ten years a generic surge of interest in working-class whites, as many cultural and political elites publicly fret that they do not understand what people in "Middle America" are thinking. But that is not the same as a national conversation about the Midwest. Whenever it suits them, Midwesterners ignore that "Middle America"—or "heartland" or "flyover country"—is frequently used outside the Midwest to refer not to a real geography but to an amorphous amalgam of cultural reference points untethered to any physical location.

To be fair, the history of these terms is confusing, and national media have compounded the muddle in their urgency to anoint various conservative white men to be their Working-Class Whisperer, even when those men have not even asked for the job.

A case in point is Ohio's JD Vance. Although Vance's 2016 memoir *Hillbilly Elegy* is well known enough to need no elaborate introduction, specifying its relation to the Midwest requires a bit of unpacking. Vance is a native of Middletown, Ohio, but the primary identification he claims throughout *Hillbilly Elegy* is in the book's title: he thinks of himself as a product of Appalachia. For Vance, his Ohioan nativity is a technicality: he recalls that as a child he mentally distinguished his "address"—the houses in Ohio "where I spent most of my time with my mother and sister, wherever that might be"—from his "home [which] never changed: my great-grandmother's house, in the holler, in Jackson, Kentucky." Most of Vance's family migrated around mid-century from Kentucky as part of a wave of Appalachians looking for better pay in the factories of Midwestern cities. "As the economies of Kentucky and West Virginia lagged behind those of their neighbors, the mountains had only two products that the industrial economies of the North needed: coal and hill people. And Appalachia exported a lot of both."[7]

But if Vance did not advertise himself as a Midwesterner, he soon began to play one on TV. Introduced frequently as a voice of the "Rust Belt," Vance's preferred self-image did not work well for an election year in which news coverage and editorial columns focused on battleground states and counties. "Greater Appalachia"—a term Vance pilfers from the journalist Colin Woodard without a citation—was not an electoral battleground. Particularly after November, Vance and his book were uprooted from their true geography and replanted in the Upper Midwest for interpretive triage. Someone had to answer the question that was being asked in a thousand different ways: how could they?

Pundits' deference to him as a MAGA interpreter may have struck Vance as more than a bit ironic. Not only had he been up to that point unequivocally opposed to Donald Trump's takeover of the Republican Party, but a close reading of *Hillbilly Elegy* yields no evidence that he wrote the book to launch a career founded on his supposed expertise about white Midwestern psychology. Vance does offer his insight into what goes through the minds of his fellow "hillbillies" in several different contexts, and he theorizes freely about Appalachia's balance of social, economic, political, and religious factors and the help or harm they do. But an attentive reader will pick up on the strain beneath this opining—it does not seem to be something Vance *enjoys* doing, let alone something he would want to continue doing full time, for a living. In fact, there is ample material in the book to make the opposite case—that Vance wrote *Hillbilly Elegy* partly as a self-purgation, a way to put a period at the end of the Appalachian chapter of his life. Until his homecoming as a candidate for the Senate, most of Vance's career looks more like a series of attempted escapes from his roots: to the Marine Corps and Iraq, to Connecticut and Yale, to California and Silicon Valley. And yet, in a strange twist of fate, he is now more Midwestern than ever, and his book can only be read henceforth as a meditation on what it means to be from the Midwest.

*Hillbilly Elegy* is an example of the kind of unflinching self-scrutiny that few Midwestern writers have ever undertaken but that appears now to be breaking out wonderfully in corners all over the region. What is exciting about this mood or vein of writing—usually expressed in the genres of memoir or creative nonfiction—is its courage, its refusal of evasions or deferrals when it comes to articulating the tumult of one's feelings about the Midwest and its history, its cultural disappointments and its compensatory pleasures, its politics, its peculiarities, its petty forms of neighborly surveillance and its almost angelic expressions of neighborly support. It stares ambivalence and alienation in the face and neither packs up and leaves nor gives in and falls in love with the Midwest.

I have already mentioned Phil Christman a couple of times, but there are many passages I have flagged in my copy of *Midwest Futures* that typify this practice of pulling at thoughts like an endless row of weeds, grasping for the root of a problem in the knowledge that one root, one weed removed is only one more than you had, and never the last you need to clear. Here is a sweeping passage that earns its grandeur.

> The Midwest became central to so many of this country's stories about itself in part because some of it is naturally rich, productive. But that is not a normal thing to be; it is precisely a gift, something generous and prodigious. That we take such a good place for granted, as though its usefulness for human life were proof of its dullness and interchangeability, allows us to misuse it, and ourselves, and each other, who are marked as boring by having come from this boringly good thing, or marked as threatening because they didn't.[8]

Alongside Christman, another essayist whose writings about the Midwest have drawn well-deserved attention is Meghan O'Gieblyn. As a kind of companion to the paragraph above, I have stitched together a few passages from O'Gieblyn's 2018 collection *Interior States*.

> [I]t's a paradox of human nature that the sites of our unhappiness are precisely those that we come to trust most hardily, that we absorb most readily into our identity, and that we defend most vociferously when they come under attack. . . . This is among the many reasons why young people leave these states. When you live in close proximity to your parents and aging relatives, it's impossible to forget that you too will grow old and die. It's the same reason, I suspect, that people are made uncomfortable by the specter of open landscapes, why the cornfields and empty highways of the heartland inspire so much angst. There was a time when people spoke of such vistas as metaphors for opportunity—"expand your horizons"—a convention, I suppose, that goes back to the days of the frontier. Today, opportunity is the province of cities, and the view here

signals not possibility but visible constraints. To look out at the expanse of earth, scraped clean of novelty and distraction, is to remember in a very real sense what lies at the end of your own horizon.[9]

I find what Christman and O'Gieblyn are doing here both lovely at the sentence level and a little daring on the conceptual level. Midwestern intellectuals have often approached their writings on the region with trepidation, as if they have only one chance to define their connection to the Midwest. They feel they must strike one time only, confidently, resonantly, articulating perfectly and on the first try the spirit of the Midwest, its geographic reality, and its place in the world. Anything else may be judged ignorant or unperceptive. Above all, one's feelings must be strong; there is no room for ambivalence. If they are estranged from the region, their alienation must be pitched at the peak of hatred and despair; if they are at home, they must emanate a feeling of being welcomed and accepted that must be so complete that it feels like a foretaste of something divine.

One traditional way to work through this problem—to generate a sense of alienation with some nuance and real uncertainty—has long been simply to leave the Midwest. Doing so allows one to write a novel or an essay or a sociological monograph from a distance that can be coded as an indefinite sojourn. If one wants to write with a sense of sophistication and nuance, it is helpful to be able to pivot from thinking that one's homeland spit you out and then to say in the next breath, "Well, of course I left—I needed something more—but I can always go back!"

There has not been very much writing that openly evinces uncertainty about how to feel about the Midwest, that admits that no amount of attachment or detachment ever feels completely natural. Christman—and many other writers as well—are willing to persist in the discomfort of alienation. Not the strong form of estrangement which borders on resentment and rejection, but a kind of alienation that can tolerate both affection and disengagement, that does not believe that one can secure inner peace simply by making oneself even more of a Midwesterner.

Here is Hanif Abdurraqib, whose music and cultural criticism has been widely and effusively praised. Relatively little attention, however, has been paid to one of the major throughlines of his work across many projects: his strong feeling for his hometown of Columbus, Ohio:

> I am wondering always how one comes to love a country. Depending on who you are, or what your background is, or what trauma(s) you've

inherited, it seems too complicated to unravel. It was not complicated for me to perform for a while, when I'd convinced myself in my teens and early twenties that my performance of love for a country would open itself up to some kind of safety for me and the people I held close. I also knew then, as I know now, that leaving felt immensely impractical. This is one of the biggest tricks of them all. You are burdened with a place, and then, by the time you realize that exit is a possibility, the options for exit can seem distant, or insurmountable. I love Columbus, Ohio, and wince when I speak the name into the air.[10]

There are other ways of writing one's way into an ambivalent but deeply felt connection with the Midwest. The depth and almost transcendental quality of some of the best descriptive prose can rival the complications of an emotionally tense, soul-baring passage. In the following passage, from the very beginning of David Foster Wallace's unfinished novel *The Pale King*, published in 2011, we find tranquility and almost an anonymity—the reader is not addressed as a Midwestern resident, a former resident, or an outsider. There is a palpably implicit belief flowing beneath the prose that anyone can understand and respond to the region's terrain and its culture.

An arrow of starlings fired from the windbreak's thatch. The glitter of dew that stays where it is and steams all day. A sunflower, four more, one bowed, and horses in the distance standing rigid and still as toys. All nodding. Electric sounds of insects at their business. Ale-colored sunshine and pale sky and whorls of cirrus so high they cast no shadow. Insects all business all the time. Quartz and chert and schist and chondrite iron scabs in granite. Very old land. Look around you. The horizon trembling, shapeless.[11]

This passage returns us to the land, to a sensation of pure presence that is more magnificent than love and that cannot truly be left behind.

LOVE IT OR LEAVE IT? Perhaps the answer for the future is . . . neither.

## NOTES

1. I do not have the space to do justice to the abundance of excellent scholarship presented since 2015 at the annual Midwestern History Conference and published in *Studies in Midwestern History* and the *Middle West Review*, both launched in the past decade. Another recent and exciting platform for Midwestern literary and scholarly

culture is the *Chicago Review of Books*, established in 2016. While I cannot survey the many terrific books that have come out from Belt Publishing since its establishment in 2013, I want to single out two of exceptional quality: Williamson, *Black in the Middle* (see chapter 5, n. 10) and Mark Athitakis, *The New Midwest: A Guide to Contemporary Fiction of the Great Lakes, Great Plains, and Rust Belt* (Belt Publishing, 2017).

2. Although recently published, Timothy Egan's *A Fever in the Heartland: The Ku Klux Klan's Plot to Take Over America, and the Woman Who Stopped Them* (Viking, 2023) is certain to bring greater attention to the history of white supremacy in the Midwest. Two valuable online resources documenting Midwestern lynchings and sundown towns are, respectively, "Lynchings," The African American Midwest, accessed April 7, 2023, https://africanamericanmidwest.com/history-racism/lynchings/; and "Historical Database of Sundown Towns," History and Social Justice, Tougaloo College, accessed April 7, 2023, https://justice.tougaloo.edu/sundown-towns/using-the-sundown-towns -database/state-map/.

3. An article that productively pushes back against some of these anxieties that the Midwest is a "lost region"—a phrase that comes from Jon K. Lauck's field-defining book *The Lost Region* (see chapter 4, n. 22)—is Klumpp, "Not a Revival" (see chapter 7, n. 11).

4. Halvorson and Reno, *Imagining the Heartland*, 1 (see chapter 8, n. 12).

5. In fact, Welles at one point in his life declared "I'm almost belligerently Midwestern and always a confirmed 'badger.'" See Patrick McGilligan, *Young Orson: The Years of Luck and Genius on the Path to* Citizen Kane (Harper, 2015), 5.

6. Christman, *Midwest Futures*, 23 (see chapter 10, n. 26).

7. J. D. Vance, *Hillbilly Elegy: A Memoir of a Family and Culture in Crisis* (Harper, 2016), 28.

8. Christman, *Midwest Futures*, 94

9. Meghan O'Gieblyn, *Interior States: Essays.* (Anchor, 2018), xiv, 5, 9.

10. Hanif Abdurraqib, *A Little Devil in America: Notes in Praise of Black Performance* (Random House, 2021), 148.

11. David Foster Wallace, *The Pale King* (Little, Brown, 2011), 3.

# CONTRIBUTORS

EMILIANO AGUILAR is Assistant Professor of History at the University of Notre Dame, where he teaches courses rooted in political, urban, and labor history, specifically on Latinas and Latinos. His manuscript in progress, *Building a Latino Machine: Caught Between Corrupt Political Machines and Good Government Reform*, explores how the ethnic Mexican and Puerto Rican community of East Chicago, Indiana, navigated machine politics in the twentieth and twenty-first centuries to further their inclusion in municipal and union politics. His work has appeared in *The Metropole*, *Belt Magazine*, the *Immigration and Ethnic History Society's Blog*, the *Los Angeles Review of Books*, and more. He published an entry about Latino labor for the *Oxford Research Encyclopedia of American History* and has research in the *Indiana Magazine of History*. A chapter of his research was published in *Building Sustainable Worlds: Latinx Placemaking in the Midwest* (University of Illinois Press, 2022).

TIMOTHY G. ANDERSON is Associate Professor in the Department of Geography at Ohio University, where he has taught courses in cultural and historical geography since 1996. His research interests focus on the historical settlement geography of the United States, especially the production of regional and ethnic cultural landscapes, governmentality, spatialization theory, and the production of cultural landscapes associated with Germanic diasporic movements and communities. He received his PhD in geography from Texas A&M University (1994) and was a Fulbright Scholar (Romania) in 2014.

CAMDEN BURD is Assistant Professor of History at Clemson University. He is the author of *The Roots of Flower City: Horticulture, Empire, and the Remaking of Rochester, New York* (Cornell University Press, 2024). His work on Midwestern environmental history has appeared in various journals and edited collections, including *The Conservative Heartland: A Political History of the Postwar American Midwest* (University Press of Kansas, 2020).

TIMOTHY DEAN DRAPER is Professor of History at Waubonsee Community College in Sugar Grove, Illinois. He received a BS and MA at Ball State University and pursued doctoral research in history at the University of Iowa and Northern Illinois University, the latter of which awarded him a PhD in American history. Draper has published various articles and reviews on religion, urbanism, immigration, the political left, teaching methodology, historiography, and the Midwest. He served as an officer and board member of the Immigration and Ethnic History Society, and he currently sits on the Illinois State Historical Society's Board of Directors. After several years as Book Review Editor for the ISHS's peer-reviewed journal, he was named the publication's Special Project Editor. Currently, Draper is researching the role of sports in postindustrial Chicago and coauthoring a study of hiking historic and natural trails in Illinois.

SARA EGGE is the Claude D. Pottinger Professor of History at Centre College in Kentucky. She received her PhD from Iowa State University and her undergraduate degrees from North Dakota State University. Her work has appeared in *Minnesota History, Annals of Iowa, Indiana Magazine of History, Agricultural History*, and *Middle West Review*. Her book *Woman Suffrage and Citizenship in the Midwest, 1870–1920* won the Gita Chaudhuri Prize from the Western Association of Women's Historians for the best book published on rural women in any time and place and the Benjamin Shambaugh Award from the State Historical Society of Iowa for the best book on Iowa history. She is currently writing a book on the history of naturalization in the United States. She served as president of the Midwestern History Association from 2020–22.

OLIVIA M. HAGEDORN is a historian of women, gender, the Black Midwest, and the African Diaspora. She received her PhD in history from the University of Illinois Urbana-Champaign. Her research explores the internationalist and feminist activism of Black women cultural workers in Chicago from the Chicago Black

Renaissance through the Black Arts Movement. Her work aims to extend the geographic scope of the African Diaspora to include the Midwest, position Black women as progenitors of internationalist thought, and highlight the importance of space and place to the articulation of Black women's diasporic politics. She is currently a postdoctoral fellow in the School of Social Work at the University of Illinois Urbana-Champaign.

ASHLEY HOWARD is Assistant Professor of History and African American Studies at the University of Iowa. Her research investigates racial violence in the Midwest. Howard's work has appeared in *Nebraska History*, *Annals of Iowa*, *Middle West Review*, the *Journal of African American History*, the *Labor Studies Journal*, the *American Historian*, *Smithsonian Magazine*, *TIME*, the *Washington Post*, the *Financial Times*, and numerous other popular and scholarly outlets. In 2023, she and co-investigator Colin Gordon were awarded a Mellon Foundation grant to examine race-based property restrictions in Iowa.

R. DOUGLAS HURT is Professor of History at Purdue University. He is a past-president of the Agricultural History Society and a current Fellow of the Society. He has served as the editor of *Agricultural History* and *Ohio History*. As the associate director of the State Historical Society of Missouri, he edited the *Missouri Historical Review*. He is the author of *Agriculture in the Midwest, 1815–1900*, *The Great Plains during World War II*, *The Big Empty: The Great Plains in the Twentieth Century*, *The Dust Bowl: An Agricultural and Social History*, and *The Ohio Frontier: Crucible of the Old Northwest, 1720–1830*.

ZACHARY MICHAEL JACK is an award-winning author of many books on his home region, including *The Haunt of Home: A Journey Through America's Heartland*; *Wish You Were Here: Love and Longing in an American Heartland*, and *The Midwest Farmer's Daughter: In Search of an American Icon*, among others. A seventh-generation Iowan, Jack is a former member of the board of directors for the Midwestern History Association and a longtime professor of English at North Central College in Naperville, Illinois, where he developed interdisciplinary courses in place studies for the Leadership, Ethics and Values (LEV) and Chicago Area Studies (CAS) programs.

JOSHUA J. JEFFERS was born and raised in Chillicothe, Ohio, and he completed bachelor's degrees in history and philosophy at Ohio State University in 2006.

He earned a master's degree in history from Northern Illinois University in 2008 and completed his PhD in history at Purdue University in 2014. His research interests include Native American history, Ohio history, and early America. His recent publications include "Colonizing the Indigenous Past: Settler-Colonial Place-Making and the Ancient Landscape of the Early Midwest" in *The Making of the Midwest: Essays on the Formation of Midwestern Identity, 1787–1900* (Hastings College Press, 2020), and "From Pipes to Pistols: Blood Run, the Pipestone Trade, and the Eclipse of the Pre-Contact Economy in the Upper Midwest" in *Heartland River: A Cultural and Environmental History of the Big Sioux River Valley* (The Center for Western Studies, Augustana University, 2022). He is Assistant Professor of History at California State University-Dominguez Hills, where he teaches courses on Native American history, early America, and environmental history. He lives in La Mirada, California, with his wife and three children.

JON K. LAUCK is the author of several books, including *The Lost Region: Toward a Revival of Midwestern History* (University of Iowa Press, 2013); *From Warm Center to Ragged Edge: The Erosion of Midwestern Regionalism, 1920–1965* (University of Iowa Press, 2017); and *The Good Country: A History of the American Midwest* (University of Oklahoma Press, 2022). Lauck is currently serving as an adjunct professor of history and political science at the University of South Dakota, as Editor-in-Chief of *Middle West Review,* and as president of the Society for the Study of Midwestern Literature. He earned his PhD in history from the University of Iowa and his law degree from the University of Minnesota.

ERIK S. MCDUFFIE is an associate professor in the Department of African American Studies and History at the University of Illinois Urbana-Champaign. He is the author of the award-winning monograph *Sojourning for Freedom: Black Women, American Communism, and the Making of Black Left Feminism* (Duke University Press, 2011). He is completing a new book, tentatively titled *Garveyism in the Diasporic Midwest: The American Heartland and Global Black Freedom, 1920–80.* Drawing from original research conducted in Canada, Ghana, Grenada, Jamaica, Liberia, South Africa, Trinidad and Tobago, the United Kingdom, and the United States, the book establishes the importance of the US Midwest to twentieth-century global Black history and the African world through Garveyism. The book received an American Council for Learned Societies fellowship and National Endowment for the Humanities fellowship. A sixth-generation Midwesterner, his family hails from the United States, Canada, and St. Kitts.

MARCIA NOE is Professor of English and Director of Women, Gender, and Sexuality Studies at The University of Tennessee at Chattanooga. Her most recent publication is *Three Midwestern Playwrights: How Floyd Dell, George Cram Cook, and Susan Glaspell Transformed American Theatre* (Indiana University Press, 2022).

ANDREW SEAL is a Senior Lecturer in Economics at the University of New Hampshire. He has published on the Midwest's history and culture in *Middle West Review*, *The Chronicle of Higher Education*, the Society of US Intellectual History's blog, and *The Sower and the Seer: Perspectives on the Intellectual History of the American Midwest* (Wisconsin Historical Society Press), which he co-edited with Joseph Hogan, Jon K. Lauck, Paul Murphy, and Gleaves Whitney.

JASON STACY is Professor of History and Social Science Pedagogy at Southern Illinois University Edwardsville. Recently, he published *Spoon River America: Edgar Lee Masters and the Myth of the American Small Town* (University of Illinois Press, 2021). His previous publications include *Walt Whitman's Selected Journalism* with Douglas Noverr (University of Illinois Press, 2015), *Leaves of Grass, 1860: The 150th Anniversary Facsimile Edition* (University of Iowa Press, 2009), and *Walt Whitman's Multitudes: Labor Reform and Persona in Whitman's Journalism and the First* Leaves of Grass, *1840–1855* (Lang, 2008).

JASON WEEMS is Associate Professor of American Art and Visual Culture at the University of California, Riverside, where he recently completed service as department chair. He is the author of *Barnstorming the Prairies: How Aerial Vision Shaped the Midwest* (University of Minnesota Press, 2015). This book received the Fred. B. Kniffen Book Award from the International Society for Landscape, Place, and Material Culture Studies and the Jon Gjerde Book Prize from the Midwestern History Association. He is also a curator for exhibitions including "Interrogating Manzanar: Photography, Justice and the Japanese American Internment" (2015) and "Out of Site: Survey Science and the Hidden West" (2024). His current research includes investigations of archaeological illustration in the Americas circa 1900, photography of and by Native Americans during the New Deal era, and tropes of soil and land connectedness in US art and culture. He grew up on a farm in Iowa.

E. JAMES WEST is Lecturer in Arts and Sciences at University College London and the Co-Director of the Black Press Research Collective, based at Johns Hopkins University. He is the author of three books, most recently *Our Kind of Historian: The Work and Activism of Lerone Bennett Jr.* (University of Massachusetts Press, 2022).

# INDEX

*References to illustrations are in italic type.*

Abbott, Robert, 67, 70–73
Abdurraqib, Hanif, 55, 56, 236
abortion, 123
Adams, Cyrus, 65
Adams, Herbert Baxter, 96
Adams, John Quincy (*Appeal* editor), 65
Addams, Jane, 122, 141
African American(s), 25, 44n3, 50–51,
    66, 113, 144; in agriculture, 8, 22;
    communities, 107, 109; culture, 56,
    80, 83; experiences, 51, 55, 73, 78,
    82–83, 155; farmers, 22–23; in film,
    220; history/study of, 2, 9, 11, 51;
    identity, 38–39, 56, 57, 81; intellectual
    contributions, 56; literature, 54–55;
    migrants/migration, 66–69, 70–71,
    155; Studies, 10, 65, 67; violence
    against, 80, 81. *See also* racism, white
    supremacy; women, 11, 78, 79, 125.
    *See also* Black(s)
African-American Heritage Association
    (AAHA), 77–78, 81
African diaspora, 10, 52, 78, 83
*The Afro-American Press and Its Editors*
    (Penn), 66

agriculture, 8, 12, 14, 22–24, 26, 27,
    39, 151–58, 187, 192; economic
    importance of, 113; and economic
    hardship, 28; environmental history
    of, 151–52; history of, 21, 29, 100, 217;
    industrialization of, 149, 170, 202,
    215; and labor migration, 25, 100;
    and Latinas/os, 25, 107, 113; Native
    American, 22, 36; policy, 8, 27, 28;
    production, 197; and small-town
    myth, 223; study of, 100; and women,
    27, 125–26
Aguilar, Emiliano, 12, 239
American Historical Association, 11
American Society for Environmental
    History, 150–51
Anderson, Sherwood, 173, 184, 217, 219,
    221
Anderson, Timothy G., 14–15, 239
Anishinaabeg, 37–38, 47n42
anthropomorphization, of land, 16, 186,
    187, 192, 193, 205–6
antisemitism, 125
Appalachia(n), 34, 142, 149, 168–69,
    175n2, 233–34; Trans-, 97–98

www.ingramcontent.com/pod-product-compliance
Lightning Source LLC
Chambersburg PA
CBHW020348100426
42812CB00035B/3391/J